PERGAMON GENERAL PSYCHOLOGY SERIES

*Editors:* Arnold P. Goldstein, *Syracuse University*
Leonard Krasner, *SUNY, Stony Brook*

---

# Survival: Black/White

PGPS-15

# Survival: Black/White

**FLORENCE HALPERN**

*New York University*
*School of Medicine*

**PERGAMON PRESS**

New York · Toronto · Oxford · Sydney · Braunschweig

PERGAMON PRESS INC.
Maxwell House, Fairview Park, Elmsford, N.Y. 10523

PERGAMON OF CANADA LTD.
207 Queen's Quay West, Toronto 117, Ontario

PERGAMON PRESS LTD.
Headington Hill Hall, Oxford

PERGAMON PRESS (AUST.) PTY. LTD.
Rushcutters Bay, Sydney, N.S.W.

VIEWEG & SOHN GmbH
Burgplatz 1, Braunschweig

---

---

Printed in the United States of America
08 016994 5 (H)
08 017193 1 (S)

# Contents

v

# *Preface*

This book is about black people. Since I am white I think some explanation for what may be regarded as presumptuous behavior on my part is indicated. My purpose is to communicate to others how I became involved in the lives of the southern black people and how my perception and understanding of them changed as the result of that involvement. My hope is that what is written here will help other white people "feel and think black."

What follows is the product of close, sustained living with the black people of the rural south. I went to Mississippi originally, not to study the black people or write a book about them, but rather to relieve the guilt I experienced when I learned through the communication media what was happening to black citizens in the south.

My first experience in the south was with Head Start in the summer of 1965. The Head Start program in that state, known as the Child Development Group of Mississippi, consisted of eighty-four centers, scattered all over the state. The program, directed by Dr. Tom Levin, a clinical psychologist, was a highly controversial one. Because of the philosophy of the project and the goals it had set for itself, the local white people in the area were very unhappy with the program and tried to hamper and do away with it. To this end they harassed the people working with the project and brought pressure to bear on local and federal politicians to have the project's funds rescinded.

What was particularly distressing to the white residents were the efforts that were being made to develop feelings of dignity, self-respect, and self-confidence in the black people of the area. One way this was being

done was by turning over authority to the black people, not only permitting them to make their own decisions but urging them to do so, rather
than constantly looking to "white authority" for assistance and direction.
So they were assured that if the solutions they found for a given problem
did not work out well, no great harm would result and a new answer could
always be reached. In this way it was hoped that their longstanding
dependence on and deference to white people and resulting negative
self-image would be overcome. Similarly, the children who initially
appeared afraid to speak to or even look at the white workers were
encouraged to engage with them in verbal exchange and spontaneous
play. By the end of the summer most of the children were quite responsive
and outgoing. In fact, several of the mothers reported that when they
took the children to the integrated school to register them for the fall
term, they were very pleased at the way the children "picked up their
heads and spoke their names," in contrast to the behavior of some of the
white children who cried and clung to their mothers during the registra-
tion.

There were actually over a thousand people in the program—teachers,
teacher-aides, cooks, social workers, psychologists, doctors, nurses,
clerks, and secretaries. Only about a hundred of these people were white
professionals from the north, while the remainder were black people
whose concepts of child development and child rearing derived solely
from their experiences in raising their own children and grandchildren.

Functioning as a psychologist in the program, it did not take me very
long to recognize that the needs, the values, and the motivation of the
black people were in almost all respects quite different from those of
middle-class white people. As a result, I had to acquire a whole new set
of concepts and values before I could communicate meaningfully with
the people with whom I was working.

Following the Head Start experience I became involved with the
people of Strike City. The residents of Strike City were a small group
of black people who, for the first time in the history of the United States,
had gone on strike, refusing to work in the cotton fields for three dollars
a day. Such unprecedented behavior on the part of black people was met
with anger and rejection by the plantation owner who promptly fired
the striking workers. This meant that they not only had to leave their
jobs, but also the shacks that were their homes. For a time they were
in dire straits as they traveled around Mississippi trying to find new homes
and the means of staying alive. Finally, they were able to procure a few
acres of ground from a black man. Here they pitched tents and lived

in them during one of Mississippi's coldest winters. They survived and even produced two new babies. By their behavior they demonstrated a capacity for independence and self-determination that few white people believed they possessed.

During the winter of 1965–1966 I visited the tent community sporadically, doing whatever could be done to ease the wretched condition of the people. Their needs at that point were very immediate and concrete, so bringing them much needed supplies was important. However, providing them with emotional support was also important. The fact that someone from the white community, someone from the north, knew about them and cared about what happened to them, helped lift their spirits and strengthen their morale. So they held on and eventually left their tents and moved into the houses that the men had built with their bare hands.

Many of the children in Strike City were going to attend an integrated school in the fall and so, during the summers of 1966 and 1967, I ran a one room class with children ranging in age from five to eighteen years. From 9 a.m. in the morning until late in the afternoon we worked on reading and arithmetic. Naturally I came to know all the children and their families very well and they learned to know me, and I was soon seen by all the members of Strike City as one of them. Thus a woman might ask me to drive her to town because she had to buy something, or she wanted to visit a relative. Another woman might ask me to go to a clinic or the Welfare agency with her. In general I was a member of the community, not an outsider.

In 1968 I became a member of Tufts Delta Health Center, a project set up by the Department of Community Medicine (later known as the department of Community Health and Social Medicine) of Tufts University School of Medicine in Boston, Massachusetts. The program was financed by OEO and served the indigent population of North Bolivar County, Mississippi in the the Mississippi Delta — about 15,000 people residing in an area of 500 square miles. Much of the work of the Center is discussed in later chapters. As staff psychologist I gave talks to professionals and paraprofessionals on issues related to mental health, "did therapy" with the patients (most of whom were black) and with members of the white staff and their families when they became discouraged and depressed, counseled and encouraged members of the black staff when they questioned their ability to carry out their assignments, visited sick and disturbed people in their homes and in the small local black hospital, and attended church and went to church sociables and picnics organized by the black community. I also taught two days a week for one semester in a small, all black college.

Briefly then, what I have learned about the black people comes from living closely with them in their homes, working in their schools, their Head Start Centers, their hospitals, churches, colleges, and other organizations. This kind of living enabled me to participate intimately in the every day experiences of the people, sharing with them their joys and sorrows, their illnesses, births and deaths, their disappointments and rejoicings when there was reason to rejoice, and more recently sharing with them the gradual realization that change might come, that there was the possibility for a better way of life for themselves and their children than they had ever known before.

Out of this living with the black people have come not only new concepts and values, but the realization that feeling guilty about the condition of the black people, being sympathetic and well-intentioned toward them, or being "liberally" oriented does not result in constructive change. What is needed is a solid understanding and appreciation of the life styles of the black people, how they came to be and what purposes they serve. Only then is it possible to consider how blacks and whites might come together with mutual trust and respect, and work toward the survival of both races.

FLORENCE HALPERN

*Mound Bayou, Mississippi*
*New York, N.Y.*

# Part I    How It Has Been

# CHAPTER 1

# *Beyond Guilt*

This book is concerned with the experiences and resulting life styles of the black people of the rural south. The question might well be asked, why focus specifically on the southern rural black population? What do these relatively quiet, God-fearing and overtly compliant people, engaged until recently in agricultural and domestic pursuits, have to tell us about the black man in America today? There are several answers to such a question, the two most significant ones being: until recently, the greatest number of black people lived in the south and their life styles were therefore the prototype for black people everywhere; and currently it is these southern black people who are "invading" the northern cities, bringing with them their century-old culture. Consequently, their beliefs and attitudes and their response patterns have a marked impact on the black city dweller.

Because the experiences of the black people have been so different from those of the white people, their ways of perceiving the world and themselves, their concepts, their goals, and their motivations differ considerably from those of most white people. Attempts on the part of the Establishment to bridge the gap that exists between the black and white worlds consist almost exclusively of efforts at teaching the black man how to think and react as the white man does, while nothing is done to enable the white man to appreciate, respect and in certain ways emulate the black man's life styles. Yet without such efforts there can only be misunderstandings and tensions.

This distance from and lack of appreciation of the black man's way of life so characteristic of the perceptions and thinking of most white people — even well-educated, well-intentioned white people — is well illustrated by their reactions to the recent tragic events at Attica State prison. Many of these people expressed a certain amount of sympathy for the prison inmates, yet were nonetheless appalled at what had happened, and were certainly not hearing what the black man was trying to communicate. Instead the white people asked, "Does anything, any form of prison abuse, justify the behavior of the inmates?" What these questioners failed to realize was that it was not a matter of justification, not a question of "right" or "wrong" at the moment, but a predictable reaction of black men in this country responding to the injustices and the mistreatment they and their ancestors had endured for centuries. While current prison conditions certainly triggered the behavior of the convicts, it was their life-long perceptions of, and experiences with the white world that they were really battling.

What white men in this country fail to recognize is that it is their way of responding to the black people that accounts for the black-white problems that exist today. What happened to the black man, from the time he was captured in Africa and shipped to America to serve the white man's needs, accounts for the personality traits that he has developed and the behavior he now manifests. Subjected to conditions quite different from those to which any white person was relegated and prevented from participating in the more positive and rewarding aspects of the prevailing culture, the black man naturally developed life styles quite different from those of the white man. So what should be asked is, "Is there any justification for the way in which the white man has dealt with the black man from the time he was forcibly and unwillingly brought to this country?" More practical and constructive, and certainly more to the point, the question should be, "Given today's conditions, the racial tensions and inequalities, how can black and white people come together in mutual respect, trust and understanding?"

The answer obviously is that, while some changes in the black man's perceptions, concepts and life styles are needed, the major change must come from the white community. Yet almost any discussion among white people about what they choose to call the "black problem" focuses on what must be done to and for the black people in order to change them; but clearly the problem is the white man's. As one young black activist put it, "I'm so tired of being told what's wrong with *us*." It was President Eisenhower who said that a solution of the black-white issue would not come from passing laws but when there was a change in the hearts of men.

This book has been written in the hope that it will help the white people gain some understanding of the way the black man really thinks and feels. For this purpose, in the succeeding pages the focus will be on the way the black man perceives and experiences his world. To the extent that a white person can convey a black person's thoughts, feelings, concepts and ideas, what is reported here will be from the black rather than the usual, traditional white orientation. This is a point of view, with a few notable exceptions, which has been minimized, overlooked, or neglected by white professionals working with black patients, white educators teaching black children, white counselors advising and training black workers, and by white researchers conducting investigations on black populations.

To acquire some meaningful understanding of the way in which the black man perceives his world requires a radical shift in many firmly established white concepts and values. When such a shift in outlook and attitude occurs, it is a startling and exciting experience. In many respects, it is like the shifts or changes in perception and feeling that take place during the course of therapy. There is nothing forced or deliberate about such changes. Rather, without having given the matter any conscious thought, there is the sudden realization that one is thinking and reacting to many situations in strikingly new ways, and one's ideas about certain matters are quite different from what they had previously been. The experiences of a white college student, working in the south with the Civil Rights movement during the summer of 1965, provide a good illustration of the changes that unwittingly occurred as a result of her exposure to a new culture with very different attitudes, needs and response patterns from her own. She explained that she had come south for ideological reasons, because she could not tolerate the thought of the injustices and the hardships that she had heard the black people were enduring. In spite of the many things she had heard about the dangers of working for Civil Rights, she experienced no fear of bodily harm. What she really dreaded was the possibility of being arrested. Her white middle-class background caused her to regard such a happening as a deep and enduring disgrace. However, after she had lived in the south for a few weeks, spending all her time with the black people, she suddenly realized that the thought of being arrested no longer disturbed her, not having a prison record no longer marked her as "respectable" nor had it the connotation of being law abiding as it once did. This change in her outlook and her feelings was certainly not something that she had deliberately thought through; rather, it was the product of what she saw and heard. As she became more and more immersed in the lives of the black people, her former ideas about law and order, her concepts of what constituted disgrace and what honor meant, as well as many other values she had long held, were markedly altered.

This is not a scholarly book in the usual sense of that term. To paraphrase Mark Twain, I have not allowed my education to interfere with my knowledge. To state it more bluntly, I have not allowed formal kinds of interview sessions, research methodology and standardized tests to come between me and the people I sought to know and understand. Lynd* puts it very well when she says, "The detachment of science may, if emphasized at the expense of other relations to the world, bring an impoverishment of experience, and in so far as it is an inadequate account of the world, a distortion of science as well." Certainly formal, rigorously controlled research does not seem an appropriate method to employ in order to gain real understanding of the black people. It would definitely not yield the kind of knowledge sought here. To know a people one need not measure them in different ways, but rather become an integral part of their community, totally living the lives they live. So the concepts offered here are based on observation, participation, conversation, some interviewing and therapy, and very occasional testing. That these concepts have validity and reliability, despite the absence of formal research procedures, is indicated by the accuracy with which, on the basis of what was learned about the black population, prediction of both individual and group behavior was achieved.

The ideas presented here have been incubating and fomenting for a long time; yet there has been great reluctance on my part to write about what I feel, think, and know about the black people of the rural south. This reluctance stems from a number of factors, the chief one being my firm conviction that no outsider, no white person, no matter how knowledgeable he may be about the black people and their life styles, no matter how understanding and compassionate he is, and how great his respect for the black man, should speak for him. Yet my sense of urgency about the need for change among the white people compels me to make the effort. Like Hersey,† I feel that "every scrap of understanding, every door-crack glimmer of illumination, every thread that may lead not just to survival of the races but to health — all should be shared as soon as possible. There is so much to be done in so little time." One has only to remember the nature of the relationship that existed between the black and white Civil Rights

*Lynd, H. *On Shame and the Search for Identity.* Science Editions, Inc., New York, 1961, p. 244.
†Hersey, J. *The Algiers Motel Incident.* Alfred A. Knopf, New York, 1968, p. 35.

workers in the early and middle sixties, when it was thought that "the Civil Rights movement will save America" and compare that relationship and that mood with the distant, ununderstanding, suspicious and distrustful mood that obtains between the two races today, to recognize how very quickly and dramatically change can occur, and how desperate is the need for speedy appreciation and constructive answers to the black-white issue.

As a further justification of this effort at presenting the black man as I came to know him is the fact that it is the white man to whom I am speaking, it is the white man I am trying to reach, with the hope of enhancing his understanding and changing some of his misconceptions about black people. And I am certainly not a stranger to the white man's way of thinking and reacting. I know his language, his moods, his concerns, his fears, his conflicts and his hopes. So I dare hope that I may be able to influence him somewhat by what follows here.

Yet even as I try to put down on paper the way in which I have come to know the black people I am overwhelmed by the impossibility of conveying, through the medium of words, what it has meant to be a black person, and particularly to be a black person in the rural south. To appreciate this incredible position it is necessary to live as the black people have lived, not only in terms of the physical deprivation and the harm and violence they have suffered, but in terms of the psychological insults they have experienced, the humiliations and injustices that have been heaped on them. What is more, one has to live this way, with uncertainty and fear as constant companions, not just for a few weeks or months, but for a long stretch of time, and above all to live this way without any hope of change or escape. Even so, the experience for the white man can never be as dire as it was for the black man. When conditions become too difficult, too frustrating and depressing to be endured, the white man can always pack up and leave, can go back to his white community and his white way of life. This escape hatch is always available to him. Only if he denies himself this opportunity, only if he blots out of awareness the possibility that there is such an opportunity, can he begin to appreciate what the absence of hope can do to an individual's outlook on life, and what hunger, sickness and despair can do to a person's perception of himself and his world. Yet the black people in the rural south have lived with extreme deprivation and little or no hope for anything better, at least on this earth, for generations. So when one writes about them every statement should be printed in red ink, in large bold letters so that nothing is overlooked or forgotten.

Northern whites who give the matter any thought rarely see the relationship between the experiences of the southern black people and the
attitudes and behaviors of the black men they know, the men who live
in the urban ghettos. When any reference is made to the experiences and
habits of the southern black people, when their traditions are cited as
possible explanations for black behavior everywhere, the northern white
refuses to recognize that these have any bearing whatsoever on the reactions of the black people as he knows them. Yet in a variety of ways the
traditions, the perceptions, and the response patterns of the northern
black city dweller are very similar to those of his southern kinsmen and
stem from the same experiences and beliefs. Obviously the black man
who goes north cannot instantly abandon all his old ways. Instead, old
customs and former modes of response still determine how the black man*
who is a newcomer to the city perceives and reacts to his new environment. Similarly, one has only to talk with northern black people, people
who have never been in the south, about child-rearing practices among
southern blacks, to win head-nodding understanding from them and
statements to the effect that they were raised in exactly the same way
that is being described as typical of their southern kinsmen. After all, as
was noted above, it is only a very short time ago that the greatest number
of black people lived in the south, and it is in the south that the roots of
black culture and black customs are to be found. Consequently, southern
life styles influence much of the thinking and the behavior of black people
everywhere, north and south.

What the white man tends to see most sharply when he observes or
interacts with the urban ghetto dweller is the aggressive, unco-operative
and sometimes belligerent stance adopted by many, though by no means
all black people. He is also very much concerned about what the influx
of southern black people into the city is doing to property values, to the
school system and to the whole educational process. His concern is
understandable, but the condition is not likely to alter until the white man
comes to appreciate why the black man reacts as he does. Only when he

---

*The experiences and the response to such experiences described here are largely taken
from the lives of the black people in Mississippi. While the behaviors of black people in other
parts of the south are somewhat different this is so only in minor matters. The basic problem,
the need to survive in the face of overpowering discrimination, deprivation and oppression,
was something with which all the black people had to cope. Although the coping methods in
Georgia for example, may have departed in certain details from those practiced in Mississippi, the overall life styles grew out of similar needs and experiences, and so produced
relatively similar defensive reactions and adjustive mechanisms.

acquires such understanding and makes the appropriate adjustments in his perceptions and his reactions in relation to the black man can the situation become a more positive and mutually rewarding one. Until this happens the black man will continue to express the frustration he experiences, as he discovers that his economic and social condition in the north is not much better than it was in the south, and realizes that northern people also regard him as "different" and "inferior," and are no more ready to accept him as an equal than the southern whites were.

Even though his condition in the north is very little better than what it was in the south, in the north the black man does enjoy a kind of freedom that he did not have in the south, a freedom that permits him to go anywhere he wants to go without question, a freedom that lets him stare at white women without fear of being lynched, the freedom to ride with white people in crowded subway trains and buses, conversing with white people and even arguing with them. This freedom to give verbal expression to his feelings, especially his angry, hostile feelings, constitutes one of the major differences between the black man's experiences, north and south. So he takes advantage of this opportunity to release his long pent-up anger; he gives voice to his frustrations with blasts against "whitey" and "honkeys," and at times angry words are supplemented with action. All this affords the black man momentary release from tension, but of course only increases the white man's negative perception of and angry response to him. Yet from whom was the black man supposed to have learned more constructive ways of coping with his feelings of injustice and outrage? From the police and the courts that, consciously or unconsciously, discriminate against him? or from the white man, north or south, who engages in many forms of lawlessness and often manifests a general disregard for anyone's rights but his own?

There are still other reasons why the traditions and the behaviors of the southern black people have importance. One is the unique psychological significance that the south, and Mississippi in particular, has for both black and white people. For the black people everywhere, regardless of where they were born and where they now reside, the south is perceived as a kind of homeland, the place from whence their elders came and where many of their relatives still live. Miserable though it may be, it is the place to go to, to learn about one's origins. as the hero says in "My Sweet Charlie." Mississippi especially stands as a symbol of the worst horrors of American slavery and subsequent pseudo-freedom. Consequently, what happens in Mississippi has very special meaning and importance for the black people, wherever they are currently living. Similarly,

for the white liberal and activist, the south, and again particularly Mississippi, represents all the prejudices and injustices against which he is
fighting. Contrariwise, for the southern white man, especially the segregationist and die-hard racist, Mississippi stands as a monument to a
treasured past and constitutes one of the last strongholds of the traditional
southern way of life; and so for the southern white man too, the area has
special importance.

Much of this book was written while I was still living in Mississippi
with the black people. At that time there were some questions in my
mind about the need to produce this material, for trying to convey to
others what I had learned from the black people about their experiences
and how these experiences led to the development of their particular life
styles. Re-entry into the urban world of the north quickly dispelled
any such doubts. Discussions with northern city people, liberal and well-
educated though they might be, soon revealed appalling gaps in their
knowledge of the black people and gross misconceptions regarding the
way the black people think and feel. No matter how a white man felt
about the black people, whether he was concerned for them, interested
in them, indifferent about them, or negative and hostile toward them, he
rarely had any real appreciation of the way the black man perceived his
world and why he reacted to his experiences as he did. Furthermore, the
white man's concepts in relation to the black people were almost never of
an objective order, but were almost always strongly colored by a variety
of emotions, positive or negative.

In addition to their emotional reactions, there are a number of other
factors that account for the limitations and distortions that characterize
the white man's concepts of the black people. One such factor, of course,
is our ethnocentricity, the tendency present in all of us to perceive and
evaluate others in terms of our own concepts, standards, and values.
Another factor is the custom employed by researchers, to point up the
differences that exist between the populations under investigation. As a
result, in studies dealing with black and white subjects, it is very often
the differences that are stressed, and although the findings are not always
discussed in such terms, the implication in many instances is that the
white way is the right way. So the black man's ways of performing, his
child-rearing practices, his familial and sexual patterns, his teaching
methods or whatever else it is that is being explored, are perceived as less
desirable than those of the white man, and indicative of some defect in the
black people and their mode of functioning. Even when the researcher
does not put it in such terms, there is always a reader who is likely to

make such an inference and quote the study to support his arguments.

Another factor that has resulted in misinformation and misunderstanding where the black people are concerned is the research methodology employed in most investigations. There is almost never any recognition on the part of the professional conducting the study that in exploring the life styles and customs of a given population his entry into the situation immediately alters it (page 199). When he gives a black man a test or asks him to respond to a questionnaire, when he interviews him or has him perform certain tasks in a laboratory, or when he observes his behavior under various conditions, at work, in school or in his own home, the subject's way of responding is inevitably different from what it would be if the investigator were not present. This is a factor that has to be taken into account in all human research, but is especially true in the case of the black people because of their sensitivity about their relationships with white people and their basic distrust of them. In many instances they are convinced that the research is just still another attempt on the part of the white man to derogate the black people, and even if they are persuaded that such is not the case, they feel that they are being used as subjects because they are perceived as "different."

A good example of the wrong kind of conclusion arrived at by white observers can be found in the myth that has been circulated and accepted by white professionals regarding the limited verbal interchange that characterizes the black communities. The individuals who report such findings clearly do not recognize that their presence, the intrusion of a white stranger into the home, the school, the workshop or the playground, accounts for what is called limited verbal output. When one lives with the black people for a considerable period of time and is accepted by them, it becomes very apparent that they talk a great deal, but are very likely to resort to meager utterances in the presence of unfamiliar white persons.

The inhibition of speech, so characteristic of the black people when in the presence of white strangers, is well illustrated by the experience of a young white woman who had taken part in the Selma march. When she arrived in Montgomery she was housed for the night with a black family. Exhausted by her experiences during the preceding days, she slept late and when she awoke it was almost noon. Yet she heard no voices, neither children's nor adult's. Subsequently she realized that because she was there, because there was a strange white woman in the area, the people in this crowded neighborhood were not permitting themselves to speak with the ease, the freedom, or the frequency that they ordinarily employed, even though her participation in the march made it obvious what her sentiments regarding the black people were. Nevertheless, the black people limited themselves to essential communications, delivered in low, barely audible tones.

Observers can always accumulate and report "facts" and there can rarely be any argument with facts as such. What is arguable is the way the facts are interpreted and the inferences that are drawn from them. An article in a recent issue of the *American Journal of Orthopsychiatry* provides an excellent example of the way in which "facts" can be presented in a prejudicial manner, that is, in a way that leads to wrong inferences and erroneous conclusions, largely because such facts are evaluated from the white man's point of view, rather than from the point of view of the black population that is being studied.

In this article Hunt* states that "when the children of the poor ask questions or vocalize their demands, their parents typically respond with 'shut up' without even saying why." This type of parental reaction is then offered as an explanation for the poor language skills and poor learning ability ascribed to black children. When the matter is left there, when no further statement about this practice is made, the reader is left with the impression that black parents are stupid, insensitive people who have no concern for or patience with their children. Telling black children to "hush" is actually a survival technique used for centuries by the black people of the rural south. Only if they and their children were quiet and deferential in the presence of the white man could they hope to stay alive. For generations the black people were convinced, and rightly so, that a careless word might well bring disaster to them and their entire family. Living in the midst of hostile whites, they constantly strove to teach their children the importance of being quiet in the presence of the white man. Black people have survived by *not* asking questions or encouraging their children to question or make demands. Only very recently, during the past decade, has the need for such docility and compliance begun to disappear in the south; and it is still safer for a southern black man to agree with a white man than to question him or argue with him. Stressing the parental behavior without giving the reason for such behavior casts a negative light on the parent-child relationship, whereas the interaction is actually of a positive, life-preserving order.

Child-rearing patterns that have been transmitted from one generation of black parents to the next cannot be changed in a few years, particularly

*Hunt, J. McV. Parent and Child Centers: Their Basis in the Behavioral and Educational Sciences. *Am. J. Orthopsychiat.*, 1971, Vol. 41, No. 1, January 1971, p. 22.

since many of the parents still believe that their children's lives depend upon the assumption of silent, docile forms of behavior. And families who have gone north and settled in northern cities have taken with them the traditions and the life styles that they learned from their parents. So in the north children are reared as their elders were, even though the restraints that are being imposed on the children, the admonitions to "be still" are no longer necessary for the maintenance of life. Nevertheless, even in the north, some black parents continue to program their children for the kind of adjustment they learned was most likely to provide them with a chance of staying alive, and for them keeping their children alive was and is far more important than the acquisition of verbal skills.

If the reasons why black people "hushed" their children and trained them not to question were better understood, if the attitudes and behaviors of the parents were recognized as part of the reality with which the black people have always had to live, and if the lack of trust that black people feel for white people, north and south, was recognized and accepted as a "fact," then perhaps some of the "remedial" and "helping" programs so much in vogue at this time might be restructured in terms of the black man's perceptions of the situation instead of those of the white educator and white psychologist. If for the sake of the children the practice of saying "shut up" without an accompanying explanation is to be changed, the first step should be one that seeks to develop trust and confidence in the parents where the white people are concerned, rather than focus on programs geared to enhance the verbal and cognitive skills of the black child. These latter efforts are often regarded with suspicion by the black community, no matter how friendly, involved and co-operative the people appear to be. Making an issue of learning when there are no jobs, no food, and life itself is precarious and threatened can only leave the black people with a deepened conviction that the white man does not understand them or their needs, and in most instances does not really care about their welfare. What is needed is a change in attitude and understanding on the part of the white population so that the black people will eventually learn to trust them and then will not feel it necessary to protect their children by training them to be still and unquestioning. As it is, much money is being poured into programs to train or re-train the black people. Where is the money to train the white people so that they will recognize the problems for what they are and then help meet them constructively, not in white but in black terms?

Even though a white person may have done nothing that can be described as an overt act of prejudice or harassment, the fact that the majority of white people have sat by and done nothing to change the condition of the black people accounts in good part for the latter's resentment and distrust of white people. Yet, as the situation stands at the moment, how many white people would really like the black child to begin asking questions, to wonder why he lives as he does when others live so much more comfortably, or why he is so often treated in unfriendly, even humiliating fashion? How many white people are ready to face such questioning and respond truthfully?

In attempting to describe the perceptions and behaviors of any group of people there is almost always a tendency to generalize. This is particularly likely to occur in discussing a population whose isolation from the mainstream of life, as practiced by the dominant group, and whose meager opportunities for learning about life styles other than their own, keep the people at a relatively uniform level of behavior. This is even more likely to occur when, as a result of the conditions imposed on them, a whole group of people has had to find and stay with modes of response that constitute almost the only way they can hope to remain alive. Such was the case for the southern black people, a condition that is only now and in a limited way, beginning to alter. Because of their circumstances and comparatively common modes of response, the white man has created certain stereotypes of the black man, and these stereotypes have been derived largely from unfriendly and ununderstanding perceptions of him. Yet among the black people, as among all people, there are definite individual differences, the same range of differences present in any population, in the intellectual, emotional, social and physiological areas.

The white man's perceptions of the black man, however, rarely take individual differences into account. His way of seeing the black people is very likely to be strongly influenced by what he has been taught about them, what he has heard others say about them, and what his general attitude toward anyone who is "different" is likely to be. Few white men are capable of maintaining an objective orientation in this regard. Thus there are some white people who consider the black man incapable of doing anything really well, while for others everything he does is just "right"; and of course there is every shade of opinion between these two extremes. Important in this connection is the way the white man experiences himself, his own self-image and his particular way of satisfying his emotional and status needs. And of course there are all the experiences that the white man has had with his fellow men, black and white.

Regardless of the factors that shaped the individual's final concept of the black man and determined the way he would react to him, consciously or unconsciously, shame and guilt have played a part. This is definitely so, even when such feelings are most vigorously denied. There is nothing wrong with feeling guilty and ashamed when such feelings are appropriate. What is harmful to both black and white is the neurotic response such feelings tend to elicit, and the consequent recourse to denial, aggression, defensiveness, or reaction formation. Unless guilt and shame become springboards for constructive interaction with the black community, they have no purpose.

In the psychological and psychoanalytic literature there is considerable discussion of shame and guilt, and efforts at defining the differences between these two concepts. There appears to be fairly general agreement that "guilt" derives primarily from thoughts and behaviors on the part of an individual that are not in accord with the values and standards he received from his parents and other authority figures, the concepts he has internalized. Guilt therefore can be seen as an internal or intrapsychic experience, the result of self-exposure or self-confrontation. "Shame," on the other hand, is the emotion experienced in response to criticism from the outside world, from exposure to others.

Individuals raised in this country have been instilled with the basic principles on which this nation was founded, namely that all men are equal, entitled to equal rights, equal opportunities, equal justice. Yet not a day goes by that we are not made aware via the newspapers, radio, and TV, that such is not the case. And so guilt takes over. Similarly, criticism is repeatedly leveled at us, both by our own citizens, at this time most particularly by the younger generation, and by people in other parts of the world. We are perceived as preaching one doctrine but practicing another. Hence our shame.

An individual's response to his feelings of guilt and shame depends in good part on the type of defense operations he has developed. There are those who rely heavily on denial and rationalization. These are the people who, in relation to the black issue, insist, "It isn't my problem," "I don't harm black people," "My ancestors weren't even in this country during the slavery period," or "I'm not prejudiced but what can I do?" Such reactions are in many ways frighteningly like the whinings of many of the German people following World War II. When they were asked why they had done nothing to stem the tide of Nazism, why they had made no effort to prevent the murder of six million Jews and three million other people, the response almost invariably was 'I didn't know what was happening" or "What could I do?" It seems that these Germans, and the Americans who use the same justifications in talking about the black people, have never heard, or having heard do not believe that if one is not part of the solution one is part of the problem.

Apparently for many white people in this country there is also no realization or no acceptance of the fact that *the problem is now*. It does not really matter where one's ancestors were more than a hundred years ago or who is responsible for what is so illogically called "the black problem" when it is really the white man's problem since it is he who created it and he who blocks efforts at positive solutions. So it is the responsibility of everyone living in this country today.

Carried to extremes, denial not only constitutes the way the white man divests himself of all responsibility for what has happened and still is happening to the black people, but the way in which he justifies what has been done to the black people, justifies all the hardships, the abuses, and degradation that have been heaped on the black man by the white man. What is actually being denied is that the black man is a human being. If he were, then according to the laws of humanity as well as the laws of the land, he would be entitled to the same treatment and the same opportunities accorded the white man. So the white man goes to almost any lengths to deny the black man's humanness. In some instances his efforts even involve violence and cause physical harm, while in other instances they are more subtle but equally destructive. In any case, underlying such reactions on the part of the white man is the need to deny his shame and guilt. If he can convince himself that the black man is inherently weak, inferior, lazy, and stupid, possessed of all the other negative qualities so often attributed to him, then the white man can perceive the black man as less than human and feel justified rather than guilty for treating him as he does. Of course this also means refusing to recognize that he, the white man, was and still is responsible for creating the conditions that have produced what is so often described as "different" and "unacceptable" behavior on the part of the black man. And along with this goes the denial of any responsibility for effecting constructive change in the black-white situation. On the whole what such white men want is for the black man to withdraw from his present stand and become once again the overtly quiet, unobtrusive worker that he once was.

Very different are the reactions of the people who experience their shame and guilt so keenly that they can only find relief by adopting a kind of breast beating attitude. So when they hear of an injustice or an atrocity perpetrated against a black person, they are immediately impelled "to do something, anything," to make up for the wrong that was committed. They are far too emotionally involved to recognize that it is impossible to "make up" for wrongs, past or present. There is no way to compensate thousands of black people, long dead, for the years they suffered in the cotton fields, for the beatings and lynchings they endured, for the heartless disruptions of families, with husbands and wives ruthlessly separated, and children torn away from parents. Neither is there any way to compensate black men today for the unequal opportunities, inadequate education, discrimination, and general degradation with which they have been forced to live. It is essential to move beyond shame and guilt and view the situation objectively and realistically for the purpose of preventing further tragedy and injustice. If this is not done, if the issues are not approached objectively, then harmful rather than constructive outcomes may well result.

The purpose of this discussion is not to criticize and certainly not to belittle the efforts of the many people who through the years, in a variety of ways and often at great risk to their own lives sought to alter the black man's condition. What is intended is twofold in nature: (1) to point out the damage that can result if efforts at resolving the black-white issue are not based on sound understanding and careful evaluation of possible outcomes of any proposed action, and (2) to help white people understand how distorted their concepts of the black people are, along with the hope that their sensitivity will be enhanced and their biases removed once they see the issues from the black man's point of view. The following stories are offered as examples of what can result when emotion rather than true understanding dictates behavior, as well as how unconscious prejudice determines the reactions of large numbers of people.

The first example is the story of Ben Chaney, brother of the murdered James Chaney, a Civil Rights worker. After his brother was killed in 1964 in Philadelphia, Mississippi by southern whites, many northern liberals, overwhelmed by shame and guilt, felt compelled to do something to atone in part at least for their sins of omission if not commission. Consequently, while he was still suffering acutely from the trauma of his brother's death, Ben Chaney was invited to come north and attend a large, mainly white private school. Thus he was removed from his familiar world and the way of life he had always known. His schoolmates now were practically all middle-class white children whose experiences, concepts and life styles were quite different from his. No amount of "kindness," no efforts at "understanding," were sufficient to help Ben bridge the gap that existed between the world he had known and the one in which he was living in the north. Bewilderment and culture shock were now superimposed on the already existing severe emotional shock he was suffering. It would have been little short of a miracle if he had achieved a good adjustment under such conditions or even been particularly "grateful" for what was being done for him. Instead, it seems very likely that the strangeness of his new life, the confusions produced by his associations with white people who reacted to him very differently than the southern whites had, who seemed to care about him and what happened to him, but who clearly did not really understand him, his feelings or his needs, all contributed to his subsequent behavior. He is now (1970) in prison in South Carolina, awaiting trial, charged with having participated in the murder of several white people.

The reactions of a northern white doctor who, for ideological reasons, was working in a southern rural health center, provide still another example of the harm that can result from an unthinking, overtly "liberal," "do-gooder" stance. One of the doctor's patients, a fifteen year old girl, had tried to commit suicide when she discovered she was pregnant. The girl was not married and the doctor indicated that she could well understand why the girl was so upset. As she put it, she did not "blame" the patient for being so miserable. Instead, she felt the girl would have been abnormal had she been less disturbed. Obviously the good doctor was evaluating the situation from her middle-class, white point of view. It was pointed out to this physician that being distraught because of an out-of-wedlock pregnancy might well be the reaction of middle-class white girls, might push them toward self-destructive behavior, but that for a number of reasons (Chapter 4) such was not the case with southern black girls. Large numbers of southern black teenagers become pregnant although they are not married, and neither they, their families, nor their community are disturbed by this. Certainly these pregnant black girls do not try to kill themselves. Therefore the reactions of this particular girl had to be regarded as a departure from the usual response of her group, had implications which required exploration and very possibly remediation. Yet all the doctor saw was an adolescent behaving as she herself would have behaved under similar circumstances. Her self-righteous response to those who tried to point out cultural differences to her was that she did not think of her patients as black or white but as "people."

This doctor's attitude and reactions are just as harmful and unscientific as those of the psychologists who assess black intelligence on the basis of test findings without giving any thought to relevant cultural factors (Chapter 5). Just as the test experts fail to recognize that test findings and the inferences drawn from them are invalid and meaningless because they fail to consider what the individual has been taught, what models he has had, what his experiences have been and what his goals are, so the doctor failed to appreciate that her patient's reactions had to be evaluated in terms of the customary reactions of her group and not in terms of some outside standard of behavior. Only then could any decision be made regarding the normality or abnormality of what she had done.

Still another incident, this time involving psychologists, highlights once again the well-meaning and well-educated liberal's inability to grasp the essence of the black issue and deal with it in objective rather than in highly emotional fashion. A few years ago, at an annual meeting of the American Psychological Association, I reported on a research being conducted in the Mississippi Delta. The study dealt with the relationship between nutrition and intellectual development, the subjects being black children under three years of age, living in that area (Chapter 5). Amazing as it may seem, this audience of highly trained specialists reacted to the report not in objective fashion, but as people strongly pushed by their emotions. There was not a single question about the substance or the methodology of the research. Instead, there were questions and suggestions like the following: "Why are you doing research?", "Give them land, houses and jobs and there will be no problems." The applause that greeted such remarks clearly conveyed the audience's affective response to the whole matter, along with an appalling ignorance about the true nature of the black issue. Certainly there is a desperate need for "land, houses, and jobs," and far too much time and money spent on research involving black populations (Chapter 11). But studies which do not focus on black-white differences, which do not invade black homes and intrude into the privacy of black families, but which concentrate on matters of health can prove beneficial to the population that is being studied.

Furthermore, there is the whole issue of "giving." "Giving" does not change basic conditions, but rather leaves the recipient in the position of the weak, the inept, the failure who has to be cared for by those who are strong, effective, and successful. Giving certainly does not help people cope constructively with their problems, but simply serves as a stop-gap to tide over unfortunates in time of crisis. Furthermore, much of the time, "giving" does more for the giver than for the recipient, more for the white man than for the black man. Through the act of giving the white man manages to reduce some of his guilt. Yet giving provides at best only temporary benefits for the black man. There actually are some small, scattered communities in the rural south where the people have been given land, houses, and occasional jobs. Yet the people living in such communities are beset with persistent monetary problems, periodically experience extreme hunger and severe health crises, and still depend heavily on welfare and whatever "gifts" are forthcoming from sympathetic white friends. Their sense of independence and self-reliance has not advanced very much under these conditions. This does not mean that there should never be any giving. Certainly the starving have to be fed and the naked clothed, but this type of response will never result in meaningful, lasting change. It has all the earmarks of charity and makes no appreciable dent in the *status quo*. What is needed obviously is the opportunity to do for oneself, not in a forced, make-work kind of situation but in the way that the white man works, at a level commensurate with ability and purpose.

Less impulsively moved by the stories of the injustices perpetrated against the black man, but still believing that they "understand the problem," are those individuals who regard themselves as liberal, but whose failure to comprehend the real issues causes them quickly to lose their liberal, concerned orientation when the black man begins to ask for privileges and rights that, without question, the white man has always regarded as his and his alone. He is "sympathetic" toward the black man just as long as the black man does not compete with him for a job, does not want to live next door to him or become a force in the community. Witness the dismay and the uproar evoked by the black man's call for black power. The creed of the white man might be stated as follows: "There shall be only one power in this land, white power."

An example of this attitude is the northern white man who, prior to the riots and other more assertive efforts at obtaining their rights, had spoken well of the black people and contributed in a small way to black organizations. However, as the black pressure for open housing, school integration, and job opportunities became more insistent he said, "You know if they keep this up they'll lose all their friends." By this of course he meant that he, and many others like him, would no longer feel sympathetic toward the black man and his cause. There was no realization on his part that the kind of "friendship" he had to offer, a friendship that existed only when the person who was being befriended reacted as his "benefactor" thought he should, had no value. He was quite amazed when the prejudiced, authoritarian nature of his attitude was pointed out to him. Yet he is one of a large group of white people who, though at least superficially well intentioned, nevertheless believes that a minority group should subordinate itself to the will of the dominant group and accept the attitudes, standards and values of that group, regardless of whether or not the expected behavior accords with the minority's needs and interests. Such a man, and hundreds like him, communicate their feelings of superiority and their perception of themselves as the final authority when they make such statements as "I like the black people and I want to help them, but I get turned off by those aggressive ones who keep pushing and making trouble." Such people not only refuse to see that "pushing" comes when the real issues are not recognized and responded to, but they are so sure of themselves and their position that they really believe if they do not like the way certain black people behave, the "black child" will be disturbed by the disapproval of white authority. On one occasion a white man with such a "superior," parental orientation was answered with the following statement: "I'm sure the black activists are upset because you don't like them. How you feel about them is of course so important to them, they probably stay awake at night worrying about what you think of them." For a moment at least this man recognized the absurdity of his attitude, and how meaningless his approval or disapproval were to people seeking to work out their destiny in an ununderstanding, hostile world.

Another incident points up the extent and nature of the blind spots that so many white people have, their complete unawareness of how they really regard the black people. In this case a well-educated white man was engaged in a conversation with a white woman who was trying to show him how prejudiced he was. His defense was, "I even have two boys working for me in my plant." Asked the age of the "boys," he indicated that they were in their thirties!

Finally, there are those who, while they insist that they are not prejudiced, are convinced and try to convince others that the black man's deplorable condition is all of his own making. They refuse to hear or see anything that might modify or alter their perceptions in this regard. To prove their point they cite the adjustments made by other groups, the Jews, the Irish, the Italians, the Chinese, and so on. They completely fail to recognize the differences in experience, background, and living conditions between the descendants of black slaves and white immigrants. The Jews, the Irish, the Italians, and all the other European and Oriental peoples who came to this country came voluntarily, with the hope of making a better life for themselves than the one they had had in the old country. Even those who came as indentured servants could look forward to a time when they and their children would be free and independent.

The black man did not come here with any such plans or hopes. He did not come of his own free will but was dragged here solely for the economic advantage of the white man. Although he had had a language and a culture of his own, he was abruptly cut off from these, and forced into a degrading way of life, a slave who was treated as less than human, regarded as incapable of learning any but the simplest concepts, and lacking the skills and the maturity that would enable him to assume responsibility. So he was treated like a child, sometimes with kindness, often with harshness; and when the black man reacted as the white man wanted him to, namely like a child, his behavior was then used as evidence of his ineptness. In fact the situation was so structured that it was impossible for the black man to win. If he tried to prove that he was adequate he was perceived as an "uppity nigger" and flogged unmercifully until such ideas had been beaten out of him; and if he accepted the role that was assigned to him he was then a "stupid, lazy nigger."

In evaluating white attitudes toward the black people, one more fact must be brought into the picture, namely the negative reaction that so many people have toward anyone who looks or acts "differently," and particularly anyone with dark skin and kinky hair. For this reason, as well as for all the others cited above, it should be obvious that any comparison of the black man with the typical white immigrant is meaningless.

The attitudes and reactions discussed here are the ones most likely to be found among northern whites as they seek to deny or justify their prejudices. Among the southern whites the perceptions of the black people and the opinions they have of them, how they regard their behavior, are of a somewhat different order. The southern concepts are particularly important for an understanding of the black people since it was among the southern whites that the majority of the black people lived, at least until recently. So to a large extent their life styles grew out of their experiences with the southern communities and constituted their response to the way in which they perceived and understood the white people of that area.

Among the southern whites, as among the northern whites, there are actually a variety of reactions to the black people. There are first of all the "gentle," educated southerners whose image of themselves would not permit them deliberately to harm a black man, physically or psychologically. Yet these are the people who were and still are largely responsible for the black man's condition. This is so not only because their ancestors were the slave owners, but because of the way they and their ancestors treated the black man. Far more important than the physical labor, the punishments, and even the lack of freedom to which the black people were subjected by these southern gentlemen and ladies was their insistence on the black man's childishness and inadequacy and consequent inability to care for himself. By their kindly, patronizing manner they frequently were able to convince the black people that what was being done to them was for their own good. Hence the black man was conditioned to become and remain dependent upon the white man; and as part of this dependence he felt compelled to present a happy, smiling face to his white master, to appear satisfied when he was anything but satisfied, to say what he did not want to say and what he did not really believe; in other words, to give up his real self or at least hide it behind a bowing, obsequious manner. What is more, most southern white men still expect the black people to respond in this manner. It was and is in this way that the black man's self-respect and self-confidence have been steadily undermined.* The white point of view was well expressed by a southern white woman, a university graduate, who stated, "We have an arrangement with our Negroes. We know what they need and what is best for them, and they in turn know what we expect of them and how they must act." When it was pointed out to her that the "arrangement" seemed to be an excellent one as far as the white community was concerned, but hardly so for the black people, judging by the way they lived, their shabby homes, their high rate of infant mortality, poor nutrition, inadequate education, etc., she was very much taken aback and insisted, as all white southerners do, that northern whites simply do not understand the black people. Because the southern white has lived all his life surrounded by black people he is convinced that he really knows them, and it is this knowledge that constitutes his justification for his treatment of them, trying as he does in every way possible to keep them from maturing, from becoming men and women rather than remaining forever "boys" and "girls."

The educated southern white man's way of dealing with the black people is an extremely subtle but effective way of keeping people in bondage without having to resort to force. It is much harder to recognize and defend oneself against harmful, prejudiced, and hostile attitudes when they are expressed in the indirect manner employed by the upper-class southern whites than to recognize and defend oneself against direct, open expressions of anger, contempt, and hostility. Consequently, many black people did not really appreciate what was being done to them and therefore did not try to protect themselves against the harm caused by this insidious, damaging treatment. Not only did the southern whites do everything they could to convince the black people of their inadequacy

---

*The fact that current events are proving that the southern whites were far less successful in destroying the black people psychologically than they thought they were in no way exonerates them from the shame and guilt of their behavior, of what they tried to achieve.

and dependency, but they constantly reinforced such efforts by denying them any opportunities for learning about better ways of life or for acquiring the skills that would enable them to improve their condition. As part of this effort schooling was limited, inadequate or totally lacking, medical care meager and generally of a substandard order, economic opportunities non-existent, etc.

Although the southern white man has constantly protested that his behavior in regard to the black people was prompted by his genuine concern for them and their well-being, any number of instances can be cited that reveal the insincerity of these claims. For example, when machinery was introduced into the cotton fields and thousands of black workers were no longer needed to carry on the work that enabled them to stay alive, very few plantation owners made any effort to help the people who now had no form of livelihood. They were generally permitted to remain in the shacks that had long been their homes, since these shacks were now also without use or purpose, but beyond this, little if any attempt was made to see that these people also had food, clothing, and other essentials. No longer necessary to the economic welfare of the white man, the black man was simply written off as a burden to be dropped at the first possible opportunity rather than as a "child" to be cared for; and among many plantation owners the hope was openly expressed that the black people would be compelled to leave the rural area and go to the city, preferably to northern cities, and in this way "solve" the black problem in the south.

Again, when Head Start was first introduced into the rural south, large numbers of plantation owners did everything they could to prevent black parents from sending their children to the Head Start schools. Apparently they feared that the children and their parents would be encouraged to think, possibly taught to read, and as a result of such "stirring up" become less tractable than they had been. Certainly the fact that the federal government and northern whites were concerned about them and interested in them might alter the image they had so long had of themselves and thus make them less passive and conforming than they had been. Consequently, in many instances, men who had jobs on plantations or who were employed as truck drivers for white men were threatened with loss of employment if they permitted their children to attend the new schools. Similarly, women who worked in white homes were advised to withdraw their children from these schools. In some instances the local whites went so far as to burn crosses in front of the homes of black families who worked for Head Start or had children attending the Head

Start school; and the small black churches in which the schools were located were sometimes destroyed by fire.

Despite these direct and indirect attacks on the black communities the southern whites are able to convince themselves that, all their hardships and deprivations not withstanding, the black people were happy. They cited the smiling faces, the ready laughter, the easy acquiescence with anything that was suggested to them, and the singing in the cotton fields as evidence of this "happiness." They could not and would not recognize that such behavior was defensive in nature and that behind the seemingly happy, agreeable facade lay much sadness, depression and hostility.

The southern whites delude themselves in yet another way, namely in their belief that the black people actually "love" them. They see nothing contradictory or absurd in this assumption, and when any mention is made of the deep underlying resentment that is the natural reaction of people who have been treated as the black people have, they look pained and incredulous. They certainly have no appreciation of the relationship between fear on the one hand and anger and hate on the other. They simply do not want to recognize that it would be both irrational and impossible for the black people to love them. Actually they cannot afford to believe this since it would shatter their image of themselves as good, Christian people and would also destroy the sense of security they have constructed for themselves on the basis of their belief in this "love."

As for the southerners who do not even pretend to be positively disposed toward the black people, the story is too well known to require repetition. In general it is the poor whites, the "rednecks" who are accused of treating the black man with violence. Yet there are certainly some among the so-called better classes, the educated and professional people, who also harbor deep hostility toward the black man and who find ways of venting this. Even the clergy has contributed their share to the racism that is so rampant in the south. Their message stated that if God had wanted the black man to be like the white man he would have made him white. Since He didn't, it is obvious that the black man is inferior to the white man and must therefore be treated accordingly.

So in the south where the black customs have their origins, there are two very different groups of people, one black, one white, each living to a very large extent in an unrealistic world and in terms of "false" selves. As far as the white people are concerned they try to convince themselves that the black man is an inadequate child who needs the support and guidance of the white man, and also that he is so ineffectual that he can be easily whipped in line if such action becomes necessary. Basically however there were always white men who did not really believe in the impotence of the black people and they certainly are no longer convinced of this, in view of what is taking place among the black people, north and south, to-day. Recognizing how he would feel had he been subjected for centuries to the abuses the black man has endured, the white man is coming to realize that the black man must also be filled with rage and hate. So the white man lives in fear of retribution, and in response to this fear seeks to impose, or have the government impose, ever stronger controlling and repressive measures.

The black people too have lived lives in which reality and unreality have been strangely co-mingled. In many instances and for long periods of time, if the white boss was at all kind, the black man also resorted to denial and tried to convince himself that his life was a reasonably good one, even though his common sense indicated that by any but black plantation standards it was not. However, no opportunities to live in any other way were available to him and so he complied with the demands of the white world. So the black people, like the white people, have lived two different lives, one a reaction to the realities of their world, an adjust-ment to white demands, the other meaningful but deeply denied and repressed, or daringly released in extreme privacy.

On the whole the black man's perceptions were more in line with the way things really were than were the white man's. Many black men, de-spite their conforming facade, had no illusions about what was being done to them nor how they felt in response to such happenings. For the white man on the other hand, it was essential that he maintain the fiction of his own superiority and of the "love" that the black man felt for him. If he could not continue to think and believe this way, how could he feel secure and maintain an acceptable image of himself?

Encouraged by much that is taking place in the world today—by the spirit and strength of their leaders, the legislation that has resulted from their efforts at establishing their rights, their successes at the polls, etc.—the outlook and attitudes of the black people is definitely changing (Chapters 10 and 11). In many instances resignation and despair are yield-ing to assertive and confident attitudes, as the black people work to secure a better kind of life for themselves and their children. With this change in attitude the black man is experiencing an increasing sense of disillusion-ment and loss of faith in the "liberal" white man. This disenchantment with liberals comes in part from the black man's realization that many white men, while well intentioned, really do not appreciate what the black man is experiencing and what his needs truly are, and in part from the attitude of some liberals who are turned off when they cannot make decisions about what is best for the black communities and when the black people are not "grateful" for what the white man is doing for him. Surely the liberal who has worked with the black people should recognize that the current effort on the part of black communities to run their own programs, to do it themselves, is a sign of growth, reflects the acquisition of self-confidence and independence; and they should be glad that this has happened, that their earlier efforts may in some way have helped this to happen.

The plan of this book is as follows: the first and by far the longer half is devoted to descriptions and examples of the way in which the southern rural black people were compelled to live from the period following Reconstruction until well past the middle of the twentieth century; and the way that, despite all the efforts that have been made and all the legislation that has been passed, some of them are still living. What is emphasized in this presentation is primarily the effect that such conditions, such pseudo-freedom, has had on the black man's emotional, social and intellectual life and on his adjustive patterns. These patterns and his general life style are contrasted in each instance with those of the middle-class white community because that is the group that determines the norms and establishes the models that constitute the "American way of life." It is to this "way of life" and not those of the poor white that the black man is expected to adjust even though very little in his experience has prepared him for this. The second half of the book explores the impact that today's economic and political changes are having on the perceptions and life styles of the southern rural black man, and finally what the recent automation of the cotton growing industry has done to the southern black man's way of life and what his migration to the cities is doing to him and the total black community.

# CHAPTER 2

# *Reality — Black and White*

In this country, composed as it is of people from many different ethnic and national backgrounds, there are naturally a variety of life styles and varying ways of responding to specific life experiences. Yet despite these differences there has developed a culture that, as noted above, is identified as the "American way of life." Basic to this culture are such concepts as universal education, equal opportunities, the importance of achieving, and the emphasis on "getting ahead." Implicit in all this is the assumption that, afforded the blessings and opportunities provided by a democracy, failure to attain success must be regarded as indicative of some inherent defect, some lack of intelligence or character. Certainly there are many who insist that since the goal of the educational and socialization processes in this country has been to "upgrade" all people, recent arrivals as well as long established residents, failure to adapt to the American way of life, failure to achieve, must be the fault of the individual, not of the system.

At one time the process of adapting was described as a blending together of different racial and national groups into one "melting pot." By means of this "melting," the unique aspects of each group were fused with those of every other group, thus producing one cohesive mass, one unitary culture, made up of but different from the separate ingredients that comprised it. More recently such terms as "salad" or "clam chowder" are thought to be more accurate descriptions of what actually occurs in this country in relation to "American culture." According to this notion, each group retains certain distinct features of its own, yet adds its flavor or spice to the final product. In the end, therefore there are certain concepts and modes of response considered to be typically American and held by all Americans, while at the same time each individual preserves certain aspects of his own particular subculture.

Over and above the concepts inherent in the American way of life or those characteristic of different national or religious groups, there are certain concepts common to all people. Primary among these is the importance of life, and the belief that life is better than death, survival preferable to annihilation. Yet while there is agreement on the need for survival, the means of achieving this vary considerably from group to group, and what may be regarded as an effective way of insuring survival in one society may be considered most ineffective, unacceptable, and inappropriate in another.

In the countries or cultures that are termed "developed" or "civilized" the idea of sheer physical survival is usually not very much in awareness or likely to constitute a cause for great concern.* Rather than sheer physical survival, the struggles in which a nation is involved take the form of power contests in which prestige and wealth, as symbols of power, are the sought-for prizes, the spoils of victory. Yet such struggles are basically struggles for survival, with each nation, each industry, and each individual competing against other nations, industries, and individuals. Such is the reality that "advanced" societies have come to accept, and in such societies the unforgivable sin is to stop struggling, to fail to move ahead and acquire ever greater strength and importance; or even worse, to lose what has already been acquired.

To attain, hold and enhance the position that he is expected to occupy, a member of a developed society is trained in the basic skills of commerce, industry, or a chosen profession. Such an individual is almost always a member of the white community and from the middle class. However, in this country it is by no means impossible for a lower-class white man or a blue-collar worker to move up the ladder, to acquire wealth and power, and so become a force in his community, provided he accepts and adheres to the "realities" that are considered typically American. Certainly this country's history and folklore abound with tales of "poor white" Americans who "made it," who even became Presidents of the United States. The realities to which one was expected to subscribe in order to enhance one's position consisted largely of a belief in the benefits that result from education, hard work, diligent study, and adherence to the law of the

---

*With the proliferation of atomic weapons and the marked increase in individual violence, especially in urban areas, this statement is probably less valid than it might once have been.

land. Each child was assured that such traits and the behavior that derives from such traits would pay off, in fact were all that was needed to win out, to "get ahead" in this world.*

The theme song for the white man was "getting ahead," achieving industrially, financially, politically, socially, scholastically, whatever his chosen field might be. Consequently every one involved in the child's training stressed this point of view. To this end, ambition, competition, initiative, daring and even ruthlessness were perceived as necessary and even desirable attributes. The competitive, junglelike nature of the world into which the young white American was expected to take his place and make a name for himself is well communicated in the saying "All is fair in love and war" and becomes particularly appropriate if one adds "and business." While Americans by and large have a certain respect for education and for cultural achievements, real success and the attainment of status and power are almost always measured in economic, financial, and political terms.

In order for the white person to function as he was expected to in a highly technical society he had to learn certain important rules, and recognize and abide by certain constructs other than those taught him in his early school days, other than those that have been described as the "sterling virtues." For example, he had to understand the importance of "contacts," the benefits that come from knowing "the right people." In this connection as in many others, there were rules to be followed and limits to be observed, while at the same time manifesting a capacity for flexibility and initiative. It was also necessary for the ambitious white man to drive himself unsparingly at certain times and under certain conditions, and while so doing to forego immediate pleasure and gain for the sake of greater reward in the future. Very early in life the white person marked for "success" was also impressed with the importance of the concept of time and the significant part that time would play in his struggles to get ahead. So in his early years he was taught that it was important not to waste time. He also learned the need for punctuality, and many other concepts associated with the matter of time. Similarly, he was impressed with the need to plan and organize his activities, and in this connection, time as well as many other attitudes and attributes were brought into the picture.

For the black man in this country, and especially the black man in the

---

*During the past decade many individuals, young people in particular, have rebelled against this whole orientation and tried to "debunk" what they regard as myths.

rural south, the realities he had to face and to which he had to adjust were of a totally different order. None of the concepts that were so important to the white man and that were such potent forces as far as much of his behavior was concerned, had any meaning or relevance for the black man. In fact his world was so different from the white man's that they might have been living on different planets. Unlike the white man, for the black man it was not a case of "getting ahead," of acquiring wealth and power, but simply a matter of staying alive, a question of sheer physical survival.

Brought to this country in chains, sick and frightened by everything that had happened to him during the dreadful voyage across the ocean, confronted by strange people whose language was incomprehensible and whose way of life was completely alien to him, brutally treated when he was not totally compliant, the black man entertained no thoughts of getting ahead, had no dreams of affluence or power. All he could hope for in view of the conditions in which he found himself was to remain alive, and he quickly learned that this was possible only if he subordinated himself completely to the white master and at all times did exactly what was required of him. Everything that he saw and heard in this new world to which he had been dragged served to impress him with his helplessness and the tenuous nature of his very existence. So he had to adapt to the conditions set up for him by the white man and these were certainly not geared to his best interests.

There was no area of importance in the white world that the black man was permitted to enter or in which he might partake except as a menial. As has already been indicated, economically he was almost always restricted to field work and in order to hold onto even this lowly job he had to submit to the serf-like conditions of the plantation system. In return for the privilege of living in a miserable little shack, euphemistically called a "plantation house," and receiving incredibly low wages, the black man and his family were expected to work in the fields from sun-up to sun-down during those periods of the year when cotton had to be planted, chopped, and picked. At other times he could only remain idle.

The nature of the house to which the black man and his family were assigned was certainly not calculated to provide him with any feeling of importance or worth. All these houses or homes were very much alike, poorly built and affording only limited protection from the elements. The houses generally consisted of two, three, and sometimes four rooms, yet they often housed as many as six or eight people, sometimes even more. In addition to the immediate members of a family, the parents and their children, there often was a grandmother or an aunt with her children, or some other relative with little ones. Sometimes a neighbor who had been burned out or who had been thrown off the plantation for some reason or other, was also housed with her entire family until she could find a new home.

Some of the houses had an iron stove in the middle, some did not. Even when there was a stove the wind was very likely to come in through the chinks and the cracks and quickly dissipate the heat. Some of the houses had the luxury of a wood burning stove for cooking, others only an open fireplace. There were even a few families who had to cook outdoors. Some houses had wooden floors, others just earthen floors. Bugs, mice, rats, and snakes shared the premises. Indoor plumbing was unheard of, and water for every purpose had to be obtained from a roadside ditch or a neighbor who was fortunate enough to have a well. Riding around the back roads of the rural south even today it is not at all unusual to come across very young children, as young as five or six, staggering down the road with heavy buckets filled with water that they obtained from a neighbor as far away as half a mile. Outhouses were the rule, but in some instances even these were lacking, and then the fields and the bushes substituted for any kind of toilet facility.

The kitchen was likely to be the focal point of the house, while the remaining rooms were generally crowded with large double beds. The children, and sometimes even the adults slept crosswise in the beds so that four or five people could be accommodated in a bed meant for two. These crowded conditions, plus paper thin walls, precluded any chance of privacy. Instead, every aspect of life, even the most intimate moments, were open to public hearing and public view. Privacy is so much a part of the white middle-class way of life that it is taken for granted by the people who make decisions about life styles, economic policy, education, and many other important matters. Yet it is not a privilege that everybody enjoys and its absence has an effect on the concepts and behaviors of those who almost never have the opportunity to be alone. Such individuals know no time of real quiet, have no chance to meditate or to do anything without an audience, and, never really feel or experience themselves physically and emotionally separate from others. On an obvious, concrete level this lack of any experience with privacy probably accounts for the behavior of the women who now come to the newly established health centers of the rural south in search of medical care. When these women use the toilets, they almost never close the doors of the cubicles in which they are sitting, and as people walk in and out of the lavatory they are not at all surprised, embarrassed or disturbed by this intrusion. They seldom remember to flush the toilets since flush toilets are certainly not part of their experience.

The entire set-up has been described over and over by fiction writers, sociologists, and anthropologists, and others. Pictures of the miserable housing to which the black people were assigned have appeared in newspapers, magazines, and on TV. For many people they have an unreal quality, like something a movie producer might dream up. But for the black people they were no dream but a grim reality, the only home they ever knew or had any hope of knowing, the place where they were born, lived, loved, and died. These shacks were often right across the road from the white man's house or at least visible to him from his windows or veranda. The fact that he could day after day, contemplate these hovels and yet do nothing to improve the condition of his workers and relieve the hardships that such living conditions imposed, once again speaks loudly and clearly of the southern white man's concepts of and feelings toward the black people. For him they were less than human, for if this were not so, he could not possibly have permitted them to live in circumstances to which he would not have subjected a valued animal.

It might be asked whether the people living in city slums are better off than the people living in "plantation houses." One answer to the question appeared on a recent TV show. A black mother had come north and settled herself and her family in a condemned building in a large city. When she was discovered and asked why she had come to the city her answer was that she wanted to improve her condition. Asked if she thought she had achieved this, her reply was an affirmative one.

Just as the white man could see the shacks in which the black people lived, so the black people could see the mansion in which the white man resided. To assume that the people accepted this state of affairs without question or resentment is taxing credibility to its limits. It is possible that the middle aged and old people had lived with this situation so long that they no longer were conscious of it or gave it any thought. It was just there and had to be accepted as so many other situations had to be accepted. But surely there was a time when they were young that they must have wondered why they had to work as hard as they did and yet live as they did, while the white people were enjoying leisure and comfort. However, when the children or the young people wondered out loud they were promptly hushed by their elders since such questioning could only bring serious trouble to the questioner and his family.

Educationally the black man was denied any opportunities that might have enabled him to evaluate what was happening to him and then devise ways of defeating the white man's schemes of exploitation. Adequate schooling might very well cause him to begin to see himself as a person with the same rights that the white man enjoyed, and he might even try to enforce his rights. This would certainly upset the system that the white man had so carefully devised for his own advantage. For the white man in the south the important thing was the preservation of the "arrangement" that had been developed with the black people. If the *status quo* that was so satisfactory to the white man was to be maintained it was essential that the black man be kept ignorant and illiterate, lest he learn something that might give him "ideas." What the white man tried to do, and unfortunately was often successful in doing, was to keep the black man in the condition of an uneducated, dependent child. Good schooling was therefore out of the question. During the period of slavery, teaching a slave to read or write was a serious crime, punishable by law, and when slavery was abolished the black man was given the most inadequate kind of education imaginable. In some states in the south there are still no compulsory education laws, and there are black children in those states who have never set foot in a schoolroom. Where education is required by law the difference between the educational facilities provided the black and white children (Chapter 6), the difference in the amounts spent on the children of the two races, tells its own story. The southern white man has justified his treatment of the black man as far as education is concerned by insisting that the schools were separate but equal, while at the same time indicating by everything he does that he does not want to educate the black child, that from his point of view doing so is a waste of time and money, and contrary to his, the white man's, best interests.

As long as the black "child," and child he was no matter how old he grew to be, did as he was told, as long as he behaved as the white man wanted him to behave, as long as he shuffled and smiled and agreed with everything that was said to him, regardless of what he really thought and felt, he had a reasonably good chance of avoiding abuse and harm; but any move on his part to act otherwise, any suggestion that he might even be considering some form of assertive behavior, any hint that he might try to change the way of life set up for him by the white people or that he might in any way at all seek to fulfill himself, would immediately elicit punishment in the form of bodily harm, economic reprisal or both. So the black man had no choice but to conform and this included accepting the highly inferior education offered his children.

The illiterate condition in which the southern black people were kept was a particularly exquisite form of deprivation. There is a subtlety about this kind of treatment that makes it virtually impossible to defend yourself against it. When a man is hungry his body tells him so and he can make some efforts to alter this condition. But unless he has had some intellectual stimulation at some period in his life, a person does not even realize that his mind is being starved and that he is being seriously deprived of the opportunity to grow and achieve his potentialities. All the pleasure and fulfillment that come from intellectual activity, from the emergence and development of ideas, from sharing in the thoughts, feelings and experiences of others, were a closed book as far as the southern black man was concerned, and so no tradition of learning could possibly develop in the black community.

Unschooled as he was, the black man was also unaware of his legal rights. He knew little if anything about these, and even when he did, such knowledge was of no value to him. He had no chance of exercising his rights as a citizen, no chance of winning a case against a white man in a southern court of law. Certainly he had no redress when a white man harmed or offended him, when he was cheated out of his hard earned wages, when he was arbitrarily turned out of his house, or when a white man raped his wife or daughter. While he was subjected to all kinds of rigid and unreasonable rules and regulations by the white man and was severely punished when he did not scrupulously follow these, he had no recourse when the white man broke the law or offended him in any way. Whatever mistreatment and injustice he suffered had to be born in silence, for there was no place to which he could turn, no authority that would deal fairly with him. And yet, given such conditions, people are surprised that many black men, once freed of the southern yoke, do not believe in justice and have little respect for law and order!

Conditioned by what happened to them and their elders and by the fact that even today a black man has little chance in court if the opposing party is white, southern black men driving cars tend to proceed with extreme caution. For example, when a black man in the south comes to an intersection, even though he has the right of way, he will stop and let the white man who is facing the *STOP* sign go through first. He does this from habit and because he knows full well that should there be an accident without the slightest question the blame would be his, even though he had been proceeding according to the law.

In the political world the black man had no place whatsoever. Except for a few years during the Reconstruction period and more recently as the result of federal legislation, the black man in the south has not exercised his constitutional rights, has not dared to register and vote. Even today in parts of the south it takes daring and courage on the part of a black citizen to appear at the polls, and all kinds of obstacles are likely to be placed in the path of the black man who attempts to cast his ballot.

Socially the black man had no standing except in his own community with his own people. The interaction that took place between the black man and the white community was one which consistently emphasized his role as a servant and the white man as the undisputed master. To this end he was always addressed by his first name, never as "Mister" or "Missus," no matter how old the black person might be or what position of respect he or she held in the black community. Recently, while paying my gas bill in a small town in Mississippi, I heard one of the clerks addressing a black man as "Sam." Turning, I saw that "Sam" was an elderly man, a preacher, and one of the few comparatively wealthy black men in the area.* Neither his age nor the fact that he was a man of God made any impression on the young white gum-chewing clerk to whom he was paying his bill. From the white community's point of view to react in any other way to a black person was out of the question. It was unheard of for a black man to be considered a real friend or a guest in a white man's home. His entrance to the white man's house was always through the back or side door. As a result, even today when black people come to a medical center set up by the federal government and intended for the care of sick indigent people in the area, many black people search around and ask for the back entrance, never dreaming that the front door is open to them.

Whether the black man worked on the plantation for wages or more recently in some instances as a share cropper, the situation was much the same. The plantation worker usually received a house, rent free, and wages for the months during which he worked, that is during the planting chopping, and picking seasons. During the winter months there was nothing for him to do, no way to earn money, and since he did not earn very much even when he and his whole family did work, he had no money put aside. So during the winter months there were times when he came very close to starvation. Generally, under such conditions the plantation owner helped the worker out, but the "loans" he gave him were usually charged against him and deducted from his earnings the next spring. Hence it was extremely difficult for a worker to get ahead or have any

---

*After the Civil War a small number of ex-slaves had moved into an uninhabited swamp-like area in the Mississippi Delta. They drained the land and farmed it and their descendants are economically comfortable today.

ready cash. If the plantation owner did not help out the black family, then the only recourse was welfare and food stamps.

The share cropper planted and harvested not as a wage earner, but as a farmer working for himself. However, he worked on land and with seed provided by the white man. So after the cotton was picked, ginned, and sold he had to share his profits with the white land owner. In many instances lack of education made it impossible for the share cropper to keep adequate accounts. As a result, many a black share cropper found himself ending up in debt to the white man rather than with a profit, despite all the backbreaking work he had put into the fields.

There was a very pathetic story in the Negro Digest a few years ago dealing with the experiences of a share cropper and his family. The daughter of this share cropper was a very alert little girl who did particularly well in arithmetic. She kept a careful record of the money expended by the land owner and a record of the money that came in when the cotton crop was sold. According to her figures, several hundred dollars were due her father. Yet when the white man came to settle with the father he so twisted the accounts that in the end the black man was in his debt. From that time on, the little girl stopped going to school, stopped studying arithmetic, for what good had her learning done her or her family? Many a share cropper, unable to free himself from the "debts" that the white man insists he has accumulated, has stolen away with his family during the night, rather than remain forever tied to the white man and the cotton fields.

Such then was the reality that the black man had to meet, namely his helplessness in the face of the white man who was in the dominant position and who used that position and the power it gave him to acquire almost complete control over his hapless victims. In fact, on the southern plantations he carried such efforts to the point where the black man was not really perceived as a human being, with the same rights as every other human being in a democratic society. Instead, he was regarded as an object to be used for the convenience and the profit of the man for whom he labored. What the white man wanted was a worker who applied himself diligently to his task, who made no demands, expected no rewards, and raised no problems, In order to create such an automaton out of human flesh and blood he tried to destroy the black man's humanness, particularly his self-confidence, his self-respect, and his hope.

Given such conditions, the black man had to develop his own adjustive techniques. He could not avoid the serf-like role into which the white man pushed him, because he had to work to live. But as subsequent events have indicated, he did not give up many important aspects of his human-ness, particularly his feelings for others, his hope for the future of his race, and with all an amazing degree of self-confidence and self-respect. What he did do was present himself to the white man as a compliant, cheerful, docile, and not too bright individual, doing what he was told, and striving to humor and please the white man in order to avoid his anger. Such behaviors became the way of life for the southern black people, their major survival technique, the one that was transmitted from genera-tion to generation. In view of the particular circumstances in which he was trapped, the black man's mode of adjustment, his recourse to docility and passivity rather than self-assertion and aggression, was at that particular time in his history the only way he could stay alive. To do otherwise, to offer offense or resistance to the white community, either as a slave or later as a type of serf, would have been extremely foolhardy on the part of the black man. He had no arms, no weapons other than farm tools, and even in areas where he outnumbered the whites, any success he might attain in a struggle with them would have been shortlived, since the armed forces of the government would soon be sent against him. In fact, any such effort might very well end in genocide.

Efforts at escape during the time of slavery involved great risks, with severe punishment and sometimes even death the possible outcomes. More recently of course, the black man was free to leave the plantation, but his lack of education and of the skills that would enable him to find a good job in today's technological society, as well as the prejudices he encountered everywhere, did not hold out a very promising economic future for him when he did move away from the land. So for generations, actually until very recently when the introduction of machinery into the cotton fields left him without any work (Chapter 10), the black man has been economically dependent upon the landed gentry of the south. It was essential that he have employment as a field hand and such employment carried with it his acceptance of a docile, subservient role, not very different from the one his ancestors had been forced to adopt as slaves. This state of affairs naturally colored the black man's perception of himself, his world and his place in that world, and correspondingly enabled the white man to convince many of the black people that they really could not survive without his, the white man's, support and guidance. Thus large numbers of the black people were brainwashed, although the extent of the brainwashing varied from community to community and individual to individual. The variations that existed between the attitudes and feelings of the black people residing on different plantations were caused in part by the attitude of the plantation owner and his manager and in part by the individual black men.

For one reason or another, some black men and women were not easily convinced of their dependency and helplessness, and their attitude and ideas in this regard certainly affected the attitudes and behavior of all the black people on a particular plantation. Again, some of the white overlords were relatively kind and considerate, others were definitely not so. As has already been indicated, (page 19) in the long run, kindness can be as detrimental and even more detrimental to the development of the "self," than harsh behavior, since it is likely to keep the individual in a dependent position rather than motivating him to seek to assert himself. In any event, no amount of kindness, no "giving" on the part of the overseer or anyone else could serve as compensation or make amends for the callous destruction of self-respect and dignity that the whole system was intended to effect. To be nursed and fed by the owner's wife might tide a black family over a bad moment, but it could only leave the recipients of such largess with enhanced feelings of inadequacy, dependency, and helplessness. Although there were and still are times when such help is necessary, it certainly never does anything to better basic conditions, but only serves to compound the damage that the whole system produces. As long as the white man maintains the role of the giver and by so doing places himself in the position of a superior being capable of doling out those things that are essential for the maintenance of life itself while the black man remains the helpless recipient of such "goodness," the picture stays essentially unchanged.

The circumstances being what they were, it is obvious that none of the qualities and life styles so important to the white man, such traits as ambition, initiative, and competitiveness, were relevant in the case of the black man. In fact, rather than having relevance and value for him, in his case their adoption would most probably have exposed him to the anger and hostility of the white community. So all such feelings and impulses had to be stifled. Indeed, in order to stay alive the black man was compelled to repress and deny the strivings that every person experiences in his search for a full and satisfying way of life. As part of his adjustment he learned very early in his life to give up any thought of living in a materially comfortable fashion. Even more important was the absence of any possibility that he might be free to live and act as he wanted to, and little opportunity to give free expression to what he really felt and thought — in other words, for the black man there was little chance to be truly free. Instead, he had to forego all such satisfactions and fulfillments, present or future. This was a very different kind of sacrifice or postponement of pleasure from that which the white man made when he gave up certain immediate pleasures or satisfactions because he believed that in the long run such "sacrifices" would pay off in the form of ultimate enhanced returns. The things the black man was denied and that he had to deny himself, the things he dared not do or even permit himself to think about, would never be his no matter how many sacrifices he made. His sacrifices were made solely in the interest of staying alive. Were he to do otherwise, were he to assert himself and seek for a better way of life, were he to act or try to act as a white man did, his fate and that of his family would be definitely sealed. So it was utterly futile for him to think about or plan for the future. His future had already been determined for him by others, a future that would in no way be different from his unsatisfactory past.

Any number of investigators have reported on the black man's failure to delay immediate gratification for the sake of future advantages. Thus, one psychologist* states that "the degraded poor are rooted in the present and indifferent to the future." And again, the same author says, "Until more direct evidence is reported, the conclusion seems warranted that participants in the subculture of poverty are unwilling or unable to defer to, or plan for, the future." Again as in the instance cited in the previous chapter (page 12), as well as many others, no statement regarding the reasons why some people are unable to learn to defer pleasure are ever offered. In this particular case the inference might well be made that it is their failure to exercise control and plan for the future that accounts for the impoverished circumstances in which some groups are "rooted." Yet the truth of the matter is often quite different. When there is no future, what possible reason can there be for denying oneself immediate gratification on the rare occasions when this becomes available? Delay for delay's sake certainly has no meaning. A person can only think and plan in terms of future benefits when such benefits truly exist, when they are *real*. Consequently, if the attitude of the black people and all other people who live in poverty is to be changed, if they are to learn about the benefits of delay of present satisfaction for the sake of future pleasures, then the entire system has to be changed so that the anticipated satisfaction is worth waiting for. Furthermore, they have to believe that this satisfaction will really be theirs, that it is not just something dangled before them like the carrot in front of the rabbit's nose.

*Sarbin, T. The Culture of Poverty, Social Identity, and Cognitive Outcomes. Chapter in *Psychological Factors in Poverty*, Vernen Allen (Ed.). Markham Publishing Co., Chicago, 1970.

Certainly the history of the black people in this country has been one which has not led them to believe that there would be any advantage for them if they did not seize whatever immediate pleasure was available to them. Denied most satisfactions, while abused and repressed in all kinds of ways, always at the mercy of the white man, the black man did not have the comfort of imagining a better way of life for himself, and so he did not think or plan very much in terms of his future. Every victim of misfortune, or hard times, every prisoner, dreams of and hopes for a brighter future, looks forward to the day when his sentence will have been served, or his luck will have turned. But for the black man in the rural south such hopes were futile. Few of them had the money which would enable them to go elsewhere, and their ignorance concerning the way people lived and functioned in other parts of the world rendered such a prospect extremely hazardous. A man had to be truly desperate to consider such an under-taking. So until automation appeared on the scene and forced the people to look elsewhere for a chance to earn a livelihood, they stayed on the plantations, resigned to their misery. As one black author put it, the worst thing that the white man had done to the black man was rob him of his dreams. To live without dreams or hope is the first long step toward utter defeat. One begins by giving up the dreams, and after a time one no longer knows what to dream about or even how to dream. This is one of the greatest tragedies that can befall any people.

When any group of people, for whatever reasons, ethnic, religious, economic, etc., is prevented from sharing in the life of the dominant or in-group, then such people inevitably develop perceptions and concepts that are quite different from those of the in-group. With such differences there go different customs and different life styles. Inevitably under such circumstances the way the deprived and rejected people perceive them-selves and think of themselves is markedly conditioned by what they are experiencing. The end result of such a state of affairs is the development of a reality, a culture and a tradition quite apart from the prevailing one.

This of course is what occurred in the black communities. While each individual's perceptions and adjustment were unique, as a group there was emphasis on passivity and compliance, along with self-hatred and hatred of other blacks because of the position into which they had been thrust. This hatred was also of course directed against the white man but had to be vigorously denied and repressed. So, much of the time every black man was playing a part, was an actor filling a role that in no way corresponded to his true feelings. Only by recourse to repression, denial, and role playing were the black people able to survive. These life styles that had their origins in the rural south have an effect on the way black people all over the country perceive, think, and respond. There was nothing innate or predetermined about the behaviors that the black people developed. Had the circumstances been different, had they been free to shape their lives in terms of their own needs and desires without external interference, their reactions would certainly have been different. They made the type of adjustment that, under their particular circumstances afforded them the best chance for physical survival. In this respect at least they shared a reality held by all people. The important fact in all this is that they recognized the nature of their reality as opposed to the white man's, and then made their adaptation and survived, despite all the hardships, deprivations and humiliations, the inadequate shelter and malnutrition that often led to serious illness, chronic ill health and death, as a race they survived.

The details of each man's adjustment naturally differ somewhat from those of his neighbor. Each person has his own uniquely personal experiences and his private world which help or hinder him in his adjustive efforts. But regardless of such differences there was among the black people a will to live* despite the miserable state to which they were relegated by the white man. It was this determination to live that also enabled them to maintain the repression and the control, or at least the appearance of control, that was essential for their survival. In fact, they were so successful in controlling and disguising how they really felt that the majority of the southern white people still do not appreciate the extent of the anger that the black people have for them.

The southern white people's inability to recognize the black man's anger is of course part of their defense system. They too resort to denial and the extent to which this operates keeps them from perceiving the black-white relationships as they truly are. The distorted way in which they view the matter until it can no longer be denied is well illustrated by the reactions of the members of the staff of a southern white college. Primarily in order to receive federal funds the college had admitted a small number of black students. On one occasion these students staged a protest and sent a dozen demands to the President of the school. The demands were actually quite reasonable, one being that the staff and the students refrain from calling them "nigger." In addition to the formulation of their demands, the black students stood as a group on the college campus and sang freedom songs. The protest was certainly a very mild

*In this connection it is interesting to note that the suicide rate among the black people of the rural south is very low, much lower than among the white people. In fact, very few black people take their own lives.

one. As one white northerner put it, "Harvard and Columbia would have been delighted to have had such a protest rather than what they actually experienced." Nevertheless the staff of the college were very much shocked and dismayed, not so much by the protests and the demands as by what they finally recognized as the intense anger and hatred that the black students had for all white people.

While some white people perceive and accept the anger and hatred of the black people, regarding it as the logical response to the many severe deprivations they have endured, others are made fearful and angry by the negative emotions they perceive among the black people. However, even many of the white people who recognize and accept the anger are unable to appreciate and understand that the intense resentment that the black man feels stems largely from the fact that he is not truly free, that people who have little or no power while living among people who do wield power cannot be really free. The way the black people experience themselves is well expressed by Bessie in *Native Son* when she describes herself as being possessed by "the feeling of being forever commanded by others so that thinking and feeling for oneself was impossible."* In some instances this need to deny and repress what one really felt was only a kind of surface conformity, but in other instances it was so strong and far reaching that it produced severe personality impoverishment. This is one reason why, when tests like the Rorschach and the Thematic Apperception test are given to certain black people, it is impossible for them to give expression to any dreams or fantasies despite the opportunity to do so with safety.

When the repression and control that the black man exercised were simply a kind of surface behavior intended to convince the white man that he was passive and compliant he had to exercise an inordinate amount of effort, judgment and mental agility. He also had to act as though he was satisfied, possibly even happy, in his humble role. Because he had learned so early and so well (Chapter 3) what was required of him, the black man was very adept at responding as he was expected to respond, anticipating just what the white man expected even before any orders were issued or any conversation initiated. This ability to "read" the white man, to know what he was going to say even before he said it, was still another important survival technique employed by the black people. Like the prisoners in the Nazi concentration camps, there was a better chance to survive if one "identified" with the enemy. For the black population it was a most

*Wright, R. *Native Son*. Harper & Bros., New York, 1940.

necessary and valuable mechanism, and the black people became so skilled in its use that it led an educated northern black man to observe, "You ought to give every southern black person a Ph.D. in psychology because they are so good at understanding the white man."

Yet there were times when the black man's inner tensions became so strong that denial and repression no longer served. At such times relief was likely to be sought through withdrawal into sleep or recourse to alcohol. Sleep provided a respite from unbearable reality, from humiliating self-concepts, and from the unrelenting emptiness and tediousness of his days. The same held true for alcohol. At least while he was "under the influence" he could be oblivious to the incredible nature of his life circumstances.

Sleep and alcohol did not always provide the answers. Instead, there were occasions when the frustrations he was compelled to endure and the hatred he felt for the white man became so intense that they could no longer be contained. However, in most such instances the black man's rage was likely to be directed back against himself or against those like himself, his relatives and neighbors, rather than against the white man who was the logical target for his anger. There were several reasons why the black man behaved in what seemed an irrational fashion. For one thing, the black man was angry with himself and with other black people for allowing themselves to be treated as they were. Furthermore, if in his outburst the black man retained any sense of reality and self-preservation, he knew that the penalty for attacking a black man was never as severe as for attacking a white one. To assault a black man, even to kill him, probably would result in a number of years in prison, whereas laying a finger on a white man might well lead to a lynching.

Dreary, frustrating and deprived as his life was, there were some aspects of the black man's reality that were of a genuinely positive order. One of the most important of these was the relationship that obtained between the people who lived together on the same plantation. There was a co-operative spirit among these plantation dwellers that stood in marked contrast to the aggression and competitiveness that prevailed among the white people. For the black people one man's good experience was everyone's good experience, just as one man's disaster was a disaster for all the black people. Neighbors cared for their neighbors in times of stress, illness, childbirth and death; and shared in rejoicings when there was cause for happiness.

As part of this co-operative spirit, neighbors could be relied on to act in protective fashion. A good example of the way in which this protective system worked is provided by the following incident. A white man went to the black neighborhood of a small southern town to tell a black resident that he had some work for him. The black man had actually applied for this work and was anxious to have the job. The white man approached a group of black men talking together in the road and asked if anyone could tell him where Mr. Jones lived. The black men looked innocently at one another, shook their heads and insisted that they had never heard of Mr. Jones. Then the white man went to a nearby house, knocked on the door and asked the woman who responded to his summons if she could tell him where he might find Mr. Jones. She too protested that she had never heard of Mr. Jones. At this point it began to dawn on the white man what was really happening. He therefore said to the woman, "Well, if you see him tell him the job is waiting for him and ask him to report for work at eight o'clock tomorrow morning." With this the woman broke into a smile and exclaimed, "Oh, you mean Mr. Jones. I'se Mrs. Jones. I'll tell him."

Similar indications of the deep distrust and fear that the black people have for the white people, and their efforts at protecting one another from the common enemy, can be learned from some of the events that took place in the deep south during the early days of Head Start. As was noted above (page 24), Head Start was most unpopular with the white communities at that time, and there was real danger for the families and the children who had the temerity to avail themselves of this opportunity. Consequently, mothers who sent their little children to Head Start often did so with fear and misgiving. As a result, when a white person appeared in a black neighborhood and asked the location of the local Head Start he was regarded with deep distrust. But the schools were not easy to find because most of them were located in little churches attended solely by black people, and these churches were on small dirt roads, well off the beaten track. So when a white person, man or woman, asked a black person where the school was the questioner was likely to be met with a puzzled look and an attitude that implied that the person being questioned had never even heard of Head Start. Still other black people, with smiling faces and every indication of affability and a desire to be helpful, gave directions which landed the white person in the opposite end of town from where the school was actually located.

Given the grim realities with which they had to cope, the black people devised any number of "games" by means of which they hoped to outwit the white man. However, for the black man these were not games but a matter of life and death. When they were able to win out in such a contest, when they could get the better of a white person and not be caught and punished, they experienced some small satisfaction, some meager compensation for all the humiliations they had suffered. And of course such triumphs were always shared with the neighbors, just as the defeats, the sorrows, and the dangers were.

In addition to the co-operative and protective attitude that prevailed on the plantations, there was the church which was a source of great comfort to these down-trodden black people. In fact, for large numbers of them religion and the church were their chief solace, the rock to which they clung and from which they gained the strength to carry on. Faith in the Lord and the conviction that they would find their reward in heaven sustained many of these people. For them the Biblical miracles, the stories of Daniel and Joshua, and the escape from Egyptian bondage, were beacons of hope in their dark night.

The church also played an important part in the social life of the black plantation people. It was the place where they gathered for any meetings they might have, for whatever affairs they could arrange. Sometimes they held a singing festival, sometimes a visiting preacher might give a talk. Black people from several different plantations might attend the same church, and so church attendance provided an opportunity to visit with friends and relatives who were not seen during the week, and a way of learning about happenings in neighboring areas.

For the black plantation people the church served still another important function. It was practically the only place where a black man could attain a position of importance and dignity, the only place where he could acquire some prestige, as a preacher, a deacon, an usher, a choir member,

Because of its importance to them, church attendance among the southern rural black people was very good. It was not only the adults who came to church, but also small children and even infants. As part of their custom of taking the children with them wherever they went (page 55), whole families from the very youngest to the very oldest, came to church together. Consequently, scattered among the singing and praying adults were many small children and babies. Most of them sat fairly quietly and were reasonably still; but occasionally a few kept moving about, walking or running up and down the aisles. No one was disturbed by this or paid too much attention to the young ones unless they became too noisy. When this happened a child would be scolded and settled down in a pew, at least for a time. Even the crying of an infant rarely annoyed the worshipers or distracted them from what the preacher was saying or from the hymn they were singing.

For the middle-class white church goer who is accustomed to a great deal of decorum in the conduct of the church service what goes on in the black church is likely to be experienced as a surprise, even a shock. Yet the activities of the black church are in many respects far more in accord with the basic teachings of all religions, far more real and meaningful, than the formal type of service that takes place in a white church. In its own way, the activity that characterizes black church service expresses the true meaning of religion and worship, where all people of all ages come together, unhampered by artificial, conventional barriers. Here among the black people of the rural south the current emphasis on "praying together" has long been in existence, and for the child as well as for the adult the church was a warm, welcoming place to which everyone went willingly and happily.

No discussion of the rural black people in the south, or for that matter of black people anywhere, would be complete without mentioning their humor and their capacity for enjoying simple little pleasures. These too were part of their efforts to cope with the realities they had to face. Most peoples can, and, up to a point, do laugh at themselves and poke fun at themselves. There are no jokes quite like the jokes that people with a common ethnic background tell to one another. And certainly some of our best white comedians have attained their fame by deriding certain of their personality traits. Where would Jack Benny be if he could not make an issue of his "stinginess" or Jackie Gleason without his self-importance? To laugh at oneself when all is well, when one is in control of one's life and fortunes, is an easy thing to do. Under such conditions one can be quite comfortable in recognizing and exploiting one's shortcomings and inappropriate, even ludicrous reactions. To be able to do this when one is the victim rather than the master of the situation, when one has been placed in an incredibly low, denigrated, and hazardous position for centuries, when one lacks all the material and psychological supports that make life bearable, takes rare courage and ability. Yet the black man's humor is famous. One might well speculate that his sense of humor, his faith in prayer and in the hereafter, his co-operative relations, his flexibility, and the joy with which he greeted every new life, have been among the forces that have kept the black man going, that have enabled him to survive.

Here then are a people who chose life. In order to survive, they had to make adaptations that in practically all respects were very different from those of the prevailing society. Instead of being helped to adjust or permitted to work their way into the dominant culture as was the case with other "outside" groups, with immigrants from other countries, the black people were deliberately, consistently, and forcefully excluded. It follows then that their view of the world and their life styles had to be different from those of the white man. In a certain sense the black people are the Pygmalions that the white people created or at least tried to mold to fit their interests. In so doing they completely ignored the needs and feelings, the human aspects of the people with whom they were dealing. Given such conditions there are actually only two possible outcomes. Either the oppressed group submits and eventually dies out as a people, or the group devises ways of surviving. It is the best endowed members of a minority group, those with the greatest physical and mental strength, who, through the exercise of their assets, endure. It is such individuals, with their own unique traditions and culture that the white man is currently trying to absorb into the American way of life. But the culture that the black people have developed, like the culture of all peoples, must be recognized and respected as is the case with other minority groups. If this is not done then conflict and a host of problems that seemingly defy solutions are likely to result.

# CHAPTER 3

# *Child-rearing Practices*

Every group seeks to train its young in ways they hope will produce the type of adults who will fit into and perpetuate the society developed by their forbears. If parents, teachers, clergymen, law enforcement officers, and other authority figures are successful in such efforts then the continued existence of the culture is assured. However, the goals of each society, the way these goals are attained and the manner in which training is implemented vary considerably.

From everything that was said in the preceding chapter it is obvious that the needs and goals of the southern rural black people and those of the dominant white group had little in common other than the determination of each to survive. Consequently, as might be expected, their methods of dealing with their young differed markedly. This difference was further aggravated by the deprived and isolated condition of the rural black people. They were totally unaware that there was such a discipline as child development and that there were theories regarding the ways in which a child should be raised, that there were, for example, studies dealing with the advantages of reward as opposed to punishment. Similarly, they did not know that there were norms indicating how a child should react at a given age, and so on. Neither had they heard of such concepts as "self-fulfillment" and "the development of a healthy personality." Even if they had had such knowledge there was nothing they could do to bring their child-rearing practices in line with these formulations. The middle-class white mother might worry about these matters, might be concerned as to whether or not she was coping constructively with her child, but the black mother was preoccupied with the need to defend her child against the aggression and hostility of the white community while at the same time earning enough to buy food and keep a roof over the heads of her offspring.

Instead of "self-realization" or "actualization," instead of opportunities for varied kinds of experiences and for learning about the world through freedom to move about and make contact with many different objects and different people, the black child was early in his life subjected to severe controls and restrictions. Once he was no longer a helpless infant the emphasis was on inhibition, on "no" rather than "yes," in contrast to the openness and the encouragement provided the white child as he pursued his exploratory activities. Almost the only thing that the black child shared with the white child was the early experiences of acceptance and love. No matter how many children were already in the home and how economically deprived the family was, the arrival of a new life was always a happy event, a cause for rejoicing and celebrating. The child was welcomed and deeply loved, not only by his own immediate family, but by all the people on the plantation and in the area.

During the early weeks and months of his life the strongly positive feeling that his people had for him communicated itself to the infant both through verbal expressions of love and through much body contact. He was likely to be talked to, held, touched, and handled by all the members of the extended family into which he was born. As the child grew older and began to move about and explore his environment, as he started to assert himself, the love that his people felt for him expressed itself in a very different way. To insure his survival and teach him how he had to live if he were to survive, those intrusted with his upbringing sought to impress him at all times with the importance of behaving in docile, conforming fashion, and also of being very much aware of the distinction between black and white. Training for these two purposes took precedence over everything else the child might be taught. As a result, very early in life he was able to differentiate between black and white with amazing accuracy. His proficiency in this respect is particularly well illustrated by his handling of one of the test items on the Stanford Binet Intelligence Scale. At the three and a half year level, the child is presented with ten black and ten white buttons, identical in every respect except color. He is instructed to put all the black buttons in one box and all the white buttons in another box. Through the years I have given this test to untold numbers of children, black and white. Regardless of how young he was or how retarded in other respects he might be, the black child was always able to carry out this assignment correctly. Among the white children, on the other hand, there were the anticipated number of failures. Furthermore, when red and blue buttons of a similar type were substituted for the black and white ones the black children also showed the expected number of failures.

How does one tell a small child that although he is prized and loved by his own people, there are forces in the outside world that definitely do not love him and would harm and destroy him should he offend them in the slightest degree? To an extent every child has to learn about harm and danger. Every child, for example, has to be impressed with the hazards of traffic. Some dangers are learned without any warning from the environment. Thus a child who puts his hand on a hot stove quickly comes to recognize the stove as his "enemy." However, the child soon understands that the stove, the traffic, and all the other misfortunes of such a nature are not directed against him personally, that he has not been singled out as the victim of their attack. What the traffic and the hot stove can do to him will also be done to everyone else who comes in contact with such objects and forces. By contrast, the harm that can and does come to the black child from the white world is not a natural happening, not the result of color blind physical forces, but a personally directed attack, the outgrowth of the warped and bigoted nature of the white man's concepts about black people. Hence the black child has to be taught that this danger exists and how he can best defend himself against it.

In the main the teaching consisted of impressing on the child that he had little worth, and to this end he was constantly "cut down." So he was frequently told to "hush," and much that he said was likely to be ignored altogether or responded to with ridicule or criticism rather than with understanding, encouragement, and praise. Likewise, he was constantly being told how "bad," "worthless," and "nothing" he was. By such means it was hoped that the child would learn to deny and repress many of his thoughts, ambitions, drives, and feelings, and so come to accept the role prescribed for him by the white community.

All of this is of course totally at odds with today's concepts of good child-rearing practices. Theoretically a mother should build up her child's confidence and self-esteem, and reinforce the desired forms of behavior by praise and encouragement. Among the families of the black plantation people just the opposite approach prevailed. To have dealt with the black plantation child by praising him and encouraging him to assert himself and explore his world would have made it impossible for him to interact with the white community as he was required to. His behavior would have been perceived by the white people as highly unacceptable, as "uppity," and could therefore very easily spell disaster for himself and his entire family. To avoid such a tragedy the child's training for survival was carried out and constantly reinforced with punishments, among which "whuppings" were prominent. The whippings were generally administered with a switch, sometimes even with the cord of an electric fixture or a clothes hanger. Even the youngest children recognized and responded to the threats of such punishment. For instance, while administering the Gesell Developmental Scales to a seven month old boy he did what most children his age do, he started to carry one of the test objects to his mouth. When this happened his mother who was holding him on her lap quickly raised her hand in a threatening manner and in an angry tone of voice said, "You put that in your mouth and I'll whup you." The child froze with his arm in mid-air and then slowly put the object down. Whether it was the mother's gesture, her angry voice or the word "whup," it was apparent that even at seven months the concept of punishment and fear of punishment had already been learned and were powerful forces in the child's life.

There were almost no limits to the parents' efforts to make the child understand that he had to do whatever the white man expected of him. The behavior of a mother of a four year old who was resisting a white doctor who was attempting to draw blood from his finger is a case in point. The child kept screaming and trying to break away from the doctor. Instead of comforting and reassuring him, the mother sharply upbraided the little boy, and when her verbal admonitions and threats of punishment had no effect, she walked to the door of the building where all this was taking place, broke off a small branch from a bush growing right at the door, and came back waving the switch menacingly at the child. If there was at that moment any realization on her part that what he needed was reassurance and love, not anger and punishment, she could not permit herself to recognize and express such feelings since they would interfere with her efforts to make the child understand that, above all else, he had to do what the white man required of him.

Much of the repressive, punitive behavior that the parents employed in dealing with their children was not the result of any conscious thought or careful consideration on their part as to why they were acting as they did. Mothers did not deliberately remind themselves that the child's survival depended on the assumption of a compliant attitude toward the white community and that it was their duty to train the child so that he would learn and accept such a role. It seems likely that many of the mothers were not really aware of the history that lay behind their child-rearing methods. Instead, they simply accepted and followed the patterns that had been transmitted to them by their mothers, patterns that had been in force for centuries. This was done without question and sometimes without any appreciation of the reasons for their importance.

In addition to the traditional approach practiced by the black plantation people in dealing with their children, there were also the usual typical reactions of parents the world over. Overburdened and deprived people need a target for their anger and frustration and the child certainly is at times the victim of the adult's despair even when he has done little if anything to elicit punishment. Black parents were no different in this respect from any other parents. They too were harassed, tired human beings who at times used the child as an outlet for pent-up feelings.

Any number of incidents can be cited to illustrate the harsh nature of the training to which the southern black child was subjected, and there can be very little doubt that in the majority of cases the lesson was well learned. To give just one example: In a rural health center, federally funded and used almost exclusively by the local black people, there is a playroom where the children stay while their parents or older siblings are being seen by a physician. On one occasion a small white girl was also left in this room. She was the child of one of the physicians who worked in the center, and for some reason her mother could not care for her that day. Being an only child and a spoiled one, she assumed that every toy in the room was hers. So she spent much of her time grabbing toys away from the other children and holding onto them as tightly as she could, apparently anticipating that the other children would try to get them back. Yet such was not the case. As she seized toy after toy from the little black boys and girls, she met with absolutely no resistance. The black children took just one look at the little blond vixen and, remembering everything that had been drilled into them regarding their behavior with white people, they sadly but unhesitatingly relinquished whatever they had been playing with. Similarly, the black lady in charge of the playroom made no attempt to stop the little white girl, although she certainly did so on those rare occasions when a black child tended to act in the same aggressive or assertive fashion.

The significance of this exaggerated emphasis on repression and control even in the very young children, what it did to their entire outlook on life and to their self-concepts and their potential for growth and learning, cannot be too strongly emphasized. While every human being certainly has to make compromises and sacrifices, has to learn to do without things he very much wants, and accept frustration, for the middle-class white child this rarely occurred so early in life or reached the irrational extremes that it did for the southern black child. Eventually this kind of experience and the internalized anger that results can only lead to the development of a depressive character, and depression was and still is widespread among the southern blacks, the smiling faces and ready laughter notwithstanding (Chapter 7).

Because of the punitive manner with which the black mother often responded to her child, many white people have found it difficult to understand why the black child did not feel resentful and hostile toward her. Yet such was rarely the case. There are a number of reasons why love rather than anger characterized the feelings of the young people for their elders. For one thing, there was the warmth and love that the child enjoyed in the early months of his life, developing in him a reciprocal positive feeling for the people around him. Then there was the universality of the child-rearing practices, the fact that all plantation children were treated in the same way. Consequently, even when he was harshly treated the child did not see himself as being discriminated against, and had no concept of any other form of mother-child relationship.

In this connection it is also important to realize that the entire culture was geared toward the old people. What the old people said and did was right and accepted as such by the young people with little or no questioning or protesting no matter what they thought or felt. In a sense, what prevailed among the black people living on plantations was very similar to the child-rearing practices that existed among white people during the Victorian era, except that instead of a stern, controlling *pater familias* there was usually a stern, controlling *mater familias*. All of this of course was once again very different from what occurred in middle-class white homes where the focus was definitely on the young people and the children. In the southern black culture infinite consideration and love were given to the elders. Everything was done to spare the old people anxiety, hurt and aggravation, to the extent that this was possible. The love and devotion that black men and women have for their mothers was and still is one of the most important and touching aspects of black family life. Even those black men who escape the south almost invariably come back to visit their mothers during vacations or at holiday time; and in the summer the back roads of the rural south are crowded with cars bearing New York, California, and Illinois license plates, all driven by black people coming home.

The fact that the southern black people always included the child in the family's councils and activities, whether they were just routine matters or special events such as birth, weddings, funerals, or church services, etc. was very probably another reason why the relationship between the generations was of such a close order. Wherever the grown-ups went the child also went; and although much of what the child said was not heeded, and even if he was spoken to in a harsh manner, he was always one of the group, he "belonged," and so never felt excluded, unwanted, or alone. He was never told to "leave the table" or "go to your room," techniques very much in vogue in middle-class white families. Likewise he was never left home with a babysitter while his parents were off on some jaunt or other, visiting, attending theater, etc. So the child did not come to see himself as different from the adults who were important to him, a feeling that develops early in the white child and is constantly reinforced by the parental attitudes and activity. For the same reason the black child rarely experienced the anxiety so many white children suffer when they wonder what will become of them "if mommy and daddy go away" or "if mommy and daddy die."

Although the training to which he was subjected taught the black child how to adjust to life on a southern plantation, how to get along and avoid trouble in a white world, it certainly did not provide him with all the food he needed for his physical well-being, did not give him shoes and warm clothing in winter, or enable his people to buy him toys and books. So his life was materially very much restricted and it did not take the black child very long to realize that the many frustrations he was experiencing, the many satisfactions he was denied, and even the harsh treatment to which he was subjected, were caused by the demands of the white man rather than reflections of what his own people really felt for him or wanted for him. Consequently, the black child soon learned to fear, distrust, and hate white people while at the same time recognizing that such emotions had to be kept under strict control, and attitudes of deference and seemingly positive feeling offered in their place.

While every child has to struggle with contradictory experiences and as a result has very conflicting concepts of himself and his world, in the case of the southern black child, these conflicts were of a more extreme order than is normally the case. Loved by his own people and feeling that he had value in their eyes, yet scorned and denied fulfillment by the white community, the black child could not help being confused, even bewildered about himself (Chapter 8). Hence much of his energy was absorbed in efforts at ignoring or repressing this conflict or in trying to reconcile the opposing images of himself that were generated by this state of affairs.

Because of the way his life was arranged for him, because ironclad rules governed the way he was expected to behave, what he had to do and what he dared not do, the black child had very little opportunity to try out different modes of response. There was relatively little chance for him to grow as a result of trial and error learning, little opportunity to test out new ideas or to implement dreams and turn them into realities. Actually, dreaming as a way of preparing and planning for the future, as a constructive force in his life, was another of the "forbiddens" as far as the black child was concerned. In fact, dreaming was strongly discouraged, since dreaming of any kind, and particularly dreams of achievement, power and status, might very easily result in a disruption of the controlled, conforming adjustment the child was required to make. So there was no tolerance for dreams or for the tall tales children love to tell as they try to win attention and make themselves important. Plantation children who engaged in such fantasies and dreams were promptly told by whatever adult was within earshot to "stop talking such nonsense or else . . . ."

For the child as for the adult the probability of escape from the future determined for him by others, namely escape from the cotton fields, was very slim indeed. His labor was what the white man needed and wanted and this was therefore what the black child had to accept. Even if by some miracle he did get away — and some few actually did — he would still find only low order jobs waiting for him, and he would still be treated as an inferior, still regarded as a "boy." Several years ago a black man who had escaped and had received his medical education at one of the better northern medical schools and who today is a professor at an outstanding medical school in the north was walking in the street in Jackson, Mississippi. Two local policemen spotted him as a black stranger, carrying himself with dignity and assurance; so they stopped him and asked him to identify himself. He showed them his papers and after studying them one policeman turned to the other, roared with laughter and said, "Hey John, what do you know, this *boy* is a doctor!"

Since all the children on the plantation were reared under very similar conditions and relegated to the same uninspiring future, there was very little competition among the black children, just as there was little competition among the adults. This absence of any strong effort to "get ahead" and achieve, to do better than one's fellow, is one of the aspects of the southern black culture that puzzles those who do not understand the reasons for this non-competitive atmosphere. As one white northern woman commented, "These people aren't aggressive enough." Others, among them the southern whites, are inclined to ascribe this lack of a competitive spirit to shiftlessness and laziness. None of these people realize or allow themselves to realize that a more assertive, forceful attitude on the part of the black people would not only have been meaningless but disastrous. Nevertheless, they criticize the black people for acting as the white community has forced them to act. Compelled to play a passive, docile role and seeing nothing ahead of them but an unrewarding future, any competitiveness, any play for achievement or power, would have been most inappropriate as well as dangerous. This lack of drive and ambition that was and still is ascribed to the black people is simply the natural consequences of the conditions under which they have been forced to live. The resulting attitude of the blacks was very well communicated by an eight year old girl who was being urged to work harder at her school work, especially her reading. Her response was, "What for we gotta learn to read? We only gonna pick cotton."

There were a number of other respects in which the child-rearing practices of the southern rural black people differed sharply from those of middle-class white families. As already noted, black mothers were not aware that child-rearing was a special area that highly trained professionals had carefully researched, and that as a result of such studies there were certain formulations regarding the treatment of children that were considered especially important in terms of their future adjustment. For example, the significance attached by some white mothers to such matters as toilet training and eating habits were of no importance whatsoever to the black mothers. In the white community toilet training was regarded as one of the important ways through which the child learns to exercise control and delay gratification. In the black community control and a lifetime's delay of many forms of gratification were learned in other ways very early in the child's life. It follows then that toilet training was not stressed and was established gradually through imitative behavior. As the children ran around together on the plantation the younger ones learned from the older ones how, where, and when to indulge their excretory needs.

The eating practices of the southern black people were also quite different from those of middle-class white people. The family seldom sat down together for a meal, partly because of the different work schedules each followed. The father might be in the fields or driving a truck, the mother working in some white woman's kitchen, and the siblings caring for neighbors' children. Furthermore, in many homes there was no table and certainly not enough chairs or enough room for everyone to sit down at the same time. Instead, there was usually a pot on the stove with some food that was being kept warm, and each member of the family came and helped himself as time and hunger dictated. Little children were fed by the older ones when they cried or when the older ones ate; and after the first few months of life they ate pretty much what the adults did, since for financial reasons there were only a few foods available, mainly beans, potatoes, and corn bread. And unless a child became markedly thin and sick, little fuss was made about what he did or did not eat.

Concern about and emphasis on the acquisition of verbal facility was, in certain respects, still another way in which the training of southern black and middle-class white children differed. Both the black and white mothers spent time talking to and playing with their children, despite the myth that has been circulated by professional white people, namely that black mothers do not talk to their children and do not play with them. This myth has actually gained such acceptance that a number of programs have been initiated and considerable money expended in order to teach black mothers how to talk to and interact with their children. People who make the assumption that black mothers do not talk to their children and do not know how to play with them have surely never lived for any length of time in the black communities. It is again an instance of not realizing that black people do not talk very much to their children or to anybody else when there are white strangers present. No matter how relaxed they may seem, no matter how natural their behavior appears to be, it is not the behavior they would engage in if outsiders were not around.

Black mothers certainly do talk to their babies with the same spontaneity and the same feelings of love that characterize the reactions of the middle-class white mother or any other mother for that matter. And as she talks to him she encourages him to respond, something that he generally does, first with excited motor reactions and a smile, and gradually with attempts at vocalization. Kagan* states that "computation of the percentage of time the mother vocalized to the infant, regardless of what else she was doing, or where she was in the house, disclosed only a slight and non-significant tendency for upper-middle-class mothers to vocalize more often than lower- or middle-class mothers to their daughters. There were even less striking differences for sons." He then goes on to point out that although the amount of verbalization that takes place between a black mother and her child may be the same as what occurs between a white mother and her child, there is one important difference, namely that because of the constant noise that prevails in the small crowded living quarters of the black people, the black child actually

*Kagan, J. In "The Child," *Saturday Review*, December 17, 1968, p. 82.

"lies in a sea of sound; like the sea the sound is homogeneous. Hence the child does not learn to distinguish the various auditory stimuli to which he is exposed." This type of situation has been reported by others.*

Still another difference between the verbal activities of black and white mothers lies in the fact that, although the white mother certainly talks to her child out of deep feelings of love, she is also in many instances well aware of the importance of such verbal activity for the development of her child. The black mother, on the other hand, rarely has such awareness, and simply talks to the child because her feelings impel her to do so.

When the black child reaches his second year, almost certainly in the majority of cases by his third year, a new baby has probably arrived in his home. It is then that his mother, overburdened as she is by household chores and the necessity to earn a living, no longer has the same amount of time or energy to devote to the older child. Much of the strength available to her is being absorbed by the care she has to give the new infant. However, when this happens the care of the one or two year old is almost always taken over by a grandmother, an aunt, or an older sibling, someone he knows well and with whom he feels comfortable, someone with whom he has already shared experiences and feelings, and this person continues to play with him and talk to him.

Still another way in which the black child's life differed sharply from that of the white child was his involvement in an extended family system as opposed to the nuclear family system that marked the white child's experiences. Although the nuclear family is the one that prevails in the white community and is considered the appropriate one in western civilization, there is much to be said for the extended family system. To begin with, there is the comfort and security that a child experiences when he realizes that he belongs to a large family with many adults filling the role of parent, and that any one of these parents is ready and willing to care for him as well as his own mother does, should the need for such care ever arise.

The extended family system also leaves the child less dependent on one person and consequently, his feelings of dependency are not as strong or as unacceptable to him as they are for the growing white child and adolescent. The black child and adolescent did not have to fight against his dependency needs nearly as hard as white children do in their struggles to separate themselves from the controlling figures in their lives. As a result, there was likely to be much less tension between the black genera-

*Halpern, F. How Things Might Be and How They Are. *The Clinical Psychologist*, Vol. XXII, No. 1, Fall 1968, p. 27.

tions than there is in many white families. In fact, the generation gap that is a matter of such deep concern in the white community was almost non-existent among the black people. There were several other reasons for this. One is the aforementioned custom of including the children in all the experiences of the adult world (page 55). Another is the unchanging nature of the customs that shaped the lives of the plantation people. These were the same year after year, decade after decade, generation after generation, and consequently, there were few if any sources of friction or conflict. Long before they were old enough to disagree with their elders or rebel against them, the black children knew only too well that their security depended on accepting what they had been taught about the way they should behave in a hostile world. No new concepts dared be introduced, and so in almost all instances (at least until recently when what is occurring in the black world has produced a split in the black communities) regardless of where he went on the plantation the black child encountered attitudes and ideas very similar to those expressed in his own home. Thus when, for economic reasons his mother had to work (and when there was no work in the fields it was much easier for the black woman than the black man to find employment) and the child was cared for by an older sister, a grandmother, or a neighbor—regardless of who the surrogate mother was—he was dealt with as all the children were and as his own mother would have if she had not had to be a wage earner. Because so many black children were raised in part at least by someone other than their own mother, it is not at all unusual when talking to a black adult about his childhood for him to make a distinction between his biological mother and "the mother that raised me."

Since every child on the plantation had several mothers, he not only was less dependent on one mother, but was less possessive of his bio-logical mother or the mother who was caring for him than most middle-class white children are. Hence the severe sibling rivalry that exists in so many white homes, that drives so many white mothers to distraction, was not nearly as frequent or intense among the black children. Rather than any sense of jealousy or rivalry, the black child very quickly learned to accept his newly arrived brother or sister. What was more, even the very young child early acquired a strong sense of responsibility where his new sibling was concerned. Toddlers held nursing bottles while the baby sucked, fetched washcloths and clean diapers, even tried to comfort and protect the baby when such action was indicated.

Older children had even greater responsibilities, not only for their own brothers and sisters, but, as occasion arose, for other children on the plantation. Older boys and girls were expected to dress, cook for, and feed the younger children, as well as keep them entertained and out of harm's way. Since all the children on the plantation had the same duties, the situation was accepted as natural and the children made no protest. In most instances they really loved the little ones, and both boys and girls adopted mothering attitudes toward their little charges. All the children ran around the plantation together. Babies were carried by the big ones and the toddlers were helped along when the going got rough. A child was almost never by himself, never without several companions. On those rare occasions when a small child was praised — and such occasions were extremely rare since praise was not in keeping with the overall child-rearing methods employed by plantation mothers — the older child who was responsible for his care would beam with pride like a fatuous mother. Her child's good health, his skills, his behavior, were all in large measure the result of her efforts, and so she enjoyed a reflected glory when his assets were recognized and commented on.

The reactions of the pupils in a one room school in the Mississippi Delta provide an excellent example of the nature of the relationship that existed among the plantation children. The pupils in the school ranged in age from five to eighteen years. In order to encourage them to work hard, all their papers, no matter how poor they were, were awarded a gold star and pinned up on the wall of the classroom. The teacher, being white and a stranger to the area, and knowing nothing about the way the children felt toward one another and how they reacted to one another, anticipated that some of the older children and some of the brighter younger children would protest at this indiscriminant dispensing of awards. Much to her surprise, the children who were entitled to stars were genuinely happy that the younger and less gifted pupils were also winning some recognition and satisfaction. They even boasted that a sibling, a cousin, or a neighbor's child had received a star. They also tried to help the younger and the slower children. Their behavior in this respect was genuine, not an attempt to deny jealousy or hostility — not reaction formation. Their positive attitude was the natural outgrowth of their total way of life, of the fact that the models they had incorporated also responded in terms of mutual support and co-operation, rather than with assertion, jealousy and competition.

All of this is in marked contrast to what takes place among white children. Almost from the day he is born the white child is competing with someone. If he has an older sibling he strains to keep up with him, and when he is presented with a younger brother or sister he struggles to hold onto the place he had previously held in the family constellation. He also competes with his father for the attention and love of his mother, and with his mother for the attention and love of his father. When he is old enough he competes with other children for school marks, for popularity, for admission to a good college, for a desirable wife, and finally spends his life competing in the business or professional world.

All such challenges were absent from the life of the black child and the black adult. All the people he knew and cared for lived just as he and his family did, in the same kind of wretched house, working as he and his parents worked, rarely if ever having as much money as was needed, and seldom giving thought to the possibility of finding a better way of life. Thus none of the pressures that shape the white man's behavior were present or relevant for the developing rural black child.

Functioning as little mothers and fathers when there were children to be cared for or working in the fields when there were no children to be watched, play as such was not given much consideration in the black community. Yet play is considered important in the child's development. It provides an opportunity for physical exercise and the attainment of muscular co-ordination, fine and gross. It also facilitates the child's cognitive development as he manipulates blocks and other objects and, in so doing, learns about height, weight, size, space, and so on. Similarly, the little girl dressing and feeding her doll is preparing herself for her future role as a mother, while group play stimulates a competitive spirit, as well as loyalty and socialization.

None of the toys considered so essential for the middle-class white child were available to the black child in the rural south. The infant knew no crib-mobile, no rattle, no cuddle toy. In fact, his ignorance of such toys was such that, when in the course of testing he was presented with a rattle, he was momentarily startled, even frightened by the noise the rattle made. Older children played with abandoned car or truck tires and with toys fashioned out of whatever sticks, stones, and rags were available.

Although the black child did not have the objects considered so necessary for the white child's intellectual, social, and emotional development, his activities nonetheless provided him with the opportunities for growth in many areas, and what he learned had far more relevance for his immediate and future life than did many of the activities of the white child. The little black girl did not have to learn how to be a mother through doll play since almost from her second year on, she had been taking care of children younger than herself. Running around together as a group that included all ages of both sexes, the black child also learned through his experience a great deal about group relationships and group interactions. In fact, he was seldom without one or more, generally more, companions. As for such concepts as height, weight, size, space, etc., the black child who had been hauling heavy water buckets, gathering firewood and weeding rows of cotton certainly had some very clear ideas about these concepts. The difference between the experiences of the black and the white child lay, not in the fact that one learned through play with a toy and the other through practical necessity, but that the white child, once he had absorbed certain concepts, had the opportunity to move on and apply these concepts in a variety of situations. For the black child there were no such opportunities, no further use he could make of the knowledge he had acquired, no transfer from his routine, daily experiences to new situations. Furthermore, no one put his learning into words, no one made a point of telling him that the empty cotton sack was "light," the full one "heavy," or that the cotton boll high up on the stem was "up," those on the lower branches "down."

In addition to the extended family system and the co-operative nature of the relationships that existed between the members of a given community, there was still another way in which the black child's experiences differed from those of the white child, namely that he was reared in a predominantly matriarchal culture.* Many authors, most recently Moynihan,† have made a great point of the fact that the black family is a matriarchal one, that many black children grow up without a father in the home. The absent father is also frequently offered as an important factor in the delinquency found among black children and adolescents living in northern cities. While the absent father may in some cases play a part in the child's asocial behavior, it is not by any means the whole answer. Fathers are also absent from southern black families, yet the amount of delinquency among the southern black children is small. Furthermore, fathers are also absent from quite a number of white families as a result of broken marriages, deaths, military duty, etc. It is not the absent father that accounts for any limitations and deviations in the black child's personality, if such actually exist, but rather the reasons for the father's absence and the child's perception of the causes for the

---

*In view of the current divorce rate, plus the number of fathers who are absent from the home because of military service or other forms of business, it is questionable if the patriarchal society is as prevalent in the white community as it is thought to be.

†Moynihan, D. The Moynihan Report. Massachusetts Institute of Technology Press, 1967.

father's absence. The black child's father is not absent because an important position of economic or political significance requires him to spend much of his time in a distant city or a foreign country. Neither is his father likely to write to him or send him gifts from wherever he may be at the moment. If his father is dead, the chances are that he did not die as the result of an industrial accident thus providing his family with compensation or a pension. His father is missing because he said or did something the white community did not like and so he had to run away to avoid being attacked or possibly even killed; or because he could no longer stand by idly while his wife worked in someone's kitchen in order that her family might eat; or because he was tired of being called "boy" and being treated like a child. It is when the child or the adolescent learns the truth about why his father is missing that his negative feelings and his anger toward the white people become so strong that some form of release is imperative. It is then that he begins to reject and oppose all the white man's standards and expectations and engage in delinquent behavior.

The matriarchal society *per se* is not necessarily bad for the growing child, even for the male child. What is important as far as the child is concerned is the kind of father he knew when his father was in the home, the type of mother he has, and the relationship that existed between the parents when they were together. Many a black mother has raised strong achieving sons without the help of a husband, just as many white mothers have. Certainly many white families are essentially matriarchal, either because the father is actually absent or because the father is weak and dominated by a strong, overwhelming woman. It is not just a matter of having a father or not having a father, but rather of all the emotional and familial components that go along with the presence or absence of the father.

For the black child in the rural south to have no father or have what might be described as a "weak" father, that is, a man who was not in a position to provide adequately for his family, a man who drank or ran away periodically, was not as disturbing as it probably was for a middle-class white child. Many of the black families were fatherless or had fathers who had no work and who appeared and disappeared sporadically. Consequently, his father's behavior or absence did not make the black child feel as different or ashamed as it probably did in the case of the white child. Furthermore, as part of an extended family system, the black child always had male models and surrogate fathers available to him.

Throughout this chapter there have been several references to siblings — younger siblings to be cared for, older siblings to be seen as surrogate parents. The number of siblings that many of the black children had constituted still another way in which his family structure and his experiences differed from those of the middle-class white child. Many families had anywhere from six to twelve children, and in one case there were twenty-one children and the mother pregnant with the twenty-second. In some instances all the children had the same father, in other instances not; but this seemed to make no difference in their feeling for one another. The traditionally large family was caused in part by the absence of any information about birth control (Chapter 4) but also by the unexpressed but ever present desire to perpetuate the race. And in view of the rate of infant mortality among the black people, and the dangers that they experienced if they lived to become adults, having many children was important. For the black child the size of his family, the many brothers and sisters he had, in contrast to the much smaller white families of the plantation owner, provided him with still another experience in community living and prepared him for the sharing and co-operation that characterized the plantation life.

Despite all the differences that obtain between the black man's and the white man's situation in life, the question is frequently raised, "Why does the black man not bring up his children as the white man does? Why does he not employ the child-rearing practices that the white man uses in dealing with his offspring?" People who raise this question also point out that many black mothers work in white homes and are therefore in a position to see how the white child is reared. They even participate in that rearing. These questioners fail to recognize that there has to be appropriateness in the modeling before modeling can occur. As Hunt* puts it, "Appropriateness of models depends upon the match between the model and the schemata already acquired." There was certainly little if any match between the child-rearing practices of the white people and the life styles of the black people. Likewise there is no match between the end product that each group was seeking to develop. Consequently, there would be nothing appropriate or even valuable had a black mother sought to bring up her children as she knew white children were being raised. Similarly, it would have been little short of ridiculous for a black father to try and present himself to his children as an independent, ambitious individual, striving to improve his condition and the condition

*Hunt, J. McV. *Intelligence and Experience.* The Ronald Press, New York, 1961, p. 198.

of his family. Even if this had been remotely possible (and in most instances it certainly was not) he would have seriously endangered himself and at the same time negated everything that he and the whole black community had been trying to instill into the black child in order that he might survive.

Given such life conditions and such child-rearing practices, no scheme based on the developmental stages appropriate for the middle-class white child is relevant in understanding and evaluating the black child. Erikson's concepts, particularly his concept of "basic trust" and "autonomy," probably come the closest to what the black child experiences. What was most significant in the development and adjustment of the black child, what provides him with the strength he needs to carry on in the face of the odds that are stacked against him are (1) the love and security he enjoys early in his life, (2) his inclusion in all the family's activities, (3) his early opportunity for the assumption of physical independence and responsibility, and (4) the security provided by the many mothering figures available to him.

According to psychological and psychoanalytic theory, early experiences are of the utmost importance in shaping the personality and determining adult behavior. Given the very marked differences that obtained, and to a considerable extent still obtain between the training and experiences of black rural children (and many urban black children) and white children, it can only be anticipated that their concepts of life, their value systems, and their overall attitudes and reactions will be dissimilar. It follows then that these differences, as well as the reasons for and the meanings of such differences must be understood if meaningful communication, effective teaching, job training, etc. between black and white groups are to be achieved.

# CHAPTER 4

# *Adolescence and Adulthood*

In all societies children grow up and become adults. However, the way in which this growing up takes place and the type of individual that emerges at the end of the growing process naturally varies from culture to culture. As Benedict* puts it, "Although it is a fact of nature that the child becomes a man, the way in which this transition is effected varies from one society to another, and no one of these particular cultural bridges should be regarded as the 'natural' path to maturity."

Until recently the literature dealing with adolescence was concerned specifically with the white youth, generally the middle-class white teenager. The problems facing the white adolescent in this culture were identified as concern about a future career, religious conflicts, and sexual impulses. There was also the whole matter of breaking away from parental control—of achieving independence. Currently the problems of the middle-class white adolescent appear to be of a somewhat different order, or at least they manifest themselves in new ways. For a large number of these white teenagers, religion is no problem whatsoever, but rather is an area which in no way concerns them and to which they give little thought. Again, planning for the future tends to be shrugged off, because a large number of these youths, male and female, have absolutely no idea how they want to spend the rest of their lives and are under no pressure to prepare themselves for the future. Many of them go to college but in some instances without a specific goal in mind. Others do not even enter college, while a number of those who do go, drop out after a year or two because they see no relevance in the courses they are taking.

*Benedict, R. Continuities and Discontinuities in Cultural Conditioning. *Psychiatry.* Vol. 1, May 1938, p. 161.

For many of today's white adolescents the sexual problems that were so pressing a few generations ago are seemingly no longer an issue. Early and apparently non-guilt evoking contact between the sexes, along with intimate living and community living, seems to have solved the matter for at least some of these white teenagers. While a good number of them still have some questions regarding their role and responsibilities in relation to sex, on the whole they do not seem as tense, conflicted, and even distraught as their peers were a decade or two ago.

As far as the issue of independence is concerned, today's white adolescent has solved this aspect of the matter in his own way. He has rejected many of the concepts, values, and attitudes of his parents, but at least in some instances feels quite comfortable relying on the parents for financial support.

Despite the changes that set off the middle-class white adolescents from teenagers of an earlier time, the excitement of adolescence still remains. For the fortunate ones in our culture it is a time for exploration, for dreaming, for romanticizing, for contemplating many possible roles and ways of life, a time to sow wild oats, to think about the future, and above all to decide what is wrong with the world and those who created that world. Along with such decisions goes the definite conviction that with relatively little effort, he, the teenager, could certainly do a much better job than his elders have done, could set everything right. Probably one of the most enjoyable and stimulating experiences that the white teenager has, consists of the "bull sessions" or "rap sessions" in which he so frequently and vigorously indulges.

While today's white teenager's reactions to adolescence may have departed from those of earlier generations, he is still subject to the pressures, inner and outer, that are part of the physiological changes he is undergoing. This is of course true of all adolescents, regardless of race. However, cultural differences produce different modes of response in the adolescent, just as they do in the adult and the child. For the white adolescent there are conflicts, stresses, strains, and even confusion, but there are also many positives in the form of basic security, guidance, along with seemingly boundless opportunities to make new discoveries about himself and his world. Although physically an adult, the middle-class white adolescent continues to enjoy all the comforts and benefits provided by his middle-class way of life. He is cared for and nurtured physically, emotionally, intellectually, and spiritually. While the guidance that is offered him may at times irritate him and provoke arguments with his parents and other members of the establishment, he also does not have to be concerned about being housed, clothed and fed, and he almost always can be sure that, despite his disagreements with authority, it will continue to provide for him and stand behind him. Although he may have some responsibilities, such as mowing the lawn, walking the dog, carrying out the garbage, cleaning his own room, these chores are all of minor importance and certainly not essential to the continuing existence and well-being of his family. Rather, they have all the earmarks of "busy work." In return for fulfilling his responsibilities (and sometimes even when he doesn't) he is provided with an allowance so that he may do the things that all other adolescents in his social class do, take a girl to a movie, go to a school dance or football game, etc. And he may even have his own car or be permitted to use the family car on many occasions. While he is certainly subjected to variable and conflicting responses from his parents and from society in general, being treated sometimes as an adult and at other times like a child, there are also many satisfactions available to him during this period of his life.

For the black adolescent in the rural south the picture was and still is quite different. To begin with, in the southern black communities the lines of demarcation between childhood and adolescence, and between adolescence and adulthood were not at all sharply drawn. For many of the black youngsters the transition was actually from babyhood, not childhood, to adulthood in one swift step. As has already been stated, as soon as the very young black child could handle himself physically, he was very much on his own, and was very likely to be pressed into service, required to care for children younger than he was. It was only a few years later, when he was six or seven at the most, that his life in the cotton fields began. A well-educated young black man, born in the south but currently living in the north, put it as follows: "Black people have no time for adolescence." What he understood so well and what he was trying to convey to a white audience was what the pressures of life on a cotton plantation did to the development of the individual, forcing the child to fill an adult role long before he was physically or emotionally ready for the part he was required to play. Certainly for the southern rural black child there was no gradual transition from a comparatively carefree existence to the assumption of responsibilities, as was the case for the middle-class white child.

Again, for the black adolescent, rather than broadening his horizons as this time of life did for the white teenager, life remained just as circumscribed as it had been. For neither the black male nor female, did the onset of adolescence produce any significant change in their lives or in their way of perceiving themselves and their future. Long before these adolescents attained physical maturity, probably from the time they were six and sometimes even earlier, they were burdened with responsibilities that, unlike those of the white adolescent, were not of the "make work" order. The duties that the black children and the black adolescents were required to perform were essential to the existence of their families. Even when, as very young children, they worked in the fields and earned less than the adults because they were necessarily slower than the grown-ups, whatever little money they brought in was important. As adolescents their contributions were generally equal to those of the adults and desperately needed. And when the adolescent was not working in the field he or she was engaged in some other essential job, caring for little children or an old, sick person, carrying water from a distant well, etc.

Certainly adolescence in no way altered the black teenagers concepts of his future. For him there was no need to plan a career since his career as a field hand, a cook or nurse to white children, had long since been determined. Likewise there was no need to train for the future since he had been doing all the necessary training and the actual work for a long time. So all the anticipation and excitement inherent in the prospect of entering upon new ways of life, all the promise of achieving mastery of himself and his future, all the things that stimulate and motivate the white adolescent, were missing from the lives of the black adolescents.

Yet not withstanding his limited education and general isolation, many of the black teenagers were aware of what was going on in the outside world. Even though there were no newspapers or periodicals, they usually had access to a radio or TV, and an alert adolescent recognized the importance of knowing what was happening in the world at large. There was also information to be obtained from friends and relatives who had served in World War II, in Korea or in Vietnam. From these returned veterans the adolescent learned a great deal about ways of life quite different from his own. Consequently, when these black adolescents living on southern plantations had their "rap" sessions they were not restricted to purely local and personal matters, although naturally the daily happenings and the relationships among the plantation people were important to them. But in addition, at least some of them thought in broader terms and so prepared themselves for the changes that eventually took place even in the backwater of the rural south.

Until such economic and political changes occurred, the only things that were in any way different for the black adolescent were his newly acquired physical strength and sexual potency, and along with this an entirely new relationship with the white community. As a child the black male had been relatively free to mingle with the white community. For instance, his mother might have taken him with her to the white man's house when she went there to cook, clean, or take care of white children. Provided he did not interfere with her work and was not too noisy or pushing, his presence in the white home was accepted. However, as soon as he reached maturity the picture changed abruptly. Southern white men were and still are obsessed by their perception of all black men as potential rapists of white women. They were convinced that every black man wanted to have sexual contact with every white woman he encountered. This fear was used by the white man as the reason for his treatment of the black man, his justification for going to the lengths he did to keep the black man "in his place." Aware of this attitude on the part of the white man, the black child learned early in life that he dare not approach a white woman unless she summoned him, and then he must present himself in subservient fashion, with his head bowed and eyes cast down. Any other form of behavior on the part of a black youth or a black adult inevitably meant lynching. Obviously then the black lad who was approaching physical maturity could no longer visit in white homes while his mother worked there. Neither could he approach white people, male or female, as he once had.

The stronger and more intelligent the black male was, the more likely he was to be regarded with reservations, anxiety, and even fear by the white man. Such a black male was therefore the one most likely to be dealt with in a harsh, repressive, even castrating fashion by the white community. In self-defense the black victim of such treatment often went out of his way to present himself to the white people as stupid and shiftless, hoping in this manner to allay the fears and avoid the hostility of the white public. This was another game the black people had to play, a game that the black adolescent was taught early in his life and at which he had to become adept.

Sex was certainly not a new concept or a new experience for the black adolescent, male or female. Living as they did in the cramped quarters of the plantation houses, they could not possibly avoid seeing and hearing the sexual activities going on around them. Every child knew about sex from the time he was very young, although the adults were likely to deny that this was really so. Certainly they did nothing to provide the young people with sex information. In the main, the attitude of the black adults was that sex was something in which one indulged quite freely, but not something that one talked about. Again, custom and tradition played an important part in shaping the black person's attitude in regard to sex. During the period of slavery and subsequently during pseudo-freedom, sexual activity was encouraged by the white man because he needed large numbers of black people to do his work and add to his wealth. Indulgence in sexual relations was also one of the few pleasures available to the plantation people. Yet they have always been reluctant to talk about sex to their children, other than to warn the boys in regard to white girls and white women. In fact, in conversations with black women on the subject of sex education they indicated that they had learned about sex from observing their parents and from listening to older children, as well as from the sex play that inevitably went on in a community where boys and girls of all ages run around together. Suggestions to the effect that sex education might be advisable, that the children and the teenagers should learn about sex, not in the haphazard way their parents had, but as one learned about other facts in nature, were promptly vetoed. Similarly, when a white doctor working in a local health clinic set up a class in sex education for adolescents the parents and the school authorities promptly demanded that it be terminated. Yet there can be no question that the black adolescents wanted such information and on many occasions when a white professional was talking to them about other matters, they would interrupt and ask questions about sex, often concerning very elementary matters about which they were totally uninformed.

Even though the majority of the southern black adolescents had been reared in very similar fashion, there were differences in the way they reacted to their developing adulthood. These differences were caused in part by differences in constitutional factors, in intelligence, strength and temperament, and in part by the differences in their individual experiences. For example, in some instances there was a father or father surrogate in the home, in other instances there was not. If there was a male model in the house, he might be a strong figure or he might be a weak one. Again, the adolescent might be an only child or he might have many siblings. He might be the first born or he might be the tenth or twelfth child in a family. Some of the lads were big and strong, others short and puny. Similarly, some of the girls were quite beautiful, others just pretty, and some not especially attractive physically.

Many other factors determined the impact of an absent father on the adolescent. For both boys and girls the nature of the relationship that existed between the child and father before he left home certainly made a difference in the way the father's departure was perceived. If the relationship had been an unhappy one, the adolescent might be glad that the father was no longer around. On the other hand, if there had been a good feeling between the adolescent and the father, he might mourn the father's absence or experience it as rejection. A boy's ordinal position in the family also affected what the father's absence meant to him. If he was the oldest child he was expected to fill the father's place and this responsibility was added to all the others he had. The way his mother and the other people in the area talked about his father and reacted to the father's absence also played a part in determining what this particular situation meant to the adolescent.

In addition to the delinquency that is so often blamed on the absent father (page 63) some writers have claimed that the absence of a father also accounts for the rather extensive homosexuality that they insist obtains in northern ghettos. In the southern rural communities this problem was not acute. As has already been noted, although the boy growing up on the plantation may not have had a man in his immediate household, there were many men in the area who served as male models and surrogate fathers. The unfortunate aspect of the situation was that these models, as well as his own father, were many times, though certainly not always, men who had been so beaten by the plantation system that they could not present themselves to the young people as strong, effective, masculine figures. Even those who were strong, physically, intellectually, and emotionally, had to be careful not to make too much of a display of their strength. Theoretically the combination of a weak, passive male and a strong, dominant female is one that might well result in a homosexual orientation in the male offspring; yet such was not the case in the population under discussion.

As was noted above (page 63), it was not actually the absence of a father in the home but the reasons for that absence that were likely to make the difference in the child's and the adolescent's perceptions of his father and his identification with him. Similarly, for the adolescent girl, the image she had of the father, what she had or had not been told about him and what she heard others say about him, went a good way toward shaping her perceptions of men and her concepts of herself and her role as a woman.

The adolescent youth with better than average intelligence sometimes found ways of adjusting to his life situation that made it a bit pleasanter, a bit more bearable than it was for the majority of the black people. Such an adolescent might devote a good portion of his time and energy to the church, and through its religious and social functions find opportunities for the self-expression and the leadership denied to him everywhere else. He might even plan a career for himself as a preacher, although all preachers were not necessarily creative or capable of leadership. Furthermore, since preaching never paid enough to provide a living for a man and his family, the preacher was not freed from the cotton fields. However, preaching did afford him some opportunity to exercise his talents. Similarly, the bright teenager might contemplate a career as a teacher in the black school. In fact, until very recently when new types of job opportunities are being opened up to the black people, there were just two possibilities for an alert, ambitious young black man — teaching or preaching.

Not all able teenagers planned such futures for themselves. In some cases their good endowment and their sensitivity made them all the more acutely aware of the position in which they were trapped, made them all the more resentful and angry because of the hardships that they, their families, and all the black people had to endure. Such a lad might decide that making any effort to improve his lot was an exercise in futility, and so he was likely to succumb sullenly to the demands of the cotton field or take off for the cities. In recent years, especially during the last two decades, such youths swelled the ranks of organizations like SNCC, CORE, and SCLC.

For the majority of the black teenagers, life held no prospects other than those their parents and their grandparents had known. They saw no escape from the soul-crushing life of the plantation, so they went along in the paths prescribed for them and became the conforming docile workers they were expected to be. Still others sought escape in alcohol, sleep, and flight from the scene of their humiliation.

The experiences of the adolescent black girl in the rural south were different in many ways from those of her brothers. While she too had a constricted and well-defined road she was expected to follow, her life was nevertheless in certain respects less frustrating and hazardous than it was for the black male, teenager or adult. For a black youth to recognize and accept the fact that the white world would never allow him really to be a man, fully to fill a masculine role, was one of the bitterest pills he had to swallow. The adolescent girl, on the other hand, while well aware that white people regarded her as inferior and that she had no possible chance of ever enjoying the opportunities available to middle-class white girls, was not denied her femininity. In fact, filling a feminine role — cooking, sewing, caring for a household, bearing and raising children, doing all the things that in an agricultural community are required of women — was exactly what was expected of her. To this end she had a model in her mother as well as in all the other women on the plantation.

Another important difference between the male and female adolescent was the fact that the former was never allowed to feel important, neither by the white community nor by his own people. This of course was equally true for children and adults, but the difference between the way the male and female adolescent were responded to was particularly striking. In general, the male teenager was cut down just as the male child was, and only rarely, and then in the privacy of his own home, did a mother convey to her son how important he was to her, how "special" she thought he was, while at the same time warning him not to get "ideas" about himself and risk offending the white people with whom he had contact. The female adolescent, on the other hand, because she was not perceived by the white community as a physical or sexual threat, was received in white homes (through the back or side door, of course); and because she was frequently helpful and co-operative, was often praised and even "loved" by the family employing her. As is well known, many a white southerner was nursed and raised by a black adolescent or adult.

Given such conditions, the black female, adolescent or adult, was able to acquire and maintain a far more positive image of herself than her male relatives and friends could. Enhancing this positive self-image, and the sense of responsibility it generated, was the female's ability to find employment and support her family even when there was no work in the fields, a condition that was rarely possible in the case of the black male. It is obvious then that the position held by black women, the style of life that prevailed in black communities and caused the black culture to be labeled matriarchal was once again the product of environmental forces, the consequence of the attitudes and behaviors of white people, not the result of any basic weakness in the black male or excessive aggression or an inordinate drive to dominate in the black female.

When the black girl became adolescent, she was naturally sought after by the black males in her area. In practically all instances she had already experienced a certain amount of sex play as she moved about the plantation in the company of other boys and girls of all ages. In many small communities — and the plantation community was certainly no exception — sex is as much a preoccupation of the children as of the adults. Stories obtained from eight to twelve year old black children attending a one room school in Mississippi certainly give indication of this interest. A dictaphone had been brought into the classroom of these children by their northern white teacher and they had been shown how the machine worked. They were quite excited when they heard the teacher's voice coming back to them from the tapes, and wanted to hear themselves. So they were told to talk into the microphone and tell a story. After some initial hesitation and some urging on the teacher's part, most of these children complied. Almost all the stories consisted of statements like "Arthur Lee wants to put it to Brenda but she don't want it" or "Pearlie Bess wants to sleep with Tyrone." Once the ice was broken, a great deal of material dealing with the sexual activities of the children came out, including their use of the school room for their sex play.

Once the girl achieved maturity the question of pregnancy came into the picture. Neither pre-marital sexual relationships or out-of-wedlock pregnancies were at all unusual among the plantation people. There were several reasons why early pregnancies — sometimes as early as thirteen years of age — occurred as frequently as they did among married or unmarried black adolescents. One of the most obvious ones, of course, was ignorance regarding any form of birth control. This was true not only for the young girl but for the older women. Even when they knew birth control and contraceptive devices were available, the women, young and old, were reluctant to use them. Many of them regarded their use as flying in the face of God and nature. When this issue was raised with a group of young mothers who had recently given birth to their first child, one mother stated emphatically that she was going to do everything she could to avoid having another baby, at least for a long time. At this, another member of the group announced that she was going to have as many babies "as the Lord puts there." To which the first mother responded, "Girl, ain't you learned yet that it ain't the Lord that puts them there?"

Many of the women, both young and old, insisted that no matter how secretive they were in their use of contraceptives, the men knew what they were doing and complained that under such conditions the relationship was not as pleasurable or satisfying to them as it was when no contraceptives were employed. What seems more likely is that the men objected to the use of birth control devices because they preferred the women to become pregnant. When this happened they were assured of their virility, had concrete evidence of their potency. For men who had so little opportunity to demonstrate their manhood, such an attitude is certainly understandable. In any event, whatever the reasons for the men's reactions, the majority of the women were unwilling to run the risk of displeasing the man and having him turn elsewhere for his sexual satisfactions. Rather than allow this to occur, the women forewent birth control and, married or unmarried, permitted themselves to become pregnant.

Still another reason for the relative frequency of the out-of-wedlock pregnancy was the overall attitude of the community toward such a happening. There was rarely if ever any condemnation of the prospective mother, and no righteous, punitive, puritanical attitude directed against her. Rather than censoring her, the prospect of a little newcomer was likely to be received with pleasure, and the grandmother of the baby or some other relative or neighbor was quite ready to take care of him if his mother planned to go back to school or to work. Only the local black school adopted a negative, punitive attitude in this regard, probably in order to appease the white school board. In any event the girl was expelled as soon as her pregnancy became known. In some instances this caused a girl to lose a whole year of schooling, and as a result a number of them, even those who had hoped to continue their education, were so discouraged that they never returned to the classroom.

As has already been noted, many of the girls who became pregnant were very young, sometimes no more than thirteen or fourteen years old. Yet once they had had a child their position in their family and in their community changed. No matter how young she might be, the girl who had had a baby was herself no longer perceived as a child or treated as one. She was a mother and she had established herself as a woman. Furthermore, she had proved that she was fertile and therefore desirable. The fact that a girl had had one or more babies out of wedlock did not reduce her prospects for marriage; in fact it might even enhance them.

In discussing their pregnancies with a number of unmarried teenagers it became apparent that having a baby had been very meaningful to them for several reasons. For one thing, having a baby had made them feel alive and assured them of their femininity. Furthermore, having the baby gave them something of their very own, an experience that many of them had never really had before.

There is still a further reason for the black community's lack of concern about the out-of-wedlock child, namely the black people's attitude toward the whole concept of marriage. This attitude is in many instances very different from that of middle-class white people. Although the church and some members of the black community believe that marriage is important, on the whole the feeling of the black people in regard to marriage is strongly colored by two considerations: one, the matter of property and the other, the attitude of the white man toward black marriages during the time of slavery. In the white community marriage is stressed in good part because of property considerations; marriage gives the child his father's name and insures an orderly transfer of worldly goods from father to son. A man wants to be sure that the material things he has acquired during his lifetime go to his own flesh and blood. Where there is no wealth, no property of any kind, the whole question of legal marriage and the child's name have considerably less importance.

The white man's lack of regard for slave marriages has also left its imprint on black attitudes toward legalized marriage. The fact that a man was a husband and a father did not deter the white man from tearing him away from his family and selling him to some distant plantation owner. In his new home he would be given a new wife and expected to sire a new family, thereby augmenting his owner's wealth. Similarly, a black woman who had been sold would be presented with a new husband and expected to produce babies who then became the master's property. In other words, the man was used as a stud and the woman as a brood mare, all for the white person's financial gain. Now suddenly, because large black families no longer benefit the white man, they are frowned upon and condemned. The white community has become very moral and is shocked when black men and women are sexually free and have children out of wedlock. Yet customs that were actually encouraged for three or more centuries and are part of the black tradition are not likely to be eradicated overnight. So many black men tend to question the importance of legal marriage and monogamy, and to regard the white man's "morality" with skepticism. It would certainly seem as though, for the white community, the economic issue far outweighs the moral one.

As far as the black adult was concerned, his condition was not very different from that of the adolescent or even the older child. Unlike many societies where entrance into manhood is marked by elaborate religious or tribal rites or by the attainment of an educational or vocational goal, there was no definite point in time when the black child or adolescent became an adult. For instance, in the white world, graduation from school or high school and entry into the work world was seen as a milestone indicating the attainment of adult status. However, no such events signaled a "grown-up" position in the world of the southern rural black people. Many of the children did not go to school or attended so irregularly that going or not going had no real significance. Similarly, as far as working and earning money was concerned, all the children had been doing that for a long time. So in many respects the child was an adult, or at least functioning as an adult long before he was physically mature and chronologically "grown-up"; while the adult, at least in the white man's eyes, remained forever a child.

To be a black man in the rural south was undoubtedly one of the most humiliating positions that a person could occupy. Being forever a "boy" meant that one was regarded as inept, dependent, and valueless except as a field hand. In no way was the black man permitted to experience himself as a mature, effective male. Even when he worked, the black man seldom earned enough to provide adequately for his family and so his wife and children had to supplement his efforts. In many instances the wife and the children, especially the teenage female children, could earn as much or more than he did. They worked as domestics and therefore were employed the year round whereas his labors were highly seasonal. In view of the stereotype of the male as the provider for his women and children — an image that prevails in almost all cultures — the black man could only perceive himself and recognize that others saw him as less than a man.

The lack of manhood and the humiliation that the black man experienced because he could not provide adequately for his family was further aggravated by his inability to be the protector of his family. Traditionally black women were regarded as fair game for any white man who was sexually attracted to them. So many a black man has had to stand by knowing that his wife, his daughter, his sister, even his mother or some other woman he knew and cared for was being sexually assaulted by a white man as she carried out her duties in his home. Were he to make any protest, were he to react as a man ordinarily would under such conditions, were he to attempt to intervene or avenge his honor, he might very well be lynched and his family thrown off the plantation and left completely homeless. Because of this state of affairs, those families that had any degree of economic independence rarely permitted their women to work in the white homes. Rather than allow their daughters to submit to such treatment, they sent them away to schools if they could afford to or to northern relatives if they had such. However, the majority of the people had no such opportunities. Furthermore, most of them were in desperate financial straits and the money that the women earned as domestics was in many instances all that stood between the family and actual starvation. It was their inability to tolerate this state of affairs or do anything to alter it that led many black men to leave their homes forever.

Living a life of such extreme frustration and deprivation, it is not surprising that most black men took advantage of whatever momentary pleasures were available to them. Unless his physical safety was involved the idea of foregoing a few current satisfactions, such as buying a pint of whiskey, sleeping with a pretty girl, etc., either for some unidentified future advantage or for moral reasons, had little meaning and made absolutely no sense to him. In view of the kind of life he led, one of the very few times that the black man could experience himself as a man was during his moments of sexual contact.

Most of the time there were no pleasures, and then alcohol and sleep offered the only avenues of escape available to the black man, unless he wanted to shake the soil of the south altogether. Sleep could always provide at least a brief respite from the intolerable realities of his life. Sleep also served certain other functions. It provided a way of passing the time when there was nothing to do, a way of escaping boredom. Illiterate or at best semi-literate, and without access to books, magazines or papers, reading was definitely not an activity in which the black man or the black woman indulged. There was no money for any other form of entertainment or recreation, and so sleep became one of the chief ways of wiling away the hours. Many well-intentioned white people who ride around the rural south are disturbed when they see black people, especially black men, sitting on their porches rocking or sleeping. They then feel compelled to agree with the opinions of the southern whites, namely that the black man is lazy. When they are told that there are times when there is literally nothing for the black man to do, they suggest that he paint his house, repair a sagging wall, or mend the front steps. They do not realize that paint costs money that the black man does not have or that he needs for such things as food, clothes, and medical expenses; that the sagging walls of plantation houses defy repair; and that before the winter is over the front steps that require mending will be chopped up and put in the fireplace to keep the family from freezing.

Sleep also was an essential bodily restoration after a hard day's work in the fields, so even in the summertime one might see black people resting after their labors. Picking cotton is not only a matter of long hours — often twelve or more, in ninety to hundred degree heat, with the sun beating down relentlessly — but the actual work of cotton picking is not as easy as it may appear to someone who has not tried it. It is not just a matter of grabbing a soft cotton boll and dropping it into a bag that is dragging along behind you. Effort and strength are often required to to get that boll loose, and in the course of such efforts the skin of the hand is very likely to be scratched and torn. By the end of a day of picking, the hands of many of the field workers were quite sore and painful. Yet wearing gloves or any other form of protective device slowed up the worker, and since he was generally paid by the pound he could not afford to be slowed down.

From everything that has been said here up to this point, as well of much in the current literature dealing with the black people, it is apparent that the black woman was and is the central figure in the black family. Economic, social, and biological factors are all responsible for this reversal of the usual male-female roles. Economically the woman could bring in more money than her husband, if only because as already noted, when there was no work in the fields, she could find work in white kitchens and nurseries. Socially she was acceptable because, unlike the black man, she was not perceived as a threat to white womanhood; and until recently, her fertility contributed considerably to the white man's wealth. One can imagine what it must have meant to the black men to know that, in many instances, he and his children were able to eat only because his wife was laboring in some white woman's kitchen. And it would be interesting to explore the feelings of the little black child who did not see his mother all day because she was caring for a white child in the big house.

There is no way to accurately gauge the strength of the southern black women and what that strength meant to the survival of the black people. That the women were, at least in some measure, aware of the position they occupied and its significance for the future of the race is obvious from the tenacity with which they struggled to hold on and keep themselves and their children functioning. In one way or another the women managed to feed their families and keep them alive. When some of the black women were asked why they stayed on the plantations and raised the children, why they did not take off and go to the cities, free from responsibilities, the way the men did, their answers reflected keen insight and empathy. As one woman put it, "I guess the man he feels bad because he don't have much work and he can't give the kids what they want. It's hard for a man to stay with that." In addition, several women pointed out that after carrying a baby for nine months and then nursing it and caring for it, something happens to you and the way you feel about that child, and you just can't tear yourself away. "A man he don't have that. He don't carry no baby."

When a husband, legally married or otherwise, left his home a woman might after a time take another "husband." Sometimes the new husband lightened her burden, sometimes he added to it. But few women liked to be alone indefinitely. So a woman often had a number of children by a number of different men. This rarely seemed to make any difference to the mother, the current father, or the siblings. Some women were more bound by religious and conventional concepts, and for them the bonds of matrimony were more meaningful and relevant but no finger of scorn was likely to be pointed at the woman who was less "proper."

Although the black women engaged rather freely in sexual activity and were often pregnant, few of them indicated that they derived any real pleasure from the sex act itself. When the matter was discussed with them, they generally said something to the effect that "I never enjoyed nature." This failure to derive physical satisfaction from sexual inter-course seemed due in good part to the fact that very few of the men engaged in any extensive or prolonged foreplay or were responsive to the woman and what she was experiencing during the relationship. For the woman, their sexual contacts were important for reasons other than physical release and fulfillment. Like women everywhere, being sought out as a sex object caused the woman to perceive herself as desirable, enhanced her sense of herself as a woman. In a world where there was very little competition for any of the things for which women generally compete —clothes, jewels, house furnishings, social position, etc.—competition for men did exist and being sought after was certainly ego-enhancing.

Many of the homes housed more than one woman and sometimes more than one family. Often two sisters lived together, or a mother with her brood and an older daughter with her young ones. In most instances one woman was the mistress of the house and although the others did their share of the work, the decisions about how the house should be run were the prerogative of the mistress. That this was recognized by all the people living together was apparent from the way they expressed the relationships that existed among the members of the household. If the daughter was the mistress then she talked about her house, and when asked where she lived the mother would indicate, "I live with my daughter." On the other hand, if the circumstances were reversed, a daughter would say, "I live in my mother's house." Many of the shacks housed three and four generations with the line of command carefully laid out and understood.

Just as there was no sharp line for the black person between childhood and adolescence and between adolescence and adulthood so there was no real demarcation between adulthood and old age. In many ways the black woman and the black man were at forty and sixty very much as they had been at twenty and even ten. Shut off from the rest of the world, any dreams or hopes that the black person may have had as a child about a better way of life had long since faded. The chief differences between what a black person experienced when he or she was middle aged as compared with earlier days was the added responsibility of many children and grandchildren, and the physical ailments that result from hard work, inadequate food and housing.

The social life of the community and the church, the many children and grandchildren, and the respect and love of fellow plantation dwellers were the chief sources of satisfaction available to the aging southern rural black people. Some men, whose sound judgment had proved effective when the people with whom they lived and worked were called on to meet a particular crisis, became the leaders of their community. Such men enjoyed considerable respect and had to assume more than average responsibilities. Similarly, black women became important figures, not only in their own immediate households, but in the entire community. Less threatened and harassed than the black men, there were many strong black women, women who were always ready to meet the circumstances that required their judgment and their action, women who were always there when their presence and their help were required. Not until they were extremely old, and sometimes not even then, were the strong black women ready or willing to yield their positions as head of the household and as a force in the community.

# CHAPTER 5

# *Intelligence*

Any effort directed toward enhancing the white man's understanding of the black man, of modifying the former's perceptions of the latter, and doing away with white prejudices and the justification for such prejudices, must deal with the whole matter of intelligence, and particularly with the arguments that claim that the black man is intellectually "different" from and "inferior" to the white man. The current disagreements in regard to black intelligence should actually no longer be an issue in view of the many studies that indicate that when the black people are given adequate opportunity they can learn and function as effectively as white people. One of the most telling studies in this connection is that of Klineberg,* undertaken more than thirty-five years ago. What he found was that black children coming to northern cities from the south showed IQ gains for each grade they completed in an urban school. Given such evidence there can be no question about the significance of environment in the determination of an individual's functioning level.

A less frequently quoted, but equally important study was reported by Montagu† in 1945. He analyzed the findings of the tests (Army Alpha and Beta) administered to black and white men in the armed forces during World War I. Once again the results demonstrated the importance of environmental factors on mental development and functioning. According to Montagu, the lowest scores on the tests were made by individuals

---

*Klineberg, O. *Negro Intelligence and Selective Migration.* Columbia University Press, New York, 1935.
†Montagu, M. F. A. The Intelligence of Northern Negroes and Southern Whites in the First World War. *Amer. J. Psychology.* 1945, **58**, 161–188.

(*regardless of race*) who came from depressed socio-economic areas. At the time the tests were administered this meant the south, and according to Montagu, the "deeper the south the lower the scores." He also reported that the median score for Negroes from the north was higher than that of whites from the south. On the basis of this data he concludes, "These findings show that, whatever inherent differences may exist between Negroes and whites, intellectual or whatever it is that was measured by these tests, was to an appreciable extent determined by external factors and that, when these external factors are favorable to one group and unfavorable to another, the favored group will excel the unfavored one."

Before embarking on any further discussion of black intelligence it would be well to consider what intelligence actually is. It is a topic that comes up for frequent discussion in scientific and professional circles, but there is rarely general agreement on the issue. Nevertheless, although we really do not know exactly what it is, we seem to think that we have appropriate and effective ways of measuring it.

Although we do not know just what "intelligence" is or even how it develops and operates, there seems to be fairly reasonable agreement that it is determined and influenced by both genetic and cultural factors. As an inherited trait, intelligence is no different from other biological traits. Take height, for example. A child whose heredity is such that he is very likely to measure well above average when he is full grown will only do so if he has adequate nutritional supplies, sufficient exercise, has been spared severe or crippling illnesses, and so on. The same holds true for intelligence. The child whose mind has not been properly stimulated and fed, who has not received sufficient and appropriate intellectual enrichment, who may be suffering from malnutrition and anemia (Chapter 7), may very possibly not develop his intellectual potential to its fullest. This does not mean that the potential for average or better than average functioning was never present and could not have been developed had the circumstances been propitious. As it is, in the case of the rural black people, considering the many physical and cultural handicaps under which they labored, it is a miracle that they functioned as well as they did, especially in view of the fact that estimates of their intelligence were and are based on tests which in many respects were meaningless to them — on tests that for them were like a foreign language. As one black man put it, "If we had the opportunities the white folks have we'd be a race of supermen."

Granted that intelligence involves genetic and cultural factors (as well as others) Wechsler's* definition probably comes as close to explaining what intelligence is as any other that has been offered. According to him, intelligence is "the aggregate or global capacity of an individual to act purposefully, to think rationally, and to deal effectively with his environment." With such a definition of intelligence it becomes necessary to know what the individual's purposes are, what is "rational" in the particular culture in which he is involved, and what the nature of his environment is. As was indicated earlier (page 29), the ultimate purpose of all human beings is survival for themselves and their group. So every human being struggles to stay alive and strives for an adjustment that not only affords life but also as much fulfillment and satisfaction — material, intellectual, and emotional — as is possible. To this end white children, and especially white children living in urban areas, are trained to think and react in ways that are considered most likely to bring them the fulfillment they seek, and that will best fit them for coping with the situations they will have to face as adults. Certain specific functions are therefore stressed and developed, while others are minimized or possibly even neglected. In particular, verbal ability and the ability to abstract and theorize, to plan ahead and envisage new approaches to old problems are given very special consideration. Among the black children of the south such was not at all the case. For them, until very recently and in many instances even today, what was emphasized was memory and manual skills. So different functions and different skills were developed, yet the same tests of intelligence are given to both blacks and whites.

Intelligence like many other concepts such as beauty, femininity, mental normality, etc. are culturally determined rather than possessing fixed and absolute values. For the black child in the south, manual skills were far more relevant than verbal ones. Had the emphasis been on the development of his verbal skills, he would undoubtedly have scored higher on formal intelligence tests, but probably have made less effective adjustment to his particular milieu.

Although standard tests are obviously then quite inappropriate as measures of intelligence for certain populations, "experts" in the field of mental measurement do not hesitate to describe and classify black intelligence on the basis of such tests. The latest effort in this regard comes from Jensen in an article that appeared in the January 1969 issue of the *Harvard Educational Review*. Using the scores made by black subjects on standard intelligence tests, Jensen concluded that the black

*Wechsler, D. *The Measurement of Adult Intelligence*. The Williams and Wilkins Co., Baltimore, 1944, p. 3.

man's intellectual endowment was very possibly inferior to that of the white man and that this inferiority was primarily genetic in nature. As he put it, "it (is) a not unreasonable hypothesis that genetic factors are strongly implicated in the average Negro-white intelligence difference."* From this assumption he goes on to another, namely that for children whose intelligence differs from that of the white child and whose mode of learning is therefore also different, there should be a "different" educational program, one that is adjusted to the black child's type of intellectual functioning. As he describes it, black children do far better on associative kinds of learning than they do on tasks involving what are considered to be of a higher intellectual order. His arguments are far from convincing. For instance there is no recognition on his part that among the white children the so-called higher forms of learning have in many cases been encouraged and inculcated from infancy, while they have been sharply discouraged among the black people. As has been indicated over and over in this book, black people were not supposed to think, to make comparisons, and arrive at generalizations. This state of affairs, combined with generations of malnutrition and generally poor health has created what Birch† calls "pseudo-genetic" inferiority. But there is certainly no evidence to show that given adequate conditions, socially, economically, educationally, and in the area of health, the black people could not learn and function just as effectively as the white people.

One of the greatest fallacies in Jensen's argument and in the arguments of those who think as he does is its reliance on tests. Neither intelligence tests nor achievement tests measure native endowment. What they measure is what an individual has learned in the course of his life, and so such tests are at best measures of learning ability. The assumption is then made that learning ability reflects native endowment, that the better one learns the better endowed one is. For a test to be a valid measure of an individual's capacity to learn, the content of the test must obviously deal with the kinds of matters the individual has had an opportunity to observe and experience. Likewise the materials composing the test must be understandable and meaningful to him, otherwise the test might as well be presented in Chinese.

On the basis of everything that has been said up to this point, it should be apparent that the standard tests in general use in this country have no validity in so far as measuring black intelligence or even functioning level

---

*Jensen, A. How Much Can We Boost IQ and Scholastic Achievement? *Harvard Educational Review*, Vol. 39, No. 1, 1969, p. 82.

†Birch, H. Paper read at annual meeting of American Psychiatric Association, May 1971.

is concerned. Yet it is still the IQ that the black subject makes that is used to evaluate his abilities, and so in many instances he ends up labeled "inferior." Yet when studies of a typical white population are pursued and low IQ's are obtained, no one insists that the subjects in such studies are constitutionally inferior. For example, during the 1940's, Goldfarb* reported a series of investigations dealing with subjects who had spent the first three years of their lives in an orphan home. In order to protect these children from infection and disease they were kept in a kind of sterile isolation, rarely having contact with another human being. The people they did see — those who came to take care of their physical needs, to feed, wash, diaper, and dress them — varied from day to day, sometimes from hour to hour. Likewise they had few if any toys and they lacked all forms of stimulation. As might be anticipated, their mental development was grossly retarded, many of them scoring in the defective range, with the severest impairment in the verbal sphere. There have been other studies which also highlight the crippling effects of adverse environmental conditions on intellectual development. Yet no one raised the question of inferior heredity in those cases. As long as the population under investigation is white, the question of poor functioning due to heredity is not even considered. Why then is it a constitutional defect when a black group that has been consistently subjected to the most severe kinds of environmental deprivation performs poorly on an intelligence test?

A study conducted in the Mississippi Delta† during the summer of 1968 certainly suggests that the black child comes into the world with as good and possibly even better potentialities than the white child. In this study 344 black children, aged one week to thirty-six months, were given the Gesell Developmental Scales. The average Developmental Quotient for the entire group was 95.9, S.D. 17.76. However, far more significant than the group average were the averages obtained when the findings for each quarter year of life were calculated. These results are reported in Table 1.

Even if, for several reasons, the findings for the first quarter year of life are disregarded, it is apparent that until they were fifteen months old the black children functioned on an average as well as the white children did. This has nothing to do with the argument that infant tests are not good predictors of future performance. Regardless of how they might perform

*Goldfarb, W. Psychological Privation in Infancy and Subsequent Adjustment. *Amer. J. Orthopsychiat.*, **15**, 247–255.

†Brown, R., and Halpern, F., The Variable Pattern of Mental Development of Rural Black Children. *Clinical Pediatrics*, July 1971, Vol. 10. No. 7, pp. 404–409.

**Table 1**    Developmental quotients at each quarter year of life.

| Age | Developmental Quotient | S.D. |
|---|---|---|
| 1 week to 13 weeks | 117.50 | 20.70 |
| 14 weeks to 26 weeks | 101.79 | 17.64 |
| 27 weeks to 39 weeks | 101.37 | 15.64 |
| 40 weeks to 52 weeks | 101.84 | 19.67 |
| 53 weeks to 65 weeks | 101.07 | 13.26 |
| 66 weeks to 78 weeks | 96.59 | 15.74 |
| 79 weeks to 91 weeks | 90.74 | 12.94 |
| 92 weeks to 104 weeks | 89.84 | 14.28 |
| 105 weeks to 117 weeks | 86.64 | 10.76 |
| 118 weeks to 130 weeks | 88.61 | 18.82 |
| 131 weeks to 143 weeks | 88.13 | 14.31 |
| 144 weeks to 156 weeks | 86.58 | 13.81 |

in the future, the fact remains that from the time they were fourteen weeks old until they were sixty-five weeks old the black children were as effective, according to test results, as the white children were.

When the test findings are analyzed in terms of the four areas specified by Gesell, namely motor, verbal, adaptive and personal-social, it becomes evident that the black child's loss of Developmental Quotient points beginning at fifteen months of age is due in large part, although not exclusively, to his relatively poor score on the verbal part of the test. At ten to twelve months the black child's verbal functioning is still in line with expectancy for his age, but by the time he is thirteen to fifteen months old he scores below the verbal age norms, and the decrements in the verbal area mount steadily from that time on. Although there were also losses in the three other areas explored by the Developmental Scales, these were not nearly as large as the losses in the verbal sphere. Furthermore, some of the losses or failures assigned to the motor, adaptive or personal-social areas should really have been chalked up as verbal losses. For instance, at twenty-four months the child is presented with a large ball and told to kick it. Many of the children looked puzzled when they heard the word "kick" and simply threw the ball or rolled it. Yet if the act of kicking was demonstrated, most of them were able to imitate it with vigor. The failure they earned in relation to this item was nevertheless treated as a failure in the motor area although in at least some instances it was a verbal one.

It is probable that on the basis of findings similar to those just reported, many investigators and professionals working with black people have come to the conclusion that black people are verbally retarded—that black people do not talk as much as white people do. Yet take the example just offered of the two year old child who did not understand what he was expected to do when told to "kick the ball." If one has worked with impoverished black children, one soon realizes that there are no balls to be kicked and no room for kicking. No one ever tells such a child to "kick" and therefore the word is strange to him. This does not mean that he could not quickly and easily learn the meaning of such a word if the circumstances permitted.

Another important factor that must be born in mind in evaluating the verbal functioning of very young black children is their dawning awareness of strangers, particularly white strangers. While the children were, with some exceptions, intrigued by the test materials and willing and able to respond to the non-verbal items, their training had been such that verbal communication with someone they had never before encountered was virtually out of the question. This of course is not a peculiarly black reaction. As every experienced tester knows, one can usually involve withdrawn, reluctant children in the test proceedings more quickly and easily by presenting them with the non-verbal items rather than those that require the testee to talk to someone he has never met before. Anyone who has had the opportunity to administer such tests as the Gesell Developmental Scales to a large number of black children, particularly black children from disadvantaged families and from rural areas, knows these children are extremely shy, overwhelmed by feelings of insecurity, distrust, and anxiety. In the study just reported, in some few instances, a relationship with a particular child was developed over a period of days or even weeks. When this was possible the child's response to the testing experience was markedly different from what it had been when he was tested without any prior introduction to the tester.

At this juncture it is important to be clear as to what is actually meant by "verbal limitations." It does not mean, as so many researchers have implied, that black people talk very little to one another and to their children. On the contrary, they talk a great deal and at great length. Visit a black family's home, go to a church social, or any other affair where black people come together, and the talk is plentiful, provided of course that you are not perceived as an outsider. The verbal limitations that are ascribed to the black people consist not in a lack of words or in an inhibition of speech, but in what by middle-class white standards would be considered a somewhat meager vocabulary, poor grammar, and nonstandard English.

The language or verbal characteristics of the southern rural black people are both historically and environmentally determined. Centuries ago, as a newcomer from Africa, the black man had to learn an entirely new, strange sounding language, and in most instances he was taught only the barest essentials necessary for the conduct of his work. Since his contacts were mainly with other slaves who also had small vocabularies and whose pronunciation and grammar were not like that of the southern white people, he soon developed a dialect of his own. This was particularly true of the field hands whose descendants are today's plantation people. Consequently, many of them speak their own language — the language they learned from their forebears — rather than the English of the white man.

In addition to the historical factors that account for the development of a black language, there was also the absence of schooling and the general illiteracy that prevailed among the black people throughout the time of slavery. After the Civil War, education for the black people in the south was most inadequate, so that the state of illiteracy continued. Furthermore, the nature of their lives, the conditions under which they lived, and the kind of work they did, were not conducive to emphasis on learning and the acquisition of literary or verbal skills. In addition, people with an average income of $900 had no money for books, periodicals, or papers even if they had been able to read and enjoy them.

As their condition changes and work in the cotton fields becomes a thing of the past (Chapter 10), there is a gradual awareness on the part of the black people that it is necessary for them to have an education and become literate. However there is little real understanding of how this is to be achieved, what the adults can do to help the children even before they go to school. The kinds of experiences that middle-class white people make available to their children right from the start are unknown to the black people. Consequently, while white children were learning to observe, to concentrate, to question, and to analyze at an early age, black children were and in many instances still are forbidden to indulge in such intellectual activities. The current feeble and pathetic attempts of black parents to provide educational stimulation for their children are well illustrated by the following episode. A father who could not read, who had once been a field hand but currently did whatever unskilled manual work he could obtain on a day to day basis, nevertheless recognized the importance of education and especially of reading. So he asked if he might have some of the books that were lying about in a summer Freedom School and were apparently not being used. He built a small bookshelf out of some abandoned lumber and then carefully placed the books on the shelves. The only problem was that, because he could not read and did not really understand how books were constructed and used, he put all the books on the shelves with the bindings and the titles facing in. It was therefore impossible to tell one book from another until it was removed from the shelf. Similarly, because they have never had books, young black children often grab them by the pages, letting the covers fall back. They have no idea how a book should be handled or even how to turn the pages. This is very different from what happens with white children who from their earliest days see their parents handling books, and have many opportunities to handle them themselves.

Given such differences in background and experience, it becomes once again clear that testing the southern black people on such scales as the Wechsler or the Binet, and drawing inferences from the test results about their innate intellectual potential is actually ludicrous, a travesty of everything that is known about tests, intelligence, and cultural influences. The same is equally true of other tests which seek to describe in quantitative terms what abilities and what limitations a man brings into the world with him. Surely there have been enough studies pointing out the importance of environmental and several other factors, such as involvement and motivation, in evaluating intelligence to discredit any study that fails to take the individual's life experiences into account.

Not only are standard psychological tests inadequate measures of black intelligence, but they can also be very misleading when they are used as clinical psychologists use them, for diagnostic purposes, for the determination of such disturbances as mental deficiency, emotional maladjustment, neurological damage, etc.* To determine the presence of pathology among black patients — adults or children — by using the same inter-test patterns that have been described as typical of disturbed white patients, can only lead to misdiagnosis, mismanagement and generally ineffective and inequitable treatment of the black subjects. Yet it seems almost certain that, despite the incorrect information that tests yield when they are used for any purpose with black subjects, psychologists will continue to administer them for all kinds of reasons. With the hope that some knowledge of the more usual patterns that are obtained from the black subjects will, at least in some instances, prevent grossly incorrect conclusions and misdiagnosis, a brief description of the way large numbers of black people score on the WAIS is offered here.

In general, the northern white people who do not know the southern black population or had occasion to test them are very much surprised

*See page 216 for further discussion of diagnostic use of tests with black patients.

when they find that such subjects, despite their verbal handicaps, score higher on the verbal than they do on the performance half of the scale. In fact, this finding is part of the argument some people use to support their contention that black people are "stupid." They are willing to concede that, because he is culturally deprived, the black man cannot be expected to score well on the verbal half of the scale where success on many of the items depends in good part on adequate schooling. But they insist that he should be able to point out missing parts in pictures portraying familiar objects, or to put blocks together to replicate a design. What these people do not appreciate is that subjects who do not have books or magazines in their homes, whose walls are without pictures, often find pictorial representations of common objects a strange experience. In fact, in many instances they do not recognize what the picture is intended to represent. Actually all the tests on the performance half of the scale are totally new kinds of tasks for the black subject, and so he is at a decided disadvantage when compared with most white subjects.

In general, the southern black people score best on the tests of Comprehension, Arithmetic, Similarities, and Digits Forward, and much less well on all the other items. The following explanations are offered to account for the successes and failures that characterize black functioning. For people whose lives are as circumscribed and deprived as those of the southern rural black people most of the items on the test of Information are totally unfamiliar. These people have never thought about or been told where rubber comes from and can hardly be expected to know where Brazil is or what the Vatican is. Again when asked the direction one must travel in going from Chicago to Panama the first reaction of the majority of the southern black subjects is bewilderment. They look at the examiner helplessly and repeat "Panama?" in a tone of voice which clearly indicates that they have never before heard the word "Panama." So they either shrug and say they do not know or, because they have friends or relatives in Chicago and know that that is north, they venture the answer "No'th."

The Comprehension test is a rather different matter for the southern black man. Although he obviously cannot answer information questions that are totally out of the range of his experience, he is able to cope with matters with which he has some familiarity. In fact, his ability to respond adequately when the material presented to him deals with issues with which he has had at least some experience is one of the most significant aspects of his functioning on the intelligence test. He can then mull over the question and frequently come up with a reasonable answer.

Thus, when asked, "Why should we keep away from bad company?" he can readily give the standard reply. Similarly, he can often handle "If you were lost in the forest in the daytime, how would you go about finding your way out?" A relatively large number of them are able to think through the reason why people who are born deaf are unable to talk. However, when asked, "Why are child labor laws needed?" they react in puzzled fashion. The question means nothing to them and from the welter of meaningless words most of the black subjects extract two that are within their experience, namely "child" and "labor." So they come back with "You mean a lady having a baby?" When the question is repeated slowly, most subjects are still unable to see any connection between "child labor" and "laws," and so they shake their heads despairingly. Some subjects zero in on "child" and "laws," overlooking "labor." Such subjects are then likely to give a response concerned with the training of children. They say such things as "To teach him right from wrong" or "So he'll mind." In general, for people whose ancestors worked as slaves and who themselves work as wage slaves, and whose children seemed destined to do the same, the idea of laws governing the conditions of employment for their children or for themselves, is an unheard of, unbelievable concept.

Again, when asked "Why should people pay taxes?" the most common answer was "To keep their houses." When urged to tell more about the tax matter, some of the subjects give answers which indicate that they vaguely know that the tax money might be used to care for the sick and the aged; and if they have a relative in the armed forces, they sometimes make reference to the war in Vietnam. However, such answers are rare. In general, they answer in terms of what they have heard happens to people who do not pay their taxes. For them it is a very immediate and personal matter, namely that if you were fortunate enough to own a piece of property you had better pay what the tax collector demanded or lose what little you possessed. Why they had to make such payments, the uses to which the tax money was put was, in the majority of instances, something to which they gave little or no thought.

Until the problems on the arithmetical reasoning test become rather difficult and the language used in presenting the problem unfamiliar to the black subject, he does relatively well. Occasionally a black person even manages to handle some of the more difficult items. In other words, they do have a grasp of the basic arithmetical concepts.

In the literature there are repeated references to the black man's difficulty, even inability to cope with abstract concepts. Certainly this is not the type of mental operation in which he has been trained or in which he is called on to engage. Nevertheless, when the means used to measure his capacity for dealing with abstractions employs matters with which he is familiar he can respond quite adequately. Thus, on the Similarities test when asked "In what way are wood and alcohol the same?" an item failed by many urban white subjects, the southern black man can answer correctly because the relationship between wood and alcohol is part of his daily experience. Even relatively young children can answer this question with "They burn." The black subject's score on the Similarities test is among his higher ones, and it surely seems to indicate that the black man can abstract and generalize. Were his horizons broader and his experiences fuller and richer, this capacity could obviously be developed. He is not only capable of what Jensen calls "associative learning" but also of "cognitive" or conceptual learning and has problem solving ability. The potential would certainly appear to be there. Obviously it cannot under the stress of an intelligence test, at a moment's notice, be developed to the point where the amount or degree of such potential can be accurately assessed.

The difficulty that the black subjects have in coping with totally unfamiliar tasks, in acquiring a new "set" when they are called on to do something altogether strange to them, is well illustrated by the scores they make when asked to repeat digits forward and backward. They almost always do very well on digits forward but have great difficulty with digits reversed. It takes them time to understand what they should do and still more time to discover the way to do it. Under rigid testing conditions this is not possible and so the disparity between the number of digits most of the black subjects can give in forward and reverse order is quite large. Yet if they are given time and some opportunity to practice, the results are quite different.

The final item on the verbal half of the Wechsler Adult Intelligence Scale is the vocabulary test. As might be expected, people who are, as a group, semi-literate, who almost never read, and whose activities and experience do not require them to use many and varied words, do not have a large vocabulary, and they actually do not need one. The result is that many of the words on the vocabulary test were totally strange to the rural black people, and even when they did know what a word meant the way they phrased their definition generally entitled them to only partial rather than full credit.

The performance half of the Wechsler Adult Intelligence Scale starts off with the Digit Symbol Test. This is of course a test of associative learning, and therefore, according to Jensen's theory, is one on which the black people should do well. Yet such is definitely not the case. The southern black man's relative unfamiliarity with written symbols and with paper-pencil tasks of all kinds definitely handicap him on this item. Furthermore, nothing in his experience has ever given him the feeling that speed is important, and so unlike ambitious white subjects, he makes no attempt to "beat the clock." The result is that his score on the Digit Symbol test is likely to be one of his lowest.

The black subject's score on the Picture Completion test is also likely to be a low one. As was noted previously, black subjects are not familiar with pictorial representations of objects, even objects and figures with which they are well acquainted. As a result they often fail to recognize what the pictures in this particular subtest actually represent. Some of them turn the pictures in various different directions, hoping in this way to make them more meaningful. Others hold them at arm's length, while still others squint their eyes, all in an effort to learn the true meaning of this strange image. However, these efforts rarely help. Furthermore, even when the subject does recognize the picture his concept of what is and is not important is very different from that of most white subjects, and from the standard response. For instance, the first picture on this test is a door with the knob missing. The black man is very unlikely to notice this and if he does he would probably not consider it important since his doors rarely boasted knobs.

As far as the rural black people are concerned, the strangeness of the Picture Arrangement Test is even greater than that of the Picture Completion Test. On this test, scrambled pictures have to be arranged in order so that they tell a sensible story. Not only do the southern black subjects fail to recognize the figures in the pictures, but they do not grasp the rather sophisticated relationships that are part of the "story." Several of the series of pictures are actually cartoons by famous cartoonists and black people who read no newspapers are totally unfamiliar with this type of humor. Even if, on rare occasions, a black subject — with much thought and effort — finally manages to figure out what it is all about and so gets the pictures in the right order, he takes so long that he far exceeds the time allowed for the particular item. Hence he cannot be given credit for what he had done. Yet the fact that he had been able to think through the task and come up with a logical solution certainly speaks well for his ability even if it took him time. However, in most cases, either because they failed completely to grasp the concepts involved or because they grasped them too slowly, most of the black people only earn credit for the first two series of pictures, one dealing with a bird building its nest, the other a man building a house. After that they rack up nothing but failures.

Again, it does not seem as though it should be too difficult for an adult to arrange blocks so they resemble a design that is placed in front of him. Neither should he have too much trouble putting a relatively simple puzzle together. But for an adult who has had no previous experience with blocks and puzzles, correctly completing such an assignment within a given time limit is more than he can do. This does not mean that with a little practice the picture would not have become quite different.

The same factors that make the Wechsler Adult Intelligence Scale an inappropriate measure of black adult intelligence apply to the Wechsler Intelligence Scale for Children. Much the same is also true of the Stanford Binet. In testing the children, regardless of what test is used, it becomes abundantly clear that the associative learning that is regarded by some psychologists and educators as the only kind of learning the black people are capable of is really a function of the type of teaching to which they have been exposed both in the home and the school. Schooling was based almost entirely on exercises in rote memory (Chapter 6). As a result, when they are asked a question, many of these children simply repeat what the examiner has said to them, and it is evident from their manner and facial expression that they think they have done what they were asked to do, that they have successfully carried out the assignment.

In testing black people, young or old, and then comparing the results with those obtained from white subjects. there is another aspect of the situation that must be taken into account, namely what the testing experience means to the person who is being tested. In the majority of instances the white testee has, from his early years, come to regard tests of any kind as a challenge to which he must respond as well as he can in order to be perceived in a positive light and get ahead. Black subjects have rarely been programmed in this way and they do not feel as strongly pressured to achieve as the white subjects do. The drive to do well, the motivation that is such an important aspect of the whole experience, is therefore quite different in the two groups.

When testing black subjects there is still another issue that should be given serious consideration, namely what does such an experience do to the child or the adult taking the test. All subjects, regardless of color, have some feeling about the testing situation. There are some few who are so sure of their mental ability that they actually look forward to and very much enjoy being tested. The majority of people however report varying degrees of discomfort at the thought of being tested. For some, this may cause just a mild and passing discomfort, for others, it can be a truly disturbing matter.

From their general manner while taking a psychological test, it seems that for the black people this is in most instances a novel and therefore somewhat unpleasant, anxiety-evoking experience. For some of the southern rural black people it is not so much a matter of concern about their intellectual level since many of them are not really aware that this is what is being assessed. Neither do they share the attitude of most white people about the importance of intelligence as measured by tests. What makes most of them uncomfortable is the fact that there are so many things they are being asked to do that they cannot do or that they do not even understand. As in the case of white subjects, this discomfort manifests itself in a number of ways. Many of the black subjects seek to deny or hide their embarrassment by laughing each time they give a response. In this way, by laughing at themselves, they seem to be trying to forestall any ridicule that they think might be directed against them because of their inadequate performance. Others try to minimize their discomfort by acting as though the whole matter was of no concern to them. Yet the lengths to which they go to express their indifference strongly suggests that such is not the case, that they are anything but indifferent. Occasionally, especially among younger subjects, there are those who defend their own poor performance by insisting that the task is impossible. Such subjects may even challenge the examiner, asking him if he knows the right answer or can correctly copy a block design. On the whole, the difference between the way black subjects and white subjects handle whatever anxiety the test evokes seems related in part to the fact that the white subject is concerned to a large extent by the outcome of the examination, the final score he earns; whereas the black subject worries over each individual item. In fact, he will often considerably prolong the testing procedure by asking questions about each item, unwilling to move on to a new matter. For him the testing experience is likely to be seen as a possible learning situation, all part of his inexperience and even naiveté in relation to psychological testing.

If tests are meaningless when used to measure black intelligence, and there can be little doubt that such is the case, how then can an evaluation of the black man's ability to "act purposefully, to think rationally, and to deal effectively with his environment" be made? One way of course would be to develop a series of tests on which a certain percentage of the items dealt with words and concepts that were well within the range of the black man's experiences but unlikely to be familiar to most white men.

Under such conditions the white man's relatively narrow horizons and informational gaps would certainly be exposed,* and the black man's ability to perform adequately under appropriate conditions would become apparent.

Actually the whole question of tests and the use of tests comes under consideration, not only in regard to the black people but all people who are required to take tests for one reason or another. For example, take the child sent to a school psychologist for "mental testing." In most instances the teacher has had the child in her class for several weeks and has a pretty accurate idea of his intellectual ability. Testing is generally simply a confirmation of what she already knows. The same is true of an employer who has had a man working for him for some period of time. Only in rare instances do the test results differ markedly from the opinions of those who have had the opportunity to see the individual make use of his capacities, not in a kind of laboratory situation, but in his daily work. When there is this difference of opinion, the question to be answered is which evaluation of the individual is the more accurate one, the teacher's or the boss's, or the test score? To understand a person, to appreciate what his abilities are and how and why he uses them as he does, much more than an IQ is needed. In fact, in many instances the test comes between the subject and the person seeking to evaluate and understand him. In general, it would seem that while there are occasions when the results of an intelligence test can be helpful for the subject or the person who has requested the testing, the test program as it operates in this country today has been over-sold and overused. In many respects the exaggerated use of IQ tests that characterizes our times is a reflection of our current deep sense of self-doubt and insecurity and our resultant need for something concrete like a number or a test score to make us feel more comfortable about what we are doing.

If we do not use tests then the black man's abilities must be judged by his performance when facing real stress during the course of his daily

---

*That white men fail to understand when the issue is not one about which they feel strongly or in which they have been involved was well illustrated by an episode that occurred during the annual meeting of the American Psychiatric Association, held in Washington, D.C. during the first week of May 1971. This was the week that large numbers of young people were seeking to halt government business by lying down in the streets and blocking traffic. During the course of a well-attended meeting of the APA, a few hundred of these young people burst into the meeting chanting "Peace now, peace now." There were murmurs in the audience, largely white and middle aged of "What are they saying? Peace what?" Had this been a question on an intelligence test it seems likely that many of these highly educated people would have failed this item of current information.

life. This is actually what tests are intended to do. By obtaining a sample of an individual's functioning, inferences and predictions are made regarding his ability to cope. Such individual examples as will be reported here will not satisfy those psychometrists with the "spic and span minds," those who have no use for data that does not follow standard procedures and produce statistically validated results. The argument will certainly be made that individual cases are no indication of the ability of a total people. Yet such examples could be multiplied over and over, as the survival of the black man testifies.

The following three incidents are offered as examples of the capacity of the black child and the black adult to function effectively under extreme and unusual conditions of stress. Given the same set of circumstances it seems doubtful that, because of his type of training and his experiences, the white child or the white adult could have performed as constructively.

The first example involves a ten year old girl whose mother had been called to Chicago because of a family crisis there. So this little girl was required to care for herself, her eight year old sister and an eleven month old brother. All had gone well for a few days, but then she thought that her brother was not well. Although she had never been to the health center in the area in which she lived she had heard of it. As her brother's condition appeared to her to worsen she walked two miles along a dusty country road, carrying the ailing child in her arms. She was right about the child being sick, and he was provided with appropriate medical and nursing care. This little girl had learned what was essential for her survival and the survival of her people, and had acted accordingly. Under similar circumstances would a middle-class white child of ten, with an above average IQ, have acted as rationally and as purposefully?

The second incident is concerned with a four year old boy attending a Head Start school. Because he was quiet and withdrawn, his teacher had requested intellectual evaluation, suspecting that he might be "dull." So he was given the Stanford Binet—the 1960 revision. One of the questions at the four year level is "Why do we have books?" The psychologist who was doing the testing stated that she felt foolish asking a child who had probably never held a book in his hand, or even seen a book before he came to Head Start, such a question. So she decided to change the question and ask, "Why does the school have books?" However, before she could do so the little boy answered, "I ain't got no books," and then quickly added, "School got books. You read 'em." Surely any child who had been as remote from books as this child had but who could grasp the situation and respond to it as appropriately as he did showed good potential for learning, was certainly of at least average and very probably better than average ability.

The final incident took place during the summer of 1965 when one of the churches that was being used as a Head Start Center was burned by irate local whites. When the news of this atrocity reached Head Start headquarters in Edwards, Mississippi, several of the northern white professional who were working with the project that summer became extremely incensed. There was a great deal of agitated pacing, handwringing, and comments to the effect that "This is outrageous," "Washington must be notified," "The people who did this must be apprehended and punished," etc. At that time the acting director of the Mississippi Head Start — generally known as the Child Development Group of Mississippi — was a young black man, a Mississippian whose formal education included a few years in a southern black college. However, his "informal" education included more than twenty years of living in a hostile white environment and adjusting to it. Consequently, when the outraged cries of the northern whites subsided he quietly said, "We'll get a tent and pitch it on the grounds where the church stood. Then we'll go to our other centers (eighty four in all) and get a few toys, books and other necessary supplies from each one. In this way we'll be operating again by this afternoon or tomorrow morning at the latest. That will show them that they can't stop us." He paused and looked around at the assembled white northerners who recognized the wisdom of his decision as contrasted with their emotional reactions. Then he spoke directly to one of the white people saying, "And when I go to the centers to get the supplies I want you to go with me. I want the workers and the community to see me riding with a white face." Can there be any doubt about this man's intelligence? As confirmation of his high ability it might be added that he is now doing graduate work in a northern university. Yet had he been given a formal intelligence test in 1965 he would not have scored very high.

# CHAPTER 6

# *Education*

Although the term "education" is usually employed to denote formal learning in the classroom, it is actually a much broader, far-reaching concept than is implied in such a formulation. Education actually begins at birth and is facilitated or hindered by everything that happens to the individual during the course of his life. Long before schooling becomes part of a child's experience, he has learned a great deal and has acquired knowledge and skills essential to him. He walks, talks, dresses and feeds himself, knows his name and the names of his siblings, knows where he lives, knows who his friends and enemies are, knows what he is permitted to do and what he may not do, how he must behave under a variety of different conditions, etc. On the basis of what they have learned, the majority of children can and do act in reasonably adequate and acceptable fashion even before they attain school age.

Defined in terms of its Latin origin, education means a leading out from the individual those abilities and talents that he possesses. However, few educational systems even vaguely approach such a concept of education. In most instances in this country the educational philosophy of the public school system is a crude patch work of age-old, outmoded ideas about education to which, with the passing years, the thoughts and suggestions of various educators have been appended. As a result, public education in this country has gone through a series of phases, as one educational fad supersedes another or more often is simply superimposed on the existing one, so that the end result is a confused and frequently senseless hodge podge. What the American system of public education has never had is the drastic overhauling and complete reorganization that it so desperately needs. There is far too much investment in the *status quo*, financially, politically, and personally, for this to occur.

One of the most important issues in regard to education is "what are we educating for?" Yet this question has never been squarely faced or well answered. In the early days in this country, education was regarded as an important aspect of a democratic way of life. Certainly everyone should be able to read, his Bible if nothing else; and he should be capable of keeping track of his income and his expenditures, if he hoped to get along and prosper in the world. The problems that are so important today, the questions of motivation and the relevance of what was being taught, played no part in the thinking of the early formulators of American education, To be able to attend school and learn the three R's was an opportunity and a blessing one took advantage of without raising questions.

Currently however, the purpose of education ranges from the early belief that everyone should be able to read to a determination to make America the leader in technological developments. In a world that is changing with incredible rapidity, and where skills and knowledge grow at an unbelievable pace, there are many who feel that it is literally impossible to convey to the student all the known facts and all the experiences that are part of his heritage. Instead, they maintain that each child should of course acquire the basic skills, should be able to read, write, and figure, and then should learn how to identify and deal rationally with important issues, including issues in the economic, political, and interpersonal arenas. The next step is to permit him to choose his special area of interest. At the other end of the continuum are those who find value in the more traditional forms of education (with possibly some minor modifications), and of course as is inevitably the case, there is every possible shade of opinion between these two extremes.

Regardless of the eductional plan that theoretically at least determines what and how a child is taught, there are two factors of major importance that affect his learning. One is what he himself brings to the learning experience, the other the teacher's skill and his attitude toward and concept of his work. Just as research in psychotherapy has demonstrated that it is not necessarily the therapist's theoretical orientation that determines how he works with a patient, but rather his experience, his innate skill and understanding in working with people that results in patient improvement, so too it is the experience and skill of the teacher, plus her motivation and her feeling for children, that count heavily in so far as pupil progress is concerned. It is the teacher who can make the acquisition of knowledge exciting or deadly dull, who can spur the pupil on to further learning, who can encourage and foster intellectual curiosity, or who, by her attitude, turns him off completely.

What the child brings to the learning situation, especially when he first comes to school, is of course a very individual matter. Not only are there the differences in intellectual endowment — the range of mental ability that can be found in any classroom — but there are all the past experiences the child has had, experiences which cause him to feel confident or timid, strong or weak, happy or unhappy, when he has to face a new situation. In addition to his past experiences and the sense of assurance or the lack of assurance with which these have left him, there are the attitudes of his parents and his older siblings and friends in regard to school and the whole educational process. Consequently, some children regard going to school as an exciting adventure, an opportunity to explore and learn, to make new friends and try out one's ideas; while other children look forward to school with dread, seeing it as a confining and restraining force, and one in which he will surely encounter many difficulties. It is rare indeed that a child coming to school with such an orientation finds any pleasure in the classroom or benefits very much from his presence there.

In addition to the child's emotional reactions to the idea of school, there is the training and the learning that went on in his home. In some instances this was probably quite extensive and of an order that prepared the child for the kinds of teaching to which he was likely to be exposed in the classroom. For instance, some parents by their interest in books have already stimulated the child's interest in reading and in other matters closely related to formal learning. However, in other cases such stimulation has been minimal or totally absent.

Obviously no system involving thousands, even millions of children can provide for the special, individual needs of each child. Instead, the system is geared to fit the norm, and in this country that means the average middle-class white child. It can therefore hardly be appropriate or beneficial for the black child. Everything that has already been said in this book points up the sharp differences that obtain between the backgrounds and experiences of black and white children. In fact, in view of these differences and the nature of the school system, it is amazing that the black child gets anything at all out of what is presented to him in the classroom. In order to learn in the formal sense that is the essence of the classroom experience, the child must already have acquired certain basic concepts, certain ways of perceiving and reacting. A brief review of what happens to black children, and especially southern black children, and white children in this regard is therefore indicated. Only then can the differences existing in their learning "readiness" be understood.

Even before the white child is born his mother is not only receiving good medical care, including a healthful diet, but she is acquainting herself with all the latest ideas in regard to child-rearing practices. She believes that the child's future welfare depends in good part on how she furthers his emotional and cognitive development. Hence Spock, Freud, Erikson, and many others are likely to occupy important places on her bookshelf.

When the white child comes home from the hospital, he has a bassinet or a crib all his own waiting to receive him. Very probably there is a crib-mobile attached to the side of the crib, and in a few weeks other toys, such as rattles and cuddle toys, make their appearance. His routine is a well-ordered one, alternating between periods of sleep and periods of calm wakefulness when he is exposed to appropriate kinds and amounts of stimulation. The atmosphere in his home is generally a peaceful one which enables him to concentrate in undisturbed fashion on one visual or auditory stimulus until he is able to recognize it whenever it appears.

When the white baby wakes up and makes his presence known, one person, usually his mother, comes to him. He therefore soon learns to recognize her footsteps or the sound of her voice as she calls to him. In this way specific auditory stimuli become familiar to him. Then as his mother bends over him and lifts him, he sees her, and so he gradually learns to associate his auditory experiences with his visual ones and in this way an integration of two sensory tracks is achieved. At the same time he is developing the habit of listening, of attending to sounds and visual stimuli for relatively long periods of time.

As he grows older the white child's experiences become more varied. Quite early in his life he sits on his mother's lap while she turns the pages of a book or magazine, pointing to and naming the objects represented there. Similarly, the objects around him are named and explained, not in a pedantic way but in the course of a day's experiences. He is also taken on outings with his family, provided the opportunity to visit new places and meet new people. While some of the experiences that are made available to the little white child are planned, in the main they are simply part of what goes on in an average middle-class white environment.

In the rural south until very recently, and in many instances even today, the black child's experiences are of a very different order from those of the white child. Even though the reality to which the southern black child has to adjust is gradually changing, the older members of the black community still think it necessary to be cautious in their interactions with the white community, and so partly from habit and partly from lack of trust they continue to raise their children as they always have. They do not really believe that the children will enjoy the same freedom and the same opportunities that the white children do, and consequently they do not adopt the white man's child-rearing practices. What is more, even among some of the better educated southern black people there is a strong belief in the effectiveness of "whuppings" as opposed to positive reinforcement as far as bringing up children is concerned.

Apart from the ideological concepts and the beliefs that determine what happens to the young southern black child, there is the economic condition in which he and his family live. In the small crowded shack in which he is born or to which he comes after a few days sojourn in a hospital there is no crib for him, and certainly no crib-mobile or toys of any description. He either shares a big double bed with other members of the family or sleeps by himself in a cardboard box. Because of the crowded conditions that prevail in most of the southern rural homes he is constantly bombarded by a cacaphony of sounds. His siblings and all the other children who live in the house or in the neighborhood run in and out, shouting and slamming doors. Adults also shout and scream at one another in order to make themselves heard over the ongoing racket. If the house has a radio or a TV it is always going full blast, from the time the first person gets up in the morning until the last person goes to bed at night. Exposed to this constant welter of sounds and moving objects, cared for by a number of different people, depending upon which member of the household has a chance to work and who stays home, the southern black baby does not have the opportunities that the white baby does to associate specific sights and sounds with specific objects. Few visual or auditory experiences last long enough or are sufficiently free from distracting influences for the baby to give them his sustained attention. Consequently, he does not acquire a repertoire of stable images, and the habit of attention is certainly not fostered. Furthermore, the objects he sees and the sounds he hears are not likely to be identified for him, and their meaning and/or use explained to him, simply because whoever is taking care of him at the moment does not realize the importance of such identification and naming. So even in the first few months of life, certainly by the end of his first year, the black child's experience has been very different from that of the white child. Although people do talk to him and do play with him, what they do with him does not prepare him for the white man's world with its emphasis on words and abstract concepts. Yet the educational system to which he is exposed and from which he is expected to benefit is determined by what has happened to the white child, by what is judged to be the white child's readiness for formal schooling. Similarly, what is taught in school is what is seen as important to the future needs of the dominant white group.

In addition to the fact that he is not at all prepared to benefit from the type of education offered him, the black child's ability to adjust to the educational process is further hampered by his inability to see any relevance between what he is being taught and what he has been led to believe his future is likely to be. In the past he envisaged himself as working in the fields just as his ancestors did, while currently because of automation, he does not even have this means of livelihood to look forward to. Instead he has the choice of living on welfare or taking off to the city and, from what he has heard, even in the city he will be involved in manual work. Consequently he does not believe that learning how to read, write, and figure are especially important. The way these subjects are taught in most black schools rarely stimulates interest and makes them worth the effort needed to master them.

At the present time the picture in regard to black education in the south, as well as in most other areas of the country, is of a very mixed order. In some instances integration has been thorough, meaningful, and constructive, in others limited and unsatisfactory, while in still others segregation is the order of the day. Where it has been truly successful the black southern child's attitude toward school is being gradually modified, but where it has not been effective the child continues to be disinterested and often markedly negative toward the whole learning process.

When the child's parents are aware and accepting of the social, political, and economic changes that are taking place today, the attitude in the home in relation to school is also changing and children are being encouraged to study and learn. Formerly the parents perceived the whole educational process as more or less useless, a waste of time, and even some of the black teachers shared this point of view. Consequently education did not begin to have the meaning and importance for the plantation children that it had for the white children who were geared to think in terms of "getting ahead." Because they saw little advantage for the children in attending school, black parents did not strongly encourage them to do so. Instead, a child might be kept home from school for any number of reasons, to fetch water from a neighbor's well, to help with a new baby, to care for a sick relative, to earn a day's pay working in the fields or in the white man's house, or he might not go to school simply because he did not feel like going that particular day. Currently however, certain parents are aware of the need for education and this idea is spreading as more and more parents come to realize that the old days are gone and previous attitudes about education must be modified.

When the black children attended the segregated schools of the south, the nature of the teaching to which they were exposed went a long way toward reinforcing their indifferent, even negative attitude toward learning. The schools the plantation children attended were all black schools, taught by black teachers. This was not a matter of where one lived but a matter of the law. Black and white children were not permitted to sit together in the same classroom or even attend the same school. Hence the black children often had to walk long distances, passing more conveniently located white schools, in order to reach the black school. These so-called separate but equal schools were certainly separate, but they were *not* equal. The black schools were almost invariably housed in old, unattractive, dilapidated buildings with outside toilets. School books and other supplies were limited and almost never new and attractive. Compounding the negative features of the system was the fact that the teachers were the products of the inadequate educational system, and so were rarely in a position really to educate their pupils or enrich their lives. Certainly they could not introduce them to the wonders and the excitement that come with a broadening of horizons and the birth of new ideas. The truly incredible nature of the curriculum and the teaching offered the black children is well reflected in the following episode. As I was riding along a southern highway with a nineteen year old who had been "educated" in Mississippi, a Missouri car went by. I read the license plate and my companion repeated the word "Missouri" as though she had never heard it before. "Do you know where Missouri is, Sue Ellen?" I asked. Sue Ellen shook her head. I then asked her about a few other nearby states, but all the names were strange to her, as were England and Europe. My next question was "Did you ever study geography?" "Gogaphy," she echoed dubiously. The matter was considered for several minutes and then she finally said, "Oh, yes. They taught us about Askemos." Further questioning revealed that the "Askemos" were a strange people who lived far away where it was cold all the time! So much for geography and the whole educational program.

Even if the black teachers had been better prepared to interest and stimulate their pupils, their dependence on the good will of the white school board and the white superintendent would have made any such venture a most hazardous one. Black children were not supposed to become too interested in or excited about learning and their minds were certainly not to be stimulated. Since none of the black teachers, no matter how long they had been teaching, were given tenure, they were most unwilling to risk their jobs by doing anything that would be unacceptable to white authority. A teacher could never be sure that his contract would be renewed another year, or even that it might not be revoked during the year if he did something contrary to the wishes of the white establishment. So if they were to know any economic security it was essential for them to go along with the requirements of the white system in which they functioned. So they taught—if it can be called teaching—in a most uninspired fashion.

The kind of teaching that went on in the black schools of the south rather than being a "leading out" might best be described as "putting in," and this was accomplished in the most unexciting way imaginable. Memory was stressed above all else, certainly to the exclusion of thinking. Consequently, when a black child was asked a question he was very likely to give an answer that he had learned by heart, without in the least understanding what he was saying. Sometimes he did not even realize that he was being questioned, but assumed that he was being "taught." He would then repeat the question, believing that repetition was all that was required of him. For example, on a vocabulary test, when asked "What is a . . .?" or "What does . . . mean?" instead of giving a definition, some black children simply say, "What is a . . .?" and believe they have done what they were expected to do.

The southern white establishment certainly did not care if the black children failed to receive a good education. In fact, for a number of reasons, they preferred their education to be poor and limited. It was not to the advantage of the white people for the black people to be able to read and learn about life styles other than their own. Clearly the white people did not want the black people to give any deep thought to their position in life and how it might be altered. There was still another reason why the southern whites considered it important to keep the black man ignorant. Having justified their treatment of the black people by insisting on their stupidity and inferiority, it was necessary to keep them uneducated. Here then was the antecedent of what more recently has been described as the self-fulfilling prophecy. In order to be sure that his predictions about the educability of the black man were correct, the white man added low quality teaching and generally poor educational opportunities to all the other handicaps the black man suffered. Poorly nourished so that he frequently felt weak and fatigued, tired because of crowded sleeping conditions and constant noise, with no privacy, not even a place to sit and do homework, how could the black child possibly learn?

Still another factor impeded the black child's ability to learn, namely the question of an open receptive mind. In order to make a new concept one's own, an individual has to look at it from different points of view, has to be flexible in considering all sides of an issue, etc. By the time the southern black child reached school age such openness and flexibility were rare indeed. What had been encouraged and developed in the child was quiet, conforming behavior. Intellectual curiosity and a quest for knowledge were not acceptable to parents or teachers, and assertive attempts at "knowing" and "understanding" were very likely to be met with rejection and punishment. For years the black child had been trained not to think or question, not to come up with any original ideas, and the dreams and fantasies that might have led to the development of new concepts had been vigorously discouraged. The child had rigidly narrowed his outlook in order to conform to the demands of the adults, and consequently, he was resistant to any effort (had there been one) to modify his orientation. As a result, he sat in the classroom bored, sometimes half asleep or actually sleeping, emptily repeating whatever was said to him, but certainly not trying to understand what he was saying or even wondering why he was saying it.

With the educational process as unimportant and uninspiring as it generally was as far as the southern black child was concerned, comparatively few of them stayed in school very long. All through their school careers they had frequently missed school for any number of reasons and often for long stretches of time. This was likely to occur particularly if work of any kind was available or if there was serious illness in the family. Most of them gradually stopped attending school and the average educational level of the southern rural black people was at about an eighth grade level. However, eighth grade in a southern rural black school was certainly not the equivalent of eighth grade in a northern school.

The situation in the all black high schools was much the same as it was in the elementary schools. While some of the teachers were sincerely and strongly motivated, the system was such that it was virtually impossible to maintain such motivation very long. Sooner or later most of the teachers became markedly disillusioned and unhappy, and if they had ever had any thought of helping their people through education, that hope was abandoned.

What was taught in the high school was of course determined by the white school board, and obviously nothing that was likely to give the black pupils any "unacceptable" ideas was permitted. Geography was not a subject that appeared in most black high school or elementary school curricula since there was no point in making the black pupil aware of a larger world than his own very immediate one; and of course American history never pointed out the contributions made by the black people to the wealth and growth of the nation. When the black high school student finally received his diploma his knowledge and his skills were more like those of an average elementary school child, somewhere between the sixth and eighth grade levels.

With a few notable exceptions, what happened in the black colleges of the south was equally discouraging. Most black students came to college with very poor preparation and no idea whatsoever what they meant to study. In many instances therefore, class attendance was highly irregular and those who did come to class were likely to wander in and out of the room at will or gaze out of the window, paying no attention to what was going on. The teacher was expected to "tell" them, to "put in," just as he had in elementary school. Similarly, just as the small child met his assignments by repeating verbatim what was said to him or what was asked of him, so many college students repeated what the teacher had said in the previous session. An assignment on any subject was dealt with by copying pages from a book, often without the least understanding of what the reproduced text was all about. In one instance, when a student was asked to read her report in class, she had great difficulty pronouncing a number of words and it was obvious that they were unfamiliar to her. Finally, when she stumbled over the word "subjective," she was asked what it meant and she shrugged and indicated that she did not have the faintest idea. Of course it had never occurred to her to look it up in a dictionary. Neither was she at all abashed by her use of words and concepts that were meaningless to her. Such had been her experience in the educational system for her entire life and she simply took it for granted that there were many things that were mysteries to her and would remain so.

Actually then, few black students in the rural south truly understood what it meant to go to college or what higher education was all about. The idea that college was a place where one not only acquired certain facts but where one engaged in independent thought, broadened one's outlook and reorganized one's ideas was not at all the way the black student viewed the experience. For many, though not all, it was simply a continuation of the memory exercises that had always marked their educational career. This was the concept of higher education that most of the black students had and they went along with it partly from lack of choice and partly because, if they did otherwise, they would not receive the diploma which gave them the right to teach. Given this kind of training, it was not surprising that the way these students taught when they received their certificates followed the traditional methods of the black educational system, thus making any change for a more constructive approach out of the question.

Rigidly tied to the things he had been taught in his earliest years, it was almost impossible to break through the concepts and superstitions that the student had lived with practically all his life. No amount of reasoning, no logical, rational approach to an issue was likely to sway him from the position that he and his forebears had held for generations. For example, in a course on child psychology, it was virtually impossible to get a class of Juniors to understand or even consider the possibility that positive reinforcement might be a more constructive way of dealing with a child than constantly focusing on the negative aspects of his behavior. Greatgrandmothers, grandmothers, mothers, and other adults were all cited as authorities who knew that the best way to bring up a child was to scold him and "whup" him. Actually such discussion and disagreement with an instructor were rare and on the whole only occurred when the instructor was someone whose concepts were very different from those of the students and who invited such response. In most instances the instructor was one of them, someone who only a short time ago had sat in the seats they were now occupying and who thought exactly as they did.

Yet these students were not without the capacity to think if thinking was encouraged and they considered the situation safe enough for them to express themselves. Thus on another occasion, in the same child psychology class, the subject of the hippies came under consideration. The entire class indicated a negative attitude toward the hippies, expressed as "We don't like them." The instructor, a northern white psychologist, was amazed at this reaction and wanted to know why. She explained to the students that, as a group, the hippies were probably more positively oriented toward the black people and their problems than any other group in the country. Although grudgingly admitting this, the class continued to express its negative feeling toward the hippies. The reason for their dislike of the hippies was finally expressed as "We don't like how they look." What they meant was that they strongly disapproved of the long, disheveled hair, the unmatched, sloppy clothing, etc. affected by the hippies. That they had given the matter considerable thought was evident from some of the statements they made in this regard. Most of them realized that the hippies were largely middle class, that they came from families that, as they put it, "had made it." Hence, according to the black students, they could afford to look as unkempt as they did although the students saw no reason why they should. They went on to point out that they, the students, were in a very different position, were trying to make it. "We'se coming up," was the way they expressed it, and as part of this effort they stressed a neat, attractive appearance, something that practically all of them achieved.

Again, when what was being presented to the black students in no way conflicted with their traditional concepts, they could grasp new ideas very readily and use them creatively. For instance, when research procedures were explained to them they immediately perceived their relevance and importance. Asked to devise ways of testing some of the child development theories that were being discussed, they came up with well-conceived and creative procedures. It is obvious then that the black student has the ability to give constructive thought to matters that concern and interest him. Unfortunately much of the time in southern black colleges such opportunities are not available.

Almost none of the teachers in the small black southern colleges had Ph.D. degrees. In fact, many of them had spent a good part of their professional life teaching in the black elementary and high schools of the south. They themselves were therefore the victims of the system that so handicaps the black people. Because they were at least partially aware of their limitations many of these college teachers tended to be defensive and rigid about what they were doing, to the point where it became impossible for them to recognize the need for innovations or accept change. Instead, they resisted change, partly out of fear of how white authority would react to any change, even a small unimportant one; and partly because the need for change carried with it the implication that they had not been doing the best possible job. For example, in one college where there was talk of introducing a remedial reading program because so many of the students read at a sixth grade level, the college staff vetoed the program as unnecessary.

Another seriously hampering factor in practically all black colleges is the matter of funds. Many of the southern black colleges are privately supported, frequently by religious organizations. However, even those that are state supported lack adequate funds, and many essentials are in short supply or absent altogether. So libraries are likely to be small, laboratories non-existent. Likewise, salaries are low and well-trained black instructors who have had the benefit of an education in a northern college are reluctant to come south, deterred not only by poor pay but by the meager facilities, the poorly prepared students and the hardships and discrimination to which they would be subjected by the white community.

Such then was the situation in regard to black education until just a few years ago. Now the picture is no longer a monolithic one, but rather one that goes from the extreme of ineptitude to highly constructive, creative forms of teaching and learning. The changes that are occurring in black communities all over the country are certainly affecting the way that the black people, adults and children, view the educational process, and these views are naturally varied and innovative.

More and more professional people are coming to the realization that the entire educational system in this country is an anachronism, regardless of whether one is considering the education of the privileged or the so-called "disadvantaged." Much of the content and the methodology are inappropriate for today's world; and even when the educational authorities are unaware of this or at least unwilling to admit that they realize this, the students know it very well. Hence their increasing disinterest and the growing number of drop-outs. If the situation is difficult and meaningless for the white students, how much more so is it for the black ones whose needs were never even recognized or considered when the system was devised.

# CHAPTER 7

# *Health — Physical and Mental*

The physical condition of the black people in the rural south is briefly discussed here, mainly because the way in which a person feels certainly has considerable bearing on the way he functions and the way he experiences himself. An individual who is hungry, weak and tired all the time, who is subject to spells of dizziness or who is in more or less constant pain, is bound to find it very hard to do the things he is expected to do, whether it be learning in school, cleaning some white woman's house, or picking cotton in the field. Furthermore, for the physically weak or ill person control of impulses and emotions is often considerably more difficult than it is for a person who is enjoying relatively good health, and certainly a suffering person is not likely to have a positive image of himself.

A very large percentage of the southern rural black people, young and old, suffered from some bodily discomfort or from an actual illness during much of their lives. The infants were the most vulnerable members of the black community, the rate of infant mortality among black babies during the first year of life being roughly four times what it was among white babies. There were many reasons for this vulnerability. One of the chief ones of course was the lack of sufficient food appropriate for a child in his first year. In addition, there was the complete lack of pre- and post-natal care, so that many children were damaged during pregnancy or during the birth process itself. Almost none of these children came into the world with the aid of a trained physician although actually, because of the poor health conditions that prevailed in the black community, their need for this was great.

The poor physical condition of the mother contributed greatly to the poor health and life hazard experienced by the child. Many of the mothers were very young, no more than thirteen or fourteen years old, in most cases not physically ready for child bearing. On the other hand, some of them were much older women who had already given birth to ten or more children and who, because of their frequent pregnancies, hard work, and poor diets, were worn out and ill equipped to bring another healthy child into the world.

Given a poor start many of these children were further damaged by everything that happened to them following their birth. Practically none of the children received milk everyday or even every week. Powdered milk with water added to the point where it was more water than milk, was available occasionally. In the main, the diets consisted of black-eyed peas, beans, occasional potatoes and corn bread, and sometimes fat back, though meat was extremely scarce. Often hungry and irritable, a large percentage of these children suffered markedly from a lack of vitamins and minerals, and the greatest number of them showed some form of anemia.[*,†]

Many of the school age children were chronically hungry. Even in homes where there was a little money, it was rarely enough to purchase the foods that would be health-producing. For instance, in one town there was a school program where, for twenty-five cents, a child could purchase a hot lunch prepared by the school dietitian and well fortified with necessary vitamins and proteins. However, relatively few families could give their children twenty-five cents even once a week, much less everyday. Instead, many of the children had at the most a dime, with which they would buy a bottle of coke. This bloated them and made them feel full for a short time, while the sugar gave them at least temporary energy. Sometimes one bottle had to be divided among two or three children. There were also children who went without lunch altogether.

Their poor physical condition accounted in good part for the many infections the children had. Running sores and other forms of skin infection were common among them. What often happened was that when they received a small scratch or insect bite, they scratched and soon developed an infection because of their lack of resistance. When bodily discomfort, itching, pain, and hunger are more or less ever present, restlessness, list-

*Brown, R., and Halpern, F. The Variable Pattern of Mental Development in Rural Black Children. *Clinical Pediatrics*, Vol. 10, No. 7, p. 405.

†Zee, P., Walters, T., and Mitchell, C. Nutrition and Poverty in Pre-School Children. *JAMA*, August 3, 1970, Vol. 213, No. 5.

lessness, and fatigue can be expected. Such conditions are certainly not conducive to learning and surely do not develop or strengthen habits of attention or concentration. The circumstances being what they are, one can only be amazed that the black children develop as well as they do and learn as much as they do.

By the time the southern rural black man or woman reached adulthood he was very likely to be suffering from some chronic disturbance or disability, some of them mild, some of them seriously handicapping. Young or middle aged, her poor nutrition left the black mother far more likely to abort, to have a premature infant, or a difficult birth than would have been the case had she had sufficient health-providing food and other physical comforts. Naturally the mother's poor condition and the difficult birth had an impact on the health of the child. So there are many children and many adults who, were they members of a more privileged group, would be receiving intensive care or in some instances even be hospitalized. Yet among the black people where the need is particularly great, adequate medical care has been woefully lacking and their poor health has been aggravated by their living conditions and their need to engage in hard labor.

It is an accepted medical fact that an organism can and often does adapt to circumstances that are basically not conducive to health. It is by means of such an adaptation that the organism manages to survive. Such would seem to be the explanation for the physical survival of the black people, just as their recourse to compliance and docility enabled them to survive in their interaction with the white community. The psychological adjustment that they made was no more conducive to mental health than was their adaptation to poor food, unsanitary conditions, limited shelter from extremes of climate, etc. conducive to physical health. Yet physically and psychologically the adaptation had to be made, and, failing this, as a group they would have perished.

Despite the very poor physical condition of many of the southern rural black people, health did not have a high priority with them. Illness and suffering were so much a part of their daily experience that it had to be markedly increased before it was given any thought or any steps taken in relation to it. While the people talked a great deal to one another about their pains and aches, how difficult it was to bend, how much stomach distress they were experiencing, etc., they had lived with such conditions all their lives and accepted them as part of living or as "the will of God." Jobs, housing, and more recently, good education were perceived by the black people as more important for their welfare than health care. In fact, when a government-financed clinic was opened in the rural south some of the people were actually distressed, since they felt this indicated that their real needs were not recognized and appreciated.

Certainly health did not have the importance or the meaning for the southern black people that it has for middle-class white people. White people have been the targets of intense educational programs which have made them very conscious of their diets, of the need for periodic checkups, and of the whole concept of preventive medicine. For the black people there was no such thing as preventive medicine, in fact, the term was unfamiliar to them. Likewise there were no periodic checkups either for the adults or the children, and relatively few of the children received the many shots that white children get. As far as diet was concerned, one ate what was available, in order to stifle hunger pangs, regardless of whether what one ate was healthful or not. Only when an adult or a child became extremely ill and the pain virtually unbearable was any thought given to the possibility of medical attention. For most ailments, most of the time, century-old, home-made remedies, recourse to prayer and in some instances to voodoo, were the cures that the local population employed.

Among an agrarian people, living and working as the black people did, accidents were inevitable. Deep cuts and broken bones were certainly not unusual. There were also wounds from beebee guns and wounds from hunting accidents. The open fire places also constituted a serious hazard. Children frequently went too close to the flames and suffered severe burns. Also among the older people who suffered from arthritis and for whom heat provided some relief, the temptation to move too close to the fire at times overcame their better judgment, and as a result not a few of them suffered from burned knees.

Among the infants, chronic diarrhea and accompanying dehydration were not at all uncommon, while among the older people, hypertension, heart and kidney ailments and the early onset of arthritis were among the major causes of poor health. Largely because of the nature of their diet the majority of the middle aged women were markedly overweight and this of course took its toll in terms of heart and kidney ailments, etc. Yet the lack of money made it virtually impossible for the people to maintain a diet that would enable them to lose weight.

In addition to poverty, ignorance and recourse to magic and voodoo interfered with constructive medical practice. For instance, a patient who came to a Health Center in the deep south and was being treated by a highly competent, northern trained white physician insisted that she could not get well because her boyfriend had put a "hex" on her. Only after the doctor consulted with the staff psychologist and then assured the patient that her "hex" was stronger than the boyfriend's, was the patient able to recover.

Until federally financed health centers were opened in the rural south the majority of the physicians practicing in the area were white southerners, and such is still the case. Although they treated black patients, there were always separate entrances for blacks and whites, separate waiting rooms and separate treatment rooms. While some of these men were humane in their attitudes and feelings for their black patients, they were also the victims of their culture and their backgrounds. Furthermore, in some cases their response to the black man's needs — and when the black man came to the white doctor the needs were almost always desperate — could hardly be described as humanitarian or in accord with professional doctrine. Many of these white doctors never touched their patients, never really examined them. All they did was sit across the room from the patient, listening to his complaints and then prescribing for him. Among the black people there were all kinds of unhappy stories regarding the way in which they were treated by the white doctors. It was claimed that in many instances, acutely suffering black patients were kept waiting for hours while white patients with minor ailments were being cared for. It was also claimed that doctors refused to see a patient who did not have the fee with him when he came into the office.

When a federally financed Health Center was opened in the Mississippi Delta late in 1967, to everyone's amazement it was not the children who came in great numbers for treatment, but the old folks. These were the people who had been suffering for years and had borne their sufferings with patience because they did not have money to pay a doctor. So they resorted to home-made remedies and lived with their afflictions as best they could. That the old people came to the clinic first was also in accord with the culture of the rural black population. Old people were greatly revered, and in most matters they came first. This does not mean that no children were brought for medical care, but rather that the needs of the old people were so great and their suffering of such long duration that they were the ones whom the community thought should be helped first. Only after the clinic had been in operation for some time and the confidence of the community in the clinic personnel well established, did the aides and the nurses initiate an educational campaign aimed at teaching the people the importance of health care for the children and something about preventive medicine. So within a year the patient population changed, with children as numerous if not more numerous than the old folks.

When the older people first came to the health center they were very unsure of what they would encounter and their behavior was marked by a certain restraint and caution. Because they had rarely been carefully and thoroughly examined by a doctor some of them became quite upset when they were asked to remove their clothes. This certainly had not happened when, on rare occasions, they had consulted local white doctors. Yet even though they appreciated the care and the concern they were receiving, at times certainly some of them were skeptical about it, and so there were occasions when advice and medicine were ignored in favor of old remedies. The majority of the people however had faith in the efficacy of pills and "shots." Consequently, a doctor who stressed diet or rest or exercise for those who had no work, but who prescribed no medicine, was regarded with disfavor, not really trusted, and definitely shunned by the patients. In fact, the word quickly spread and as a result patients resisted assignment to such a physician.

Whether they followed the advice and/or took the medicine given them or in the end went back to more familiar ways of coping with illness, the majority of the people who came to the clinic began to enjoy their visits and to regard the clinic as a satisfying force in their lives. Among other things, it was concrete evidence that the government, in some form or other, knew they existed and was concerned about them. Furthermore, there were educated white people, professional people, working at the clinic who treated them with respect, who saw them as human beings with feelings and rights. In addition, as time passed, the clinic offered much more than just medical care. There was a social service department that explained to the people how they could get food stamps and supplementary food when it became available; that took care of immediate needs when there was not a morsel of food in the house, or that provided clothing when a child had to be kept home from school because he literally had nothing to cover his nakedness. The social service department was also helpful in relation to the welfare bureau and in getting aid for dependent children, all matters which for many of the black people had been most difficult, even nightmarish. Training programs intended to prepare people for jobs such as typing, nursing aide, etc. also came into being. In fact, many of the local people were working at the clinic in such capacities.

One of the most important contributions of the clinic to the welfare of the area was the sanitation department. Run by well-trained sanitarians, the members of this department visited homes in the area, screening houses, eradicating vermin, mice and rats, setting up privies where there were none or where they were in unbelievable condition, examining the water supply, etc. A number of local men had been trained by the professional sanitarian and worked as aides in the department. Some of them learned so quickly and well that they were encouraged to become full fledged sanitarians and several of them had been accepted by northern colleges for such training.

Many of the towns had serious problems in relation to sewage and garbage disposal, particularly in that part of the town where the black people resided. The white officials of these towns seemed unaware of or indifferent to the fact that, should an epidemic result from these health hazards, the white community would be as vulnerable if not more vulnerable than the black one. In one instance, when the matter was brought to his attention, the mayor of the town in question arranged for a meeting between the town officials and certain members of the clinic personnel to evaluate the situation and see what could be done to remedy it. In addition to the mayor, the town was represented by the chief of police, the fire chief, and one or two prominent citizens. The clinic personnel consisted of two physicians, a fourth year medical student who had been working at the clinic for about a month, the staff psychologist, and the chief sanitarian. The medical student who was within a week of graduation and the sanitarian were black.

Although the mayor and the police chief were obviously somewhat disturbed when they realized that they were sitting down with a professional group that included black men, and that these black men were being addressed and dealt with as equals, they managed to accept the situation with reasonably good grace. Not so the fire chief. He immediately demanded the reason for his presence at the meeting, since, as he put it, he could see no connection between the functions of his department and the matters under discussion. So the black sanitarian carefully instructed him concerning the fire hazard inherent in accumulated waste and garbage. At this point, quite irrelevantly, the fire chief wanted to know from the psychologist what she was teaching the people in regard to their activities in their homes at night. When the psychologist said that what people did in the privacy of their own homes was their business and no one else's unless what they did in some way harmed others, he launched into a long tirade about the size of black families, pointing out that many of them were fatherless and without any means of support and therefore a heavy burden on the taxpayer. In the course of this diatribe all his negative, racist feelings for the black people found expression. It was then that the medical student who was definitely middle

class and from the north, and had never before been in the south and
certainly had not been subjected to the kind of repressive upbringing that
black children in the south received, felt compelled to respond. He made
an impassioned speech about the way black people had been and still
were being treated. Among other things he said, "The white man has
been castrating the black man for three hundred years." At this, the fire
chief's face and general manner reflected hurt pride and injured inno-
cence. He leaned forward in his chair and earnestly protested, "Boy, I
ain't never castrated no nigger." The mayor and the police chief hastily
explained to him that the term castrate was being used symbolically,
but it did not seem that the fire chief really understood what that meant.

Once the clinic was well established training became one of its most
important functions. Every department employed aides, local people who
until the coming of the Health Center had either picked cotton or depended on Welfare. The clinic actually became the major employer in the area,
thus supplying not only much needed medical resources, but economic
and educational ones as well. Aides who manifested any interest or ability
were given special training, and helped to secure the formal education
that would enable them to move up the economic ladder.

Other spin-offs from Health Centers have been such organizations as
Farm Co-operatives and Health Councils. Any resident of the area serviced by the Health Center could join the Farm Co-operative. This
membership entitled the individual and the members of his or her family to
farm products at minimal cost. It also provided work for many of the members who had no means of earning a living. Although the work was agricultural and meant laboring in the fields, those doing it felt they were
working for themselves rather than for the white boss, and this naturally
affected their attitude toward the work and their image of themselves.

Health Associations were formed in various areas served by the
Health Center. Wherever there was a concentration of people a Health
Association was set up. Each association held periodic meetings where
the health problems of the people in the area were reported and ways
of meeting these problems arranged. Sometimes it was a matter of nursing care, other times of notifying the Center of the need for transportation
or the need for shelter, food, and clothes for a family that had lost everything in a fire. Each Association elected two members to represent the
area in the Health Council, a body that met twice a month and dealt with
all the policies and health problems of the entire area serviced by the
Health Clinic.

When the Health Associations and the Health Council were first established the members constantly turned to whatever white personnel—doctors, nurses, social workers, psychologists, etc.—were present at the meeting seeking guidance in making decisions and very much concerned lest the response of the black members to the issues under discussion be unacceptable to the whites. In less than a year the people learned that they ran the Associations and the Council, that the issues under consideration were their problems to be dealt with as they saw fit, that they were in charge and free to make whatever decisions they thought were appropriate. So in a short time, Association and Council members were conducting their own meetings in their own way, deciding on all health and related issues associated with the Health Center, hiring and firing the people employed by the Center, and making determinations regarding the general conduct of Center affairs. Currently, if a white person attends an Association or Council meeting out of interest or because some issue on the agenda is of special concern to him, he is welcomed as a friend, but informed that there is an agenda, so if there is some matter he wants to bring up he is free to do so under new business. In other words, in polite fashion he is being told that the meeting has been organized by the Association or the Council and will be run accordingly, and that he as an outsider will be permitted to participate when the time is appropriate. This is a far cry from earlier days when the members of the two organizations were afraid to voice their opinions until they knew how the white people felt about the issue.

In many respects then, the Health Center was of prime significance in the area in which it operated. It not only provided much needed medical, economic, and welfare functions, but it was highly educational and ego building for the black people. Unwittingly, certainly unplanned, it also served a "social" function. The "social" aspects of the Center's operation took place primarily in the waiting room. While the patients sat there waiting to see the doctor or other clinic personnel, they encountered many of their friends and relatives whom they had no other way of meeting. Although the professional staff was concerned when a patient had to wait any great length of time before he was seen by a physician, nurse, psychologist, social worker, etc., many of the patients actually enjoyed such a wait. If their stay extended past the lunch hour they were given a sandwich and a drink, and in all instances transportation to and from the clinic was provided by the Center. Naturally there were some patients who did not want to wait, who had small children or old folks at home, people who needed their care; but even such patients enjoyed a brief visit with someone they had not seen for quite a time.

Medically then, the black people of the rural south experienced all the illnesses common to white people in the area, plus the illnesses caused by their particular economic and environmental conditions. For instance, diarrhea and severe dehydration in the young children and arthritic and hypertensive conditions in the adults were conspicuous.

As far as psychological and psychiatric factors are concerned, it should be born in mind that our concepts of what constitutes mental and emotional well-being are derived largely from case studies of middle-class white patients even though mental health, like physical health, is closely related to social, economic, and cultural factors. Hence the norms for the behavior of people other than those who subscribe to what is known as western European culture are of a highly different order, and what is regarded as acceptable and "healthy" in the prevailing white group is not necessarily seen in this way by other communities.

Despite the importance of cultural factors certain conditions can of course be evaluated in all groups. Brain damage is brain damage all over the world, just as hypertension or cardiac failure can be recognized no matter where they occur. The difference lies in the fact that the reasons for the existence of brain damage, hypertension, and cardiac failure may differ considerably from community to community.

Even if there is an awareness of cultural factors when diagnosing mental disorders, there seems to be no greater number of schizophrenics among the black population of the rural south than anywhere else. What is prominent is the tendency toward hysteria, while reactive depression is almost universal. That this is so is not surprising, since according to today's concepts of what conditions contribute to or hinder the attainment and the maintenance of mental health, the black people are in a very adverse situation. According to Bone,* the need of all people is to achieve "actualization"—defined by him as "the process by which personality originates and grows." Implicit in his definition is the assumption that in every human being there is an ongoing, unfolding process—psychological as well as physical—a push toward self-fulfillment in all areas of experience. Such fulfillment requires a propitious physical, mental, and interpersonal climate. If any of the elements essential to such growth are absent or negatively oriented, actualization cannot be achieved.

Among the factors essential to healthful growth and self-realization are the feelings of security that result largely from a sense of acceptance and "belongingness," along with adequate opportunities for being oneself. In

*Bone, H. The Inter-Personal and the Intra-Personal. Presidential Address, William Alanson White Psychoanalytic Society, May 26, 1959, New York, N.Y.

his own community, among his own people, the black child and the black adult generally did experience a sense of belonging. This did provide him with a degree of comfort and security, but it was not as effective a force as it might otherwise have been because of the absence of sufficient opportunities to be and realize the self. The persistent need to be other than himself in the presence of the white man and the awareness of the dangers inherent in recourse to other than "role playing" behavior made it difficult, even impossible, for the black child and black adult to truly pursue his own ideas, feelings, and interests—ever to feel secure enough to seek his own satisfactions and his own identity. It is of course true that for all people there are "outsiders" who are regarded with caution, possibly even suspicion, but these rarely intrude deeply or consistently into one's every day life, rarely keep one perpetually aware of their power to do harm.* Yet such awareness, from infancy on, such recognition of danger, has been the constant lot of the black man. There was no time in his life when the existence and the power of the white man could be forgotten, and with this awareness went the need to placate him. This need constituted one of the major concerns—in fact, the major concern of the black man's life— overshadowing all others.

The condition in which the black man was placed naturally generated an inordinate amount of fear. Again, all people have fears, fear apparently being an inevitable part of the human experience. There are the childhood fears such as fear of the dark, fear of abandonment, fear of loss of parental love, fear of punishment, and fear of death; and adult fears which include fear of loss of self-esteem and self-respect, fear of loss of love, fear of loss of economic security, etc. Fear brings with it an undue amount of anxiety, a perpetual sense of uneasiness, and with this there also goes anger and rage. For the black people, conditions being what they were (Chapter 2), any expression of their anger and rage was impossible. Instead, it had to be contained and turned back against the self while the facade that was presented to the outside world stressed compliance, docility, and co-operation. Because of their efforts to contain and repress their rage, the depression that is so rampant among the black people has been ascribed to this unreleased hostility. Yet as is so often the case, the reasons for the black

---

*The current situation in regard to the muggings taking place every day on the streets of most large cities has produced in many people this sense of fear and anxiety, and to an extent is affecting the conduct of their lives. However, what these white citizens are experiencing is quite different from what the black people have known, partly because the street victims have the public and the law on their side, and partly because they had acquired self-realization and feelings of security long before they were exposed to street attacks.

man's concepts and feelings are not similar to those of the white man's.

According to psychoanalytic theory, anger that cannot be expressed, that is contained and self-directed, produces depression particularly if the object against whom the anger is directed is someone who is emotionally important to the angry person, someone society expects him to feel kindly toward. Unable to recognize and accept the way he really feels toward an individual who plays such an important part in his life, the angry person represses his anger, and than ends up feeling guilty and depressed. For such a person, the relationship between aggressive feelings and his depression must be kept out of awareness at all costs. *

The anger and rage that the black man feels for the white man is certainly not the same as the anger that the white man feels for someone he is expected to love. His anger is not pointed against someone emotionally close to him, but against someone who has made his life a living hell. His anger is justified and he certainly does not feel guilty for being angry. What he does feel is fear lest his anger gets out of hand. His contained rage is not the major cause of the black man's depression. His depression is on a far more conscious level, like the depression experienced by a prisoner condemned to a life in jail, someone who sees nothing ahead of him except continued frustration and deprivation. And along with this sense of frustration go all the questions related to purpose, direction and the achievement of a real identity. It is the sense of futility and hopelessness that cannot always be denied or repressed that accounts for the depression that is so rampant in the black population. Everything the black people do and say, their songs and their poems, their prayers and their art, all communicate their misery and the depressive feelings that they suffer.

Living all their lives with an overwhelming sense of frustration and futility, the black people had to learn how to cope with their despair and with the anger that that despair produced. So they resorted heavily to denial and reaction formation, presenting a seemingly happy facade to the outside world. Accordingly, Kardiner and Ovesey† state, "It is a consistent feature of human personality that it tends to become organized about the main problem of adaptation, and this main problem tends to polarize all other aspects of adaptation toward itself." In the case of the rural black people, their main problem of adaptation was to hide from the white man the extent and intensity of their feelings of frustration and the anger that went along with this.

*Storr, A. *Human Aggression*. Atheneum, New York, 1968.

†Kardiner, A., and Ovesey, I. *The Mark of Oppression*. The World Publishing Co., New York, 1962.

Given this state of affairs, any problem that a black patient presented when he came to a clinic or a therapist for help was inevitably tied in with the general condition of the black population. In addition to whatever personal difficulties he might have, the sense of frustration and the resulting anger that every black man experienced was there, making a solution to his disturbance just that much more difficult. Correspondingly, it was essential that in the course of treatment both the patient and the therapist recognize this issue and the sooner this was done the better. The problem for the therapist is what to do with justifiable frustration and anger, and therapy often becomes an exercise directed toward acquainting the patient with the opportunities for working in a Civil Rights or some similar organization.

The following are examples of the kinds of problems that bring black patients to a mental health clinic. A man of twenty-seven asked for help because he was convinced that he would one day kill himself and/or someone else because of the way he drove. He explained that he not only drove at incredibly high speeds, but that he practically never stopped for red lights or stop signs, but went crashing through them. Although he drank a great deal he did not feel that his reckless driving could be attributed to alcohol since he drove the same way when he was not drunk. What ultimately developed was that he was consumed by feelings of frustration and rage, feelings of which he was well aware but which he could not handle. What he did not recognize was that he was just as angry at himself and those like himself, namely other black men and women, for permitting themselves to be treated as they were, for submitting to the degradation they were forced to endure, as he was at the white man. His rage was such that it pervaded all his experiences and was directed against everyone, himself included. His driving was the reflection of his intense desire to eliminate everyone who crossed his path as well as to kill himself in the process.

Given this kind of situation, and the feelings and the realities that are the logical result of such a situation, it is these feelings and these realities that the patient and the therapist must face right at the outset of the treatment. Until this is done, no constructive effort at coping with other problems is possible. In therapeutic work with black people what is primary is the whole question of their place in a white society. Until the patient and the therapist, especially the white therapist, have come to terms with this issue, progress in treatment is impossible. Failure on the part of those concerned, north or south, to face this matter, and then ascribe the inevitable lack of treatment success to such things as "resistance," only avoids the basic question.

Even when the black-white issue, and particularly the issue of the black man's role in a predominantly white society, has been explored, the question of how to cope with the anger and humiliation that the black man has suffered is a very individual matter. In some instances the patient's abilities, temperament, and opportunities may permit him to channel his frustration and rage into constructive activities geared toward altering the position of the black people, rather than continue to use them in destructive fashion. In other cases, for a variety of reasons, this is not possible. But once again, it must be emphasized that, regardless of the opportunities open to a black man for altering his circumstances, the true nature of those circumstances must be recognized by him and his therapist.

Depression that tends to focus on immediate realistic issues was nevertheless often related to long standing, deep seated feelings of anger. Such was the case of a twenty-eight year old woman, the mother of five and eight months pregnant with the sixth. She had come to the clinic with vague physical complaints but because she kept crying throughout her visit with the doctor she was described as depressed and sent to the clinic's therapist. She was in tears when she came into the therapist's office and it was impossible to get her to explain why she was so upset. She did state that she did not know where her husband was and that she was concerned about herself and her children. When she was asked about housing she indicated that she lived in a house in which she could stay indefinitely because it was in such bad shape no one else would live in it. In response to further questions she stated that she had food and food stamps. Through all of this, her weeping continued and the therapist had just about decided that her distress was not, as was so often the case, the result of every day practical needs, but due to some emotional problems, when the patient indicated that although she had food she had no money for gas and therefore could not heat or cook the food she had. When the matter was discussed with her it became evident that fear and anger were both operative, fear of the outraged feelings that she experienced because she had been placed in such an unhappy position, and anger at herself, her husband and society in general for allowing this misery to occur. She was furious because of the helpless position in which she found herself, trapped by her pregnancy and five young ones. She recognized that although she certainly needed a way of cooking the food she had, this could have been accomplished without gas. Certainly some black families in the area resorted to open wood-burning fireplaces (page 32). Her weeping was basically a response to her feelings of despair and anger, rather than the fact that she had no money for gas. Yet when the necessary small sum required for gas was provided, her weeping stopped and she left the clinic, momentarily at least smiling and grateful. Although she was urged to return for further discussions of her problems she never did come back.

In another case, a young man came to the clinic for help because he had been arrested and had served time for molesting small children, and he was afraid that he would do so again. In time, during the course of therapy, his feelings of inadequacy stemming from his experiences with the white community were uncovered. With this came the resentment and rage that he felt for white people. His recourse to child molesting was not only his way of dealing with his doubts about his manhood but also of coping with his rage. Had he really felt like a man it seems questionable if he would have been able to act in the passive, inadequate, impotent manner that the white people expected of him.

The bottled-up rage that each black person carried around within himself was thought by one physician to account for some hypertensive patients' failure to benefit from the medical treatment they were receiving. The possibility of group therapy that would help the patients express their rage was discussed with various members of the staff. Although from the medical point of view the idea appeared to have merit, after considerable study it was vetoed. The reason for this negative action was the absence of any channel into which the rage could be drained once it was released, nowhere it could be safely directed. The idea that it be directed into constructive activities, geared toward improving the condition of the black people, was certainly considered; but because opportunities for doing this in that particular area were extremely limited, almost non-existent, the whole matter was dropped. It was concluded that the experiment would be too hazardous for the black patients. Had their rage been released, it seemed very probable that they and their whole community would have been seriously endangered. Unfortunately there is no way of ascertaining whether or not this decision was correct.

Some patients focused on physical symptoms in order to get the care and the attention that they were sure would not otherwise be forthcoming. At times this recourse to somatization was purely unconscious, at other times quite deliberate. The latter was the case of a young woman, the mother of four, whose dependency needs had never been adequately met. In fact, they had rarely even been recognized. She came to a Health Clinic rather frequently, presenting all kinds of minor ailments which ordinarily would have been unnoticed. However, coming to the clinic and telling a doctor about herself, having his undivided attention and concern even for a short time, was very satisfying to her. One day while she was sitting in the waiting room she observed a patient having an epileptic spell. She was impressed with the amount of attention this spell elicited, and so she began having "spells" whenever she felt she was not getting all the response she so desperately wanted. When she was thoroughly examined and it was established that there was nothing neurologically wrong with her, that her spells were indeed self-induced, the patient was sent to the therapist. She was barely seated in the therapist's office when she announced that she was going to have a spell. At that moment the therapist took her hand and said, "I know you have a lot of troubles and that you need help. That's why we're here. I'm your friend and I'll help you, but I can't help you when you act like this." The patient responded with incredulity. "Are you really my friend? You'll help me?" she asked. Once a trusting relationship was established, the patient began to talk about herself, about the things she needed and had never had. Regular visits to the therapist, with the opportunity to be the focus of attention while feeling that the therapist really did care about her and what happened to her, made the recourse to "spells" as an attention-getting device less and less frequent. While she still has a long way to go to become a truly mature woman, she is far less dependent and childish than she once was. Once again there was much unexpressed anger in the picture, anger at those whom she felt should have met her needs more adequately, as well as anger against the power structure which made it virtually impossible for any black person to be fulfilled and happy.

Anger played an important part in still another case. This is the story of a ten year old girl who became mute when her underlying anger and hostility were reinforced by what was going on around her. She was the oldest of six children, all the others being boys. Whenever her parents went to work she was left in charge of her brothers, a responsibility that she took very seriously. She became especially distressed when any argument developed among her siblings or when they scuffled with one another. On one occasion the two older boys engaged in a fist fight and one of them received a bloody nose. The sister was extremely upset by this because, according to her story, the parents would blame and punish her for what happened. Actually this was not at all the case, but rather a response to her own aggression and anger arising from her resentment at having to care for her brothers, as well as the frustration and anger she had always known because of the deprived way in which her family lived and the compliant role she was compelled to fill. When she saw her brothers fighting, all her own aggression was mobilized to the point where she could barely contain it. During the night following the bloody nose episode she could not fall asleep and when she wanted to call her mother she suddenly realized that she could not speak. In a panic she went into her parents' bedroom and with gestures managed to convey to them what had happened to her. They were so upset that, although it was past midnight, they took her to a local white doctor. He gave her some pills to "relax" her, and she did finally go to sleep and was able to talk. Nevertheless, the next morning she was brought to the local Health Clinic. With therapy she gradually became aware of the intensity of her hostile feelings both for her own family and for the white family on whose plantation she lived. In the final analysis the two families were for her one and the same, the cause of her deprivation and anger and therefore the targets of her rage.

Even in cases of schizophrenia, the rage that the black man inevitably feels for the white man holds an important place. For the black schizophrenic the content of his psychosis is inevitably bound up with the ever present black-white problem as well as with his particular conflicts. So once again the issue of anger and aggression comes to the fore. In one instance, a very well-endowed nineteen year old who was attending a high powered northern university became so agitated that he had to leave school and he came home to the sleepy southern town where he had previously lived. Even back in familiar surroundings he remained convinced that people were after him and he hid in his room for days. In interview and therapy sessions the reasons for his paranoid ideas became clear. He stated that he thought the Black Panthers were after him because he was not radical enough. What was really happening was that, because of the relative freedom he enjoyed in the north many of his long repressed impulses and feelings of rage were making themselves felt, were very much in consciousness, but this emergence of his true feelings was accompanied by fear and guilt. To allay this fear and guilt he projected his hostility onto others, in this instance the Panthers. So it was they not he who were angry and hostile. Now he feared the Panthers rather than his own hostility. Another factor in this case was the conflict and guilt that the patient experienced because while attending the university he was in many respects living the life of a white man, learning and adopting many of the white man's ways and values. For many young black students this is a serious problem, and in this case reinforced the patient's convictions that people who dedicated themselves to the black cause, people like the Panthers, could only see him as indeed he saw himself, as a deserter of his people.

This patient's experience is by no means unique. Several other students who went to northern colleges developed severely depressive or paranoid reactions. All of them were exceptionally well-endowed intellectually. However, their transfer to a culture which no longer required them to repress their true feelings and that did nothing to reinforce the controls they had so long been exercising, left them very vulnerable, even defenseless, under the onslaught of forbidden emotions. That many black students have such experiences to a greater or lesser degree raises a number of important questions. How much preparation for what lies ahead should the black adolescent going to a northern college be given, not only in terms of courses of study but in regard to the emotional experiences he will have? What selection criteria should be employed when a southern black high school graduate plans to go to a northern school? Surely many factors other than intellectual level and grades come into consideration. Finally, how much support and help can a college counselor or psychiatrist who knows nothing of the student's culture possibly provide for him?

With an ever increasing number of southern black students being admitted to northern colleges this matter of understanding and guidance becomes increasingly pressing. What is required is not only understanding of a student's emotional problems but also of his learning difficulties. Take, for example, the case of a young man who had graduated from a southern black college and was going for a graduate degree in a northern school. His field was sanitary engineering and he was apparently having a great deal of difficulty, even facing failure, because of his poor marks on tests. Yet this man had worked with great effectiveness in the sanitation department of a southern Health Center. He certainly knew what a sanitation engineer should know and also how to use that knowledge in the field. In an effort to find out just what was going on, why this man could not handle on an examination what he dealt with so well in practice, it became quickly apparent that the difficulty arose from his inability to put his ideas into words and write them down on paper. There was no question whatsoever that he knew, and knew well, what a sanitary engineer had to do under various conditions, and he had any number of times demonstrated his ability to put his knowledge into action. But he could not convey his knowledge to others through the medium of pencil and paper. This of course is a problem for many black students educated in the south. But very few professors or guidance counselors realize this. And so for the black student resentment at being misunderstood and loss of self-esteem because of impending failure take over.

In general, the attitude of the black community toward any form of mental disturbance was an accepting one. If a person acted strangely, if he seemed "different" or "slow," if he was constantly troubled by unhappy or frightening thoughts and feelings with which he could not cope, this was perceived as a condition that just "happens," part of living, "the will of God." Certainly it was not seen as a cause for ridicule or shame, something to be hidden from one's neighbors. In most instances friends and neighbors tried to "talk him out of his sickness." For example, in still another instance, the friends and relatives of an agitated young man sat with him for the better part of a night, well into the early hours of the morning, trying to reassure him and cure him by means of verbal logic.

In general, the southern rural black people, especially the older folks, are totally unaware of current theories regarding the causes of mental and emotional disturbance or the ways of dealing with these. They have not heard of dynamic concepts, and the idea that any individual, child or adult, was acting in deviant fashion because of his early experiences with the significant figures in his life was totally alien to them. They had perhaps heard the word "psychotherapy," but it meant little or nothing to them; and although they knew, without necessarily putting the idea into words, that one obtained relief just from talking about one's problems with a relative or friend, the thought of doing this with a professional, as a form of treatment, was very strange to them. Yet when such help became available, word quickly spread through the area that such an opportunity was being offered and that the experience was often quite helpful. So gradually all kinds of psychological and psychiatric problems were brought to the clinic.

In one instance a grandmother who was taking care of her son's two daughters found the behavior of both children very strange. The son was working in a northern city but had brought his children south to his mother because his wife did nothing but lie in bed all day, never caring for or feeding the two little girls or doing any of the things that might reasonably be expected of a wife and mother. The girls were five and six years old, but they did not talk intelligibly, did not respond to their names and in general acted in a bizarre fashion. There seemed no doubt that one or both of them were suffering from childhood schizophrenia. The question was whether they were both sick or whether it was a case of *folie à deux*. It was difficult to separate the girls in order to make such a determination because there was no one other than the grandmother to care for them. However, some partial separation was achieved and they were seen by different therapists. In a relatively short time it was established that the older girl was the sick one. So arrangements were made for the younger child to be returned to her father in the north once the obviously disturbed mother was hospitalized and a housekeeper installed in the home. As far as the older girl was concerned, it was felt that the less pressureful rural life would be better for her, and so she remained with her grandmother. She came to the clinic every day and was seen by a black lady, a nurse's aide, a woman who had seven children of her own and had a very definite "feel" for children. She was instructed and supervised by the staff psychologist, and in a comparatively short time this autistic child was responding to her name and reacting in somewhat more organized fashion than she had.

In another instance no highly trained professional advice or care was needed. Instead, a black lady, a fifty-five year old grandmother working as a teacher's aide in a Head Start Center, did by "instinct" or the application of common sense what a professional might have advised her to do. A four year old boy was brought to the school by his mother who explained that he needed special attention because he could not walk up and down stairs by himself. The aide assured the mother that she would watch the child and give him whatever help he needed. It happened that in this particular Center it was necessary to go up eight steps in order to get to the toilet. During the first week of the little boy's attendance at the school the aide always held his hand and helped him up and down the stairs. Then, once he felt at home in the school situation, she gradually let his hand go as he reached the top steps, and finally the day came when he was on the top step and she was at the bottom smiling up at him. For a moment the child looked very anxious and shouted, "But I can't do this." The aide smiled and said, "But you did," and from that time on the little boy scrambled up and down the stairs just as all the other children did. As someone remarked, he was a very lucky little boy. Had he been a white middle-class child he would probably have been sent to a therapist for a number of years in an effort to explore the reasons for his difficulties.

There are then any number of factors, over and above the more usual ones, that the therapist working with black rural southerners must consider. In particular there are the reality factors that these patients have to face, and the therapist who does not recognize these but remains firmly bound to his traditional concepts of the importance of intra-psychic experience can go sadly astray. Take for example the case of an attractive fifty year old widow who lived with her ninety year old senile father. Her complaints were depression, sleeplessness, and rapid heart beat. A psychiatrist who was visiting the clinic the day that the patient appeared was consulted because of the nature of her complaints. He did not ascribe her difficulties to her current dreary, taxing circumstances, to the fact that her father was incontinent, that he frequently got out of bed during the night and walked about without any realization of where he was, thus making it impossible for the daughter to relax and enjoy a good night's sleep. Instead, following an interview with the patient, he suggested that her depression might very possibly be related to some difficulties she had had with her husband, some unresolved problems in that relationship. As he saw it the hostile feelings the patient harbored against the dead husband were responsible for her present depression. So the staff therapist was urged to work with the patient, and particularly to explore this aspect of her life with her. However, the therapist was more familiar with the local people than the visiting psychiatrist was, and so this was not done. Instead, an internist was brought into the picture. He prescribed medication, not for the daughter but for the aged father so that he would sleep during the night. This enabled the daughter to relax and sleep well, and as a result her tension and her depression were greatly alleviated.

For the black patient in the south there are in a sense three possibilities, at least in so far as the realities of his life situation are concerned. He can accept, deny, or try to escape from the situations that are generating the anger that he cannot handle constructively. Each possibility and its meaning for the individual has to be explored, as well as the reasons for his acceptance or rejection of a particular line of action.

There are several other factors that make therapeutic work with southern black people rather different from what it is when working with relatively sophisticated white patients. With the black population, sporadic recourse to prayer, to voodoo, or other magical operations can be anticipated. Furthermore, what the patients want, or what they see as a "cure," is symptom reduction. Consequently, as soon as the individual feels a little better, as soon as his depression lifts a bit, he stops coming for treatment. Telling the patient that stopping his visits so soon will probably cause an early recurrence of his disturbance makes no impression on him. He feels better, so why keep going to a doctor. The same attitude prevails in regard to physical problems. Once the symptom that led the individual to seek help no longer troubles him he ends his visits to the physician even though he has been told that he needs more treatment. In most instances then, the psychotherapist must recognize that his contact with the patient will be short-lived and that what he feels he can do must be accomplished in a brief time span. He can also be relatively sure that his patient will reappear sporadically. Such was the situation with a sixteen year old girl who was having serious problems with her mother. When her problems were discussed with her and she felt somewhat better she would fail to show up for her appointments, but would inevitably reappear in a few months time, ready to reopen the issues that had never been adequately resolved.

The absence of the resources available in cities, especially in northern cities, the kinds of agencies that can provide temporary or permanent shelter, that can provide training or specialized treatment, etc. constitute still another problem for the therapist in the rural south. For example, for a southern black family that is being literally destroyed by the presence of a grossly defective child, there are no institutions that would care for that child, certainly not in a way that might produce some improvement, however slight, in his condition. On the other hand, this lack of agencies and institutions is markedly counter-balanced by the black community's acceptance of the individual with a mental or emotional disturbance. Most members of the community can and do provide support and comfort to the disturbed individual and his family, and this is a great help to the troubled patient and those involved with him. For example, an adolescent who was having difficulty with her mother and a new stepfather, and who was therefore making life miserable for herself and everyone in her house, soon found a warm accepting home with a neighbor.

In recent years the picture in regard to both physical and mental health has changed appreciably. This change is the result of the change in the nature of the problems that the southern black people have to face as they move away from the plantations and the life styles that they pursued when they lived on the land. Consequently, what problems come to the therapist and what options are open to the patient are different from what they had been just a few years ago. These matters will be discussed later as part of the overall change that has taken place in the lives of the population under discussion (Chapter 12).

# CHAPTER 8

# *Identification, Identity, Self-concept, and Role*

As the individual engages with life, an inner as well as an outer world develops for him. The outer world is in good part determined by the expectations of the environment and the individual's effort to meet these. Such efforts inevitably require varying degrees of control and repression, of displacement, projection, intellectualization, sublimation, and role playing. The inner life, on the other hand, is one in which the individual can give way to his real feelings, positive or negative. However, because many of these feelings and fantasies are not in accord with what the environment requires, because they have to be contained in the inner world, they can become tension and anxiety provoking should they threaten to get out of hand.

Because the individual's outer world, his adjustment to his culture, is at times very much at odds with what he really thinks and feels, this outer life is sometimes described as the "false self," while the inner world is perceived as reflecting the "true self," or the "real self." In order to cope with his two selves the individual develops various techniques which enable him to keep his inner world secret, hidden not only from others but from himself. Were he unable to do this, were the true nature of certain of his feelings, impulses, and fantasies clearly apparent to him, his resulting anxiety might be greater than he could tolerate.

The mechanisms that a person employs in his efforts to establish some equilibrium between his two worlds play a most important part in shaping what we call "personality," defined as "the product of the intelligence and the emotions, prefaced by constitutional factors and conditioned by the

137

environment."* Personality is then a highly individual matter, although we tend to talk about people in broad, general terms, such as Italians are volatile, the English are reserved, the Germans methodical, etc. But such generalities tell us little about the person other than that he does or does not conform to the norm for his particular group. Each individual has his own unique history, his own experiences, his own techniques for getting along in the world, his own store of resources, plus all the behaviors he has learned from his contacts with the members of his culture and the larger world. Hence the importance of individual case studies, and for black people there are such in the literature.†‡ In this text however rather than the individual study, some of the processes that shape personality development will be the focus of attention. Specifically the concepts of identification, identity, self-image, and role will be explored.

In the literature the meanings ascribed to the four concepts under consideration vary considerably, depending upon the particular author's theoretical formulations. Consequently, it is necessary to define each of these words in line with the way they will be used here. Although each concept will be defined and dealt with as an entity by itself, it should be recognized that these are by no means totally independent of each other, but rather interact in very specific ways with one another.

In the ensuing discussion the term "identification" will be used to denote the process concerned with internalizing or incorporating the attitudes and values of the group of which the individual is a member by reason of his birth. Thus identification means an acceptance of the models presented to the individual. This process begins very early in life and provides the individual with a sense of "belongingness" that permits him to experience himself as part of the community on which he is dependent and to which he looks for guidance and support.

In contrast to identification "identity" carries with it the connotation of separateness or "individualism." A person begins to acquire an identity when he starts to think about, question, and possibly even challenge the models he is supposed to emulate and incorporate, when his concepts begin to diverge from those of his elders and acquire uniquely personal aspects. When this happens a degree of independence and autonomy is established, the beginnings of an "identity" are manifest.

---

*Bochner, R., and Halpern, F. *The Clinical Application of the Rorschach Test*. Grune & Stratton, New York, 1942.

†Grier, W. H., and Cobbs, P. M. *Black Rage*, Basic Books, New York, 1968.

‡Kardiner, A., and Ovesey, L. *The Mark of Oppression*. World Publishing Co., Cleveland, Ohio, 1962.

"Self-concept" is the way the individual perceives and experiences himself. It is a highly personal matter, partly conscious and partly unconscious, and largely a reflection of the way he thinks others perceive him.

Finally, "role" is the part an individual feels he must play in order to elicit from his environment the particular responses he needs or wants. Thus in adopting a particular role at a particular time and in response to certain circumstances the individual is playing a kind of game.

Identification begins shortly after birth, largely because of the individual's need for and dependence on those who provide him with the physical and emotional support essential for his survival. As defined above, identification involves the individual's "acceptance" of the attitudes and behaviors that his immediate environment expects him to adopt. At least in the very earliest stages of the identification process "acceptance," as ordinarily defined, is too active a concept. It implies cognitive activities, a weighing of the issues under consideration and a final decision to "accept." For the infant, and even for the toddler, such is not actually the case. When the baby conforms or protests or even resists certain external pressures, such a response is "instinctual," a reaction to bodily needs, not a carefully considered evaluation of the behaviors he is being asked to assume. However, "acceptance" soon becomes a part of the identification process as the child begins to make a decision between compliance and rebellion, between conformity and resistance.

For almost every child there is a paucity of models to be "accepted" during his early days, and so once again he has really very little choice in the matter. He is born into a particular culture and what that culture expects of him is what he has to accept. And his acceptance is being constantly reinforced not only by his dependency needs and his helplessness, but by the environment's recourse to a system of rewards and punishments. It is in this manner that all groups strive to make their young a part of their culture, the way in which they bind their offspring to traditional values, standards and modes of behavior, the way in which they program them to think and act as their forebears did, and so carry on the customs of a particular society.

Different cultures naturally present different models to their young and so children from one culture internalize values and modes of behavior that differ considerably from the values and behavior patterns adopted by children from a different culture. Some cultures remain static while others change with time, and what was required of the children in a certain group at one point in their history is no longer the current model. For example, a hundred years ago middle-class white children were generally expected

"to be seen but not heard." At the present time, however, such docile behavior is very likely to be interpreted as a sign of some emotional problem
and so be a source of concern to the modern white parent who has been
taught that it is good for the child to express himself, to be heard as well
as seen.

In his early years the child's identification develops mainly through imitative behavior. He does what he sees those about him doing, copying
their mannerisms and repeating their conversations, frequently not in the
least understanding what he is parroting. For the young child whose experiences with his elders have been relatively positive and whose feeling
for them is a trusting one, what they say and do has the value of absolute
truth as far as he is concerned. How often one hears a five year old shout,
"My father says" or "My mother knows" as he tries to win an argument
with a child whose parents have taught him different concepts. In most instances the child accepts what the parents say and do, and so he develops
in their image and becomes one of the group. The greater his acceptance
the stronger his sense of belonging.

As the child grows older his imitative behavior becomes practically
automatic. He no longer has to try and remember what his parents did or
said under certain conditions. The way they react has become so much a
part of himself, is so closely woven into the very fabric of his response
patterns, that the expected reaction is right there waiting to be released.
Consequently, in familiar, routine circumstances there is very little likelihood that a child will vary from his customary behavior. Such a departure
is most likely to occur when a new element is introduced into the situation,
something for which he has not been programmed, while the ease and speed
with which he gives the expected response in the ordinary course of
affairs is a measure of the extent and intensity of his identification.

Identification has been described as the most primitive way of recognizing and responding to external reality. As such it can be considered a
form of defense, an alignment with the external forces that exercise control and mastery. In developmental terms identification is the first step in
the acquisition of a "self." If there is no identification then there are no
roots, no basis on which to build, no place where one belongs and for all
these reasons no further growth is possible. Everything a child experiences either reinforces or weakens his identification.

In advanced sophisticated societies, an individual almost inevitably acquires a number of identifications. For example, he may be identified with
one religious group, with a political group, with a professional group and
so on. These different groups may have very different precepts, values,

and beliefs and a person has to be able to handle these contradictions. Age, sex, marital status, socio-economic class all demand their special identification. In less complex societies, in cultures where the life styles, the religious practices, and the occupational pursuits are relatively in accord with one another, the individual not only has to make fewer identificaions, but he is less likely to be troubled by ideational contradictions. However, even in simpler societies there are identifications determined by age and sex if nothing else.

Obviously the variety of models available to the child has an impact on his efforts at identification. In this country the middle-class white child very early in his life almost always has opportunities to observe and even participate in behaviors that differ in varying degrees from those he observed in his home. For instance, he may go to a playground or visit the child of a family friend and discover that the children he is interacting with on these occasions respond differently from the way he has been taught to behave, and that the praise and punishment meted out to them is not in line with what he has been led to believe is "good" or "bad." So he begins to recognize that there are behavior patterns other than his own that are acceptable to some adults if not to his elders. This leads him to think about and very possibly question ideas and attitudes that he has previously taken for granted. As a consequence of this questioning he may start to modify his own concepts, explore new ways of perceiving certain relationships or events. In so doing, he begins to achieve a degree of autonomy, an "identity" or a "self" that is separate from his traditional background.

In the middle-class white child this questioning and searching for meanings and values other than those he acquired in his earliest years generally reaches its climax in adolescence. In fact, at this period of his life the white teenager may turn his back almost completely on his early models. Then gradually, partly through trial and error learning as he attempts to implement his own ideas, partly through observation and association with members of groups very different from his own, and definitely through a great variety of interpersonal experiences, some compromise between his early response patterns and his early concepts on the one hand, and his subsequent ones on the other, is effected.

The southern rural black child goes through the same process of identification that the middle-class white child does. The difference between them lies not in the nature of the process, but in the kind and variety of models available to the black child as compared with the opportunities that the white child enjoys. Because of the very restricted nature of his culture, of the life styles that his forebears have established in their search for survival, the black child's identification is also far more "fixed" than that of the white child. This is due to the fact that, in order that he might live, those concerned with his well-being constantly stressed and reinforced the behaviors characteristic of the group as a whole. So the black child rarely had an opportunity to try out behaviors that differed in any significant ways from those that were being constantly and vigorously drummed into him, and even if such had not been the case he had very few chances of observing or learning about different response patterns. Almost everyone with whom he had contact thought and responded much as he and his parents did. The religious beliefs, social concepts, and general views that his friends and neighbors voiced were virtually identical with those he heard in his own home. Most important of all, although there were arguments among the adults, in the final analysis there was rarely any significant disagreement among the plantation people on any basic issues, on such matters as how to behave in the presence of white people, how to raise children, etc. And growing older rarely if ever made a difference in the black child's outlook. As has already been noted, adolescence which made such a difference in the white lad's life, which opened so many doors for him, produced little change in the black teenager's prospects or way of life.

There are a number of other reasons why the black child's identification was as restricted as it was and why it remained as fixed as it did. One of course was the ever present white man and his expectations in regard to black people's behavior. Another is the custom, found among all minorities and especially minorities whose situation is precarious, to follow with few exceptions those modes of response that enabled them to survive. In this way, group solidarity is established and maintained, and survival hopefully insured. This is important because if one member of the minority group fails to conform the whole group may be attacked and exterminated. Among the black people this was particularly relevant, since they were easily identifiable because of their color. So it was not only in order that each child might survive but in order that an entire community might survive that the identification process was so important.

Given the conditions that characterized the lives of the black people, it is obvious that as an "out-group" their adaptation and identification had to be very different from that of an in-group. In particular, in any discussion of the development of identification and identity, there is the difference that results from feeling secure as opposed to what happens when one constantly feels insecure and threatened. The in-group is comfortable enough to examine in critical fashion many of its models, to experiment with new ones and reject old ones. The members of such a group can permit themselves the luxury of disagreeing with one another. In this connection it is interesting to note that even an in-group is likely to revert to older, long established modes of behavior in the face of a crisis. Certainly at such times disagreements tend to be far fewer than when times are calm. A people waging a war for survival or facing a ravaging epidemic are inclined to forget their differences and forego experimentation with new life styles. Under such conditions they close ranks in the face of the common enemy, and one of the most successful ways of doing this is a return to what once were the universal beliefs and behaviors of the group. For the time being at least those who moved away from identification as they developed an identity are ready to forego their autonomy in favor of identification. In a sense what happens with the group is very like the Freudian concept of what occurs with an individual when he regresses because of his inability to meet some obstacle or crisis. Since the black people in the south were living in what amounted to a constant state of crisis, identification as a survival technique was far more important to them than identity.

There were of course among the black people, as among all peoples, individuals who did not make a strong identification with the group, did not adopt the passive conforming stance that enabled the black race to survive. Such individuals, either because of their earliest experiences or possibly because of certain physical causes, could not or would not curb their primitive feelings. Instead, they repeatedly released these in ways that were very likely to arouse white anger. So such individuals were not only a source of danger to themselves but to the whole community.

In the literature the terms "identification" and "identity" tend to be used interchangeably. So a great deal has been written about the black man's lack of identification and this lack is generally attributed to his failure to know who his forebears were and from whence they came. It should be obvious that in the way that the term has been used here, the black man has a strong identification, while his opportunities for achieving a strong identity have been much more limited than in the case of the white person. The white child may have a teacher whose ideas and ways of perceiving his world are very different from those that his parents taught him. Even a close relative or friend may expose him to entirely new ways of looking at himself and his world. While this is not impossible in the case of the black child, it is certainly far less likely to happen and far less frequent than in the case of the white child.

Although relatively little opportunity for change was available to the black child, the conditions under which he lived did not totally preclude the attainment of an "identity," "the feeling of being a self-contained unity, regardless of situation, group or activity."* Obviously where group pressures are particularly strong and external pressures unfriendly this is difficult. Yet in addition to his identification, his sense of belongingness, each individual also creates for himself a private, inner world, rich or barren, dull or exciting, mature or immature, as the case may be. The natural ongoing, unfolding activities of the growing human organism make the attainment of an identity practically inevitable. However, the degree of autonomy that the individual attains, the strength of his identity, depends on many factors, internal and external, and consequently varies from individual to individual and from culture to culture. Certainly the conditions under which the black people lived were far less propitious for the attainment of a strong sense of identity than was generally the case in the white population. In existential terms the black man has had much less opportunity to be himself and fulfill himself than practically any other group of people in the modern civilized world, certainly far less opportunity than the white man in this country has had.

The black man's responses to such tests as the Rorschach and the Thematic Apperception Test are sometimes interpreted as indicating a weakness or even absence of a sense of "identity." On the Rorschach the absence of human interpretations is perceived as evidence that the black man does not have a strong identity, a firm sense of himself. Similarly, the fact that his heroes on the Thematic Apperception Test are not very stimulating figures is likewise regarded as evidence of his weak identity. However, once again such interpretations must be considered in the light of what is known about the people under consideration. For individuals who throughout their lives have had to deny themselves indulgence in fantasy it is almost impossible for them suddenly to produce richly imaginative stories filled with exciting figures. Although the southern black people can talk warmly and at length about some incident in which they participated, can describe it in detail and with emotion, the life-long taboos on engaging in flights of fantasy render story telling a very different matter. As for interpreting inkblots, from the black man's point of view this is just another of those strange mysterious tasks that the white man comes up with periodically. The end result of all this is that, even when he wants to co-operate with the test assignments, the black man is likely to

*Ruesch, J. *Therapeutic Communication.* W. W. Norton & Co., New York, 1961, p. 283.

find the task most peculiar and certainly most difficult. So using projective tests with a black population and interpreting them in the same way that one analyzes the productions of white subjects can prove very misleading. To assume that the black man has not made an identity or that he is "empty" because of what he does or does not produce on the Rorschach or the TAT can result in a totally distorted picture of the patient.

There is however one aspect of the black man's reactions to the projective tests that is unequivocal, and that is the evidence that they provide for his very marked feelings of depression. This depression not only communicates itself in the subject's relatively frequent use of black in describing the figures or objects he is interpreting, but in the depressive tone of what he actually interprets. His use of the adjective "black" may be largely a reflection of his hyper-awareness and sensitivity to the blackness of any stimulus that is presented to him, but his interpretations of "dead trees," "dying flowers," etc. and his relatively infrequent use of the chromatic colors speak for themselves. Similarly, the people he talks about on the TAT are seen as "sad," "crying," "sick," etc. Another rather consistent finding in the productions of the southern rural black man is the absence of aggressive activity. His characters practically never assume assertive stances, are never on the offensive. Rather, if they are engaged in any kind of action, it is of a defensive nature.

The figure drawings obtained from the rural black population also have to be evaluated in terms other than those used in interpreting the productions of the white population. In particular, among the older people, unfamiliarity with tasks involving paper and pencil. results in the production of very immature figures. Many of the drawings from both young and old subjects have rather strikingly bizarre aspects. Had they been obtained from white subjects the possibility of neurological damage would certainly have been raised. Specifically, quite a number of the black people produce figures that show a mixture of profile and full face. The figure is standing sideways, yet the face is given two eyes and a full mouth. In other instances the head is enormous but is imposed on a vague, small almost non-existent body. In still other productions the bizarreness is more like what is seen in the drawings of schizophrenics. Yet the individuals who produce such drawings are not schizophrenic and as far as could be determined, the people who draw pictures that suggest organic impairment are not neurologically damaged,* at least not to a degree that would explain

*Many physicians working with the southern rural black people are strongly of the opinion that, as a result of the severe malnutrition many of them suffered during the first

the production of such strange pictures. Rather, the drawings suggest a certain "primitivity," along with a striking lack of experience in dealing with paper-pencil tasks and expressing the self through graphic media. So once again, the productions should not be interpreted as they would be if they had been obtained from white subjects.

Those southern rural people who did develop relatively strong identities were often those who had opportunities for observing and participating in experiences not available to the bulk of the black population. This was likely to occur particularly when the individual who had special opportunities was also intellectually well-endowed and possessed what, for want of a better term might be called an "assertive temperament," that is the individual who tended to be less "accepting" and passive than most of the people were. When such a person, for example, had a chance to visit a relative or friend in a northern city he might very well come back to the south with many new ideas and many questions about the black people in general and himself and his role in particular. For such an individual the kind of conformity that was expected of him and that had been part of his identification could well become distasteful and difficult to maintain.

As far as "temperament" is concerned, the black man who was well identified with his culture but who, because of innate and environmental factors, was not overly passive and compliant was the person most likely to recognize opportunities for constructive change and in many instances such an individual did what he could to bring about such change. While such opportunities were extremely rare, almost non-existent, in the past, during the last few decades the situation has changed. Now there are black women and men in the south who no longer are the victims of their fears in relation to the white man. So they are able to consider, initiate and pursue new and constructive ways of coping with old problems.

A person's self-concept is a private matter, and although the environment certainly plays an important part in its formation, it is essentially an intrapsychic experience. It develops from the individual's subjective way of perceiving and interpreting his relationships with others, particularly with those who are emotionally important to him. As Sullivan† puts it,

two years of their lives, they have a degree of brain damage. In experimental work with animals the absence of protein has been shown to be especially important in this connection, and protein is certainly conspicuously absent from the diets of the black people. Such effects in humans have only been inferred, but such a possibility surely exists and is sometimes offered as part of the reason for the learning difficulties that many black children manifest.

†Sullivan, H. S. *The Collected Works of Harry Stack Sullivan*, Vol. 1. W. W. Norton & Co., New York, 1951, p. 23.

"The self may be said to be made up of reflected appraisals." It is therefore a concept that has its roots in the child's early experiences with his environment, but depends in large measure on the way he interprets those experiences, which aspects of them are stressed and which neglected. While subsequent experiences and relationships can, up to a point, modify the original self-image, once a certain perception of the self has been developed, the individual tends to cling to it tenaciously, struggling to preserve it even when it is an image that has caused him to be unhappy, even miserable much of the time. It is the image of himself with which the person has lived and around which he has built his life style. To change all that is not only extremely difficult but most anxiety-evoking. As every therapist knows, modifying the individual's self-concept is a most difficult and time consuming business, meeting with constant strong resistance on the patient's part. Each individual, patient or "normal" person, focuses primarily on those aspects of his experiences that confirm and reinforce his picture of himself, whatever that picture may be, while brushing aside anything that contradicts that image.

Rather than "self-concept," the term should actually be "self-concepts," since each person's image of himself varies in accordance with the nature of the particular environment in which he finds himself at any given moment. For example, a man who from early childhood was convinced that women did not like him would very probably have one image of himself in his contacts with women, but a different one when he was involved in an experience in which women played no part.

For the black child who was often severely punished for doing the things that almost every healthy, growing child engages in, who was frequently told to "hush," and repeatedly reminded that he was worthless, the likelihood of acquiring a negative self-image was strong. Certainly such was the result of their experiences for many of the black people in the rural south. No black man in that area could escape the repressive training that was part of the black tradition, nor was he spared the hate looks, the humiliations, the abuse and the danger that were the white community's contribution to his development.

Naturally the effect of the white man's attitude toward the black people varied from individual to individual. The self-image that the black child had before he was involved in any meaningful exposure to whites was of the utmost importance. In spite of all the inhibitions and cutting down to which the black child was subjected, some of them, either because of the mother's basic attitude or for any number of other reasons, were able to maintain a positive self-concept. On the other hand, where a strong negative image was already in existence, the attitude of the white community certainly strengthened this.

Where a relatively positive self-image prevailed the black man might try to maintain this by denying or rejecting what he perceived regarding the white man's attitude toward him and focus on whatever few positives there were in his relationships with white people. In some instances, the black individual had the strength to recognize that the prejudice and hostility of the white people was their problem not his. In other instances, the attitude of the white people might eventually wear away the black man's efforts to maintain a positive picture of himself.

In general, it can be said that the black person with the predominantly negative self-concept was likely to be quite conforming in his interactions with the white man. For many of them such conformity was the only means they could think of to avoid the abuse and the harm that they were sure they would otherwise suffer. The other possibility for such an individual was that in response to his feelings of worthlessness and hopelessness he could only see a retreat into sleep or alcohol as the answer to his situation. The individual with the more positive self-concept might also behave in docile, subservient fashion in his contacts with the white community, but for him this was a front, a show put on to appease the white man, a very conscious, deliberate act, not at all a valid reflection of the way he saw himself or felt about himself.

The ability to play a part and to act in conformity with the way he knew he was expected to act has enabled the black man to survive without necessarily impairing his positive image of himself. A great deal has been written about the black man's negative self-concept, his disgust with himself and with those like himself. In some instances this is certainly true, with self-hate paralleled by hatred for other black people. Yet there were and certainly at this time are strong indications that the image was by no means as strongly negative and as firmly fixed as many white people thought it to be and hoped it was. One such indication was the love that the black people had for their children. Had they been completely negatively oriented toward themselves they would not have had such a strong desire to perpetuate the race, nor would they have welcomed and loved each succeeding generation as they did. Had the black man been completely without self-love and self-respect the love, care, and respect that he lavished on his children would have been impossible.

Along the same lines, the positive interaction that obtained between the members of the black community, the care and love they gave one another, would have been out of the question if they had not perceived black people as having worth. Certainly there were times when their fatigue and their despair, in conjunction with the frustrations they were constantly encountering, caused the black people to become angry, even enraged at whomever was present at the moment. However, this was displaced anger that should have been turned against the Establishment, but which in the interests of survival, had to be directed elsewhere. So there were occasional angry exchanges among the plantation residents, but these were mainly of a verbal rather than a physical order. Furthermore, they seldom lasted very long and were soon forgotten as habitual relationships were quickly resumed. Such angry exchanges had a certain cathartic value, relieving unendurable tension in a safe fashion. The significant and basic aspect of the relationships that existed between the plantation people was the understanding and the support that they provided one another, and because of this they did not have totally negative images of themselves. Certainly there were some people who respected them and saw them as having worth.

Two other forces in the black man's life served to militate against a totally negative concept of himself. One was his firm belief that in the eyes of the Lord he was worthy and that no matter how much the white man might despise him and derogate him, an all-seeing, all-knowing God understood. So in the long run he would come into his own, would have a seat in Heaven and very possibly the white man would not.

The second experience that went a considerable way toward modifying the negative picture of himself that the white man constantly sought to instill in the black man were the conversations and activities that took place in the privacy of the black homes. Few white people, and especially southern white people, appreciated how well the black people understood them and laughed at them and their pretensions, how they ridiculed and mimicked them, while all the time presenting themselves as humble and docile. In line with their well-developed ability to "read" the white man (page 41), the black people had an amazingly clear perception of the white man's weaknesses and his illogical, at times irrational behavior. Although he dared not openly express the contempt he felt for the white man, the fact that he could do so both with humor and with anger when no white people were present certainly rendered the white man far less superior, far less god-like than he wanted the black man to think he was. And this lack of stature on the part of the white man naturally enabled the black man to think better of himself than he would have had the white man been as overwhelmingly powerful as he tried to appear.

Still a third force affecting the black man's self-concept was what went on in his own home, between himself, his wife, and his children. Although many of the black men felt humiliated and powerless when they were unable to care adequately for their families, some of them nevertheless enjoyed the respect and love of their wives and children. Many of the women were sufficiently understanding to try and help a man experience himself as a man, and when the mother did this the children naturally followed suit. Such a relationship in the home also had a positive effect on the child's developing self-concept. A man who respected himself for whatever reasons, possibly because when he was a child his mother had helped him develop a belief in himself or because somewhere, at some time, something had happened that made him feel like a man, could and did win the respect of others. Such a man was often a leader in his community, a force that was felt by others, someone to whom others turned for advice and guidance; and this position naturally reinforced the man's positive self-image.

If, despite everything that has been done to them, large numbers of the black people had not had positive concepts of themselves, none of the events of the past decade could have occurred. All his ability and charm notwithstanding, Martin Luther King, Jr. would never have been able to enlist the support that he did among the downtrodden black people and could never have rallied enough of them to last out a bus boycott that went on for months and months and months. Neither would the many sit-ins that took place in the south and put an end to segregated eating places have occurred; nor could Charles Evers have been elected mayor in a southern town. These are just a few of the self-fulfilling activities in which the black people have engaged in the last two decades, and they surely indicate that the black people did not perceive themselves as hateful and worthless. While it can certainly be argued that most of these enterprises were initiated by well-educated, middle-class black men, not by the rank and file, and certainly not by the uneducated rural people, it is equally true that the programs that were initiated could never have succeeded had the people been as crushed and hopeless as the white people wanted them to be or as helpless and negatively oriented toward themselves as they were thought to be.

As far as the self-concept is concerned there is still another important aspect to be considered in trying to understand the relationships that obtained between the black and the white worlds, namely the fact that the individual sees others largely in terms of the way that he perceives and experiences himself. The man who enjoys a positive feeling about himself looks for and finds positive qualities in others, and conversely, the man who feels negative toward himself will surely find negative attributes in those with whom he has contact. So in the long run the white man's efforts to make the black man feel small and ineffective could only act as a boomerang, causing the black man to perceive the white man in a negative light.

Obviously, generalizations about the black man and his self-concept can only lead to distortions and hinder any effort at understanding the individual. He is as complex as any other human being and has as many "selves" as anyone else has. Sometimes the question is asked, which is the real self? The answer has to be that each self is real in the particular context in which it occurs. The negative self-image that was so often evoked in the black man when he was interacting with the white man was as real as was the positive self-concept he enjoyed in other relationships. The difference between the black and the white man once again lies in the fact that the conflicting self-concepts were generally more extreme in the case of the former and that the intensity of the negative image did in some cases pervade all areas of their lives.

The role that an individual plays derives from a combination of his own needs and his perception of the environment in which he is operating at any given moment. If the environment is seen as hostile and negative he is very likely to adopt a role that he hopes will reduce that hostility and negativism. To this end he may present himself as overly agreeable and compliant, or he may strive to be entertaining, strong, seductive, etc. Roles are often adopted simply because when acting in a certain way the individual feels more comfortable, more secure, more important, more powerful, less conspicuous or whatever it is that he thinks will work to his advantage. The child who plays the role of the father, the teacher, the president for the moment at least enjoys the feeling of being in power. A role that is played almost continuously is likely to become so much a part of the individual, so dictate the way he acts and ultimately the way he thinks and feels, that the role may become "he."

On the other hand, when an individual is compelled to adopt a particular role but struggles to be himself at least part of the time, he generally experiences a great deal of stress and strain. Keeping the role and the self separate is not an easy task and requires considerable concentration and effort. Certainly it is not a condition that is conducive to "mental health." Mental health concepts stress the importance of providing the individual with opportunities for self-actualization or in current terms for "doing one's thing," rather than doing what someone else wants, acting as others dictate. The current trends in child-rearing practices, the move away from excessive conformity to a belief in self-expression, are indications of the current stress on self-realization as opposed to role playing geared to please others. So once again the white community's attitudes and expectations have placed the black people at a serious disadvantage since they expect the black person to be quiet and submissive, conforming and subservient.

As long as a person plays games or persistently assumes a role that does not express his true thoughts and feelings, it is impossible to form a meaningful relationship with him. If the person is not "himself" the relationship cannot be real or true. While it is very probable that no individual can ever be totally himself or able to reveal himself fully to another, the gap between any two people is unbridgeable as long as the real self remains hidden behind a role.

In all his relationships with the white community the black man was forced to play a role, to fill a part assigned to him by the white people. He was expected to fit the stereotype that the white man had of him, that is, to be slow-witted, dull, and obsequious, and he had no choice but to go along with the game according to the rules laid down by those in control. Furthermore, he knew that the rules could be changed at any time, according to the whims and the needs of the white people. In this whole situation there was nothing of a positive or constructive nature for the black man, yet he had no choice but to accept this state of affairs. Only recently have the black people begun to discard their traditional adjustive techniques and replace them with more assertive and self-realizing forms of behavior (Chapters 10 and 11). As they go through this process of change many of them are unsure, tense, and even confused about how they should react. As a result some of them over-react with emphasis on aggression and excessive demands, partly because they are convinced that they are justified in asking for the changes they seek and partly because by putting on a show of strength they feel strong. Others are less assertive, but in the greatest majority of instances regardless of how they do it, the old role is being rapidly shuffled off.

Obviously the four concepts discussed in this chapter, identification, identity, self-concept, and role, do not exist in isolation but rather they have a strong impact on one another. In general terms it might be said that the stronger an individual's identification, the less likely is it that his identity, his sense of separateness and autonomy, will be strong. Rather, the relationship that exists between these two facets of his personality tends to be of an inverse order. However, in relatively simple and fixed cultures, whatever identity the individual acquires is not likely to be in great contrast or opposition to his identification. What the individual in a simple culture wants for himself, wherever his hopes and plans lead him, is probably very much in line with what the society expects of him and plans for him. In more complex societies such close congruence between identification and identity is likely to be less common. Rather, the relationship between these two facets of the personality tend to vary, depending upon what aspects of the individual's experiences and reactions are under consideration at a given time.

Among the southern rural black people identification was in most instances stronger than identity. This of course was inevitable in view of the the way they were required to live and adjust. Yet once again it must be emphasized that the black man did achieve an identity, though the strength of that identity and his ability to maintain it when he was under pressure naturally varied considerably from individual to individual.

As for the relationship between identification and self-concept, the possibilities are even more varied than between identification and identity. The markedly subjective nature of a person's self-concept accounts in large part for this. One might speculate that the more restrictive and punitive the early training process, the process that led to identification, had been the more negative the resulting self-concept was likely to be. However, the interaction between these two concepts is not that simple. Certainly what the child experiences in his formative years has a great deal to do with the way he perceives himself later in life, but in most cases there are experiences both within and without the immediate family interactions that may modify the early perceptions. Likewise, a stern, restricting, even punitive mother can also give warmth and love, and such was frequently the case among the southern black families. In addition, there were the attitudes of the many surrogate parents the child had, and among these there was almost always at least one who was especially fond of a particular child and who singled him out for special attentions. So there were many factors, some known and some unknown, which determined the way the individual perceived himself, regardless of his identification and his sense of identity; for each individual, black or white, the "atoms" that make up the whole arranged themselves differently.

As for the relationship of role to identification much depends upon the age of the individual and of the nature of the particular circumstances confronting him. For example, in the case of a child the role he adopts will be determined in part by his acceptance or rejection of the attitudes and values of his group and his own sense of security or his lack of security should he decide to oppose that group. In certain respects the same is of course true in regard to identity and self-concept. In the case of the black people both the adult and the child were compelled to play a part designed for them by the white community, and for survival considerations acceptance of this role was supported by the black community. In fact, playing a role has become second nature to the majority of black people, certainly far more so than is the case among white people. However, this need to present himself in ways that did not at all accord with the way he actually felt did not necessarily interfere with the black man's attainment of a sense of identity or a positive self-image. In fact, his ability to role play and to fool the white man was seen by the black man as evidence of his effectiveness, as a victory over the traditional enemy; and this tended to strengthen both his sense of identity and his positive concept of himself.

# CHAPTER 9

# *Recapitulation*

Recently a colleague consulted me about a member of her family who was seriously disturbed. Being well trained and with years of experience in the field of clinical psychology, this therapist was keenly aware of the importance of certain aspects of the patient's early history. Consequently, she spent considerable time telling me her relative's life story, stressing the hardships, the rejections and humiliations that this woman had endured during her childhood. After the matter of the patient was discussed and appropriate recommendations and referrals made, my colleague began talking about other matters, including the changes that were taking place in the neighborhood where she lived. She insisted that it was the black people who were responsible for the deterioration that was occurring not only in her area but all over the city, and she made a number of disparaging remarks about the blacks. When I pointed out to her that the behavior to which she was so strongly objecting was just what might be expected from people who had suffered the "hardships, rejections, and humiliations" to which the black people had been subjected she became quite angry, saying, "I'm tired of those excuses. What happened before is in the past. That's over with. What they're doing today is taking place now." Obviously this experienced, highly intelligent and essentially kindly person saw no similarity between her relative's condition and the condition of the black people. In the case of the former she could recognize and emphasize early experiences, but brushed off such considerations as explanations of what she termed maladjusted and unacceptable behavior on the part of the black population.

It is because this lack of perception in relation to the black man is so rampant among well-intentioned, well-educated, thinking people that the previous eight chapters have described in such detail the experiences and resulting responses of the southern black people. The black people have lived lives so different from those of other American citizens that to expect them to react as white people do is highly unrealistic. To begin with, the black man was ruthlessly torn away from his homeland and his traditional way of life and forced into slavery of a kind that deprived him of all hope. This alone was sufficient to render his perceptions and his general outlook totally different from that of all other Americans. Compounding this difference was the fact that he was excluded from every important aspect of the white man's life.* So his only choice was to develop a culture and a life style of his own. Obviously the way the black man in this country has lived and continues to live, be it north or south, is not because he is essentially "different" from other people, but because he has been treated differently.

Given his particular circumstances, his lack of opportunity and his ostracism, it is amazing that the black people have survived and have achieved as much as they have. That they react very differently from the way the white man would react under certain conditions is only to be expected. Certainly scientists who have been trained to appreciate the connection between behavior and antecedent experiences, as well as much of the thinking public, should not be at all unprepared for the reactions that black people are currently manifesting. There seems no doubt that had the black people the opportunity to live as other people did, had they been permitted to share in the prevailing culture and become a part of American life in the fullest sense of the word, their functioning would be of a different order than it currently is, more in line with that of the white group. As it was, their efforts and energies were devoted to remaining alive, to surviving.

In the struggle for survival there are certain areas of human development that can be considered crucial. In very simple terms these can be designated as physical, mental, and spiritual, or as the body, the mind, and the soul or the "self." If the individual is to survive and really live, these aspects of the human experience must be nourished. Yet in all three areas the black man was deprived and rendered extremely vulnerable.

---

*The only thing the black man shared with the white man was a common religion, taught to him by the white man in order to insure his passivity and compliance. But he was not permitted to worship in the white man's church except in rare instances and then of course he had to sit apart from the white people. As some black people perceive the religious experience "they taught us the religion they disgraced."

As far as his body was concerned, that is simply staying alive, the black man was doubly vulnerable. There was danger to his life because of his highly inadequate living conditions and the ever present danger from the hostility of the white community. During the last hundred years the threat to the life of the black man in the south has probably been greater than at any time previously. While he was a slave he had value for his master and his ill health or death constituted a monetary loss for the white man. Now he no longer has that value. If he gets sick and cannot work or if he dies he can be replaced by another worker. As a result, the white man has been much less concerned and helpful to the black man in regard to health and matters related to health, such as food, medical care, etc. In fact, currently the white man does not consider the care of the black man and his family to be his but rather the responsibility of the government.

While most human beings appear to have unexpected strengths and recuperative powers, there is a minimum of health providing experiences that each organism must have in order to survive. When these are absent, sickness or death inevitably result, and the vital statistics in the southern states indicate that the average life span of the black man is considerably shorter than that of the white man.

In addition to the hazards inherent in the physically unhealthy way that the black man has been compelled to live, there was also the threat to his life because of the hostility that the white people harbored against him. Many white people did not regard the black man as a person, a human being whose life was as sacred and important as their own. So at the least provocation, and frequently without any justification, the black man might be tortured or killed. Even today in the south there are occasional completely senseless, wanton killings of innocent black people.

The black man whose body survived was nevertheless the victim of still another form of trauma, namely the mental starvation to which he was subjected. He had none of the educational opportunities available to the white people, no chance of broadening his outlook and enriching his concepts. The greatest majority of the southern black people had had little or no schooling, and those who had had some education had been exposed to such a poor brand of teaching that many of them were at best semi-literate. As a result, many of their ideas were naive and of little value to them when they had to come to terms with the realities of the world beyond the confines of the plantation.

Finally, in addition to the insults to his body and his mind, there were the constant severe insults to the black man's psyche, to the "self." Dealt with in the denigrating fashion in which he was treated by the white population, it was most difficult for the black man to achieve a positive and satisfying image of himself. Every individual has to struggle in order to find himself, to achieve autonomy and arrive at a state in which he enjoys self-confidence and self-respect. And throughout his life each person has experiences that threaten to undermine the self-confidence he has achieved and disrupt the adjustment he has made. In the case of the black man, however, such threats were especially strong and ever present, making the acquisition of the "self" far more difficult than in the case of the average white man.

Despite the many handicaps imposed on them by the environment, despite the many obstacles they have had to overcome and the many traumas they have suffered, as a race the black people have survived. A reasonably safe assumption that might be made in this connection is that those who survived were the physically toughest and strongest, the mentally most alert and flexible; and those who acquired true ego strength were most likely those who, in addition to positive constitutional factors, had the benefit of warm, strong parental models.

Now once again the rural black people are faced with the necessity of adapting to new conditions and to develop a whole new way of life (Chapters 11 and 12). Instead of living in rural isolation, dependent on the good will of the white plantation owner they are now confronted with the complex, competitive life of the city, expected to deal with this in independent fashion or, failing this, to accept what the Establishment decides is best for them. That the new circumstances to which they are required to adjust are in some respects of a more positive order than those they had previously encountered does not make the task an easy one or something that can be achieved in a few months or even years. Yet in the long run, the opportunities provided by the new environment in which the black people now find themselves should eventually lead to true emancipation and self-determination. The intervening steps, the transitional period that is part of any change process, will undoubtedly be fraught with frustration and conflict, both for the blacks and the whites. The black people are being catapulted out of their centuries-old life styles, and without any real preparation are expected to adjust quickly and easily, as well as willingly, to today's technological society, to a way of life that actually in many ways has little appeal for them. When they do not promptly acquire the response patterns that the white man feels they should have and that so many programs are geared to produce, the white community becomes impatient and then focuses on all the negative attributes it can discover in the black man, all the unpleasant things it has heard in regard to him.

Certainly the black people's initial reaction to their new life circumstances will not be in line with white concepts. Eventually, however, mainly because he is possessed of many strengths and potentialities, the black man will evolve a new life style which will most probably combine features of his own culture as well as those of the culture he must now come to terms with. His presence in the American mainstream will surely have a strong impact on white culture. In fact, it already has had an effect; witness our dress, our dancing, our literature, our language, our politics, our educational policies, our eating habits, to name just some of the areas where black influence can be seen.

The remainder of this book will be devoted to a description of the changes, social, economic, psychological, and political, that have resulted from the disruption of the plantation system and where these are likely to lead.

**Part II**  How It Is

# CHAPTER 10

# *The Awakening*

Throughout the more than three hundred years of slavery and pseudo-freedom that the black people in this country endured there were sporadic attempts on the part of the victims to throw off the yoke that pressed down so fiercely on them. Names like Denmark Vesey, Nat Turner and many others come to mind, the more recent ones being Martin Luther King, Jr., Medgar Evers, Malcolm X, and a host of others, some known and some unknown. During the time of slavery the record of successful escapes was pitifully small. Although some few among the many thousands of slaves "made it," the majority of black men and women who longed to get away from their inhuman way of life knew too little about the world beyond the circumscribed area in which they lived, were too lacking in skills other than those needed on the plantations. and too conspicuous because of their color to succeed in winning the freedom they sought. Since emancipation, the same obstacles — fear of the unknown, lack of skills, and the negative, prejudiced attitudes of many white people — have prevented large numbers of southern rural black people from abandoning their familiar way of life despite its highly unsatisfactory nature. Yet there have always been some efforts in this direction. There was always a trickle, a small stream of rural blacks headed for the cities, north and south, and currently that stream has become a mighty river. There were also a few daring souls in the 1870's who found that they did not enjoy their freedom when they had to live among white people — in the white people's town. So they left the city and built a town of their own.* There

*Mound Bayou, Mississippi, the first all black town to be established in this country.

163

have been other actions of this nature, but the majority of the black people have continued to live in white towns, albeit in the poverty stricken, segregated areas assigned to them.

The changes that are taking place in the black world today are the result of many different forces, legal, political, economic, social, educational, and humanitarian, all operating together at a given point in time. Certainly no one factor by itself can explain what has happened and continues to happen in connection with the black people in this country. While right now technology seems largely responsible for the migration of the southern rural black people and their changing image of themselves, other factors were operative in this regard long before machinery was introduced into the cotton fields. There was Truman's order in the late forties, integrating the armed forces, and the Supreme Court school desegregation decision of 1954. Then came the Civil Rights Acts of 1964 and 1965. While to date these laws have given the black people more legal than practical benefits, their presence on the books has at least provided them a foothold from which to operate. In particular, the reaffirmation of the black man's right to vote, and the encouragement and support he has received from certain groups to avail himself of that right, has made him a force in the political arena. Hence he has some leverage in his efforts to win a decent way of life for himself and his people. As politicians woo his vote, he can set forth the terms under which he will throw his support to a given candidate or party.* Jobs, decent housing, and good education for his children are the issues highlighted by the black voter.

The political response to black demands has consisted in good part of the establishment of a variety of programs, such as Head Start, Health Clinics, etc. These have usually been set up and supported by state and federal governments, the most active agency, at least until recently, being the Office of Economic Opportunity. The nature and the conduct of these agencies and the programs they have initiated have not been everything the black people hoped for, and more and more they tend to be regarded as sops. Nevertheless, their very existence proves to the people that their voices are being heard and that the pressure they are bringing to bear on the government has not gone totally unheeded.

Paralleling the legal and political activities of the forties, fifties, and sixties went the humanitarian concerns of black and white people all over

---

*There is also of course the other side of the coin, as politicians solicit white votes by appealing to the fears and prejudices of a frightened white world.

the country. The success of Martin Luther King's non-violent protests and marches gave considerable impetus to the efforts of many people interested in building a truly just and democratic America. It was during this time that organizations like SNCC and CORE came into being, as well as SCLC. In particular, during the early sixties many idealistic white youths and many young people who were deeply dissatisfied with the white middle-class way of life, the middle-class attitudes and values, were seeking to find and fulfill themselves. Some of them perceived alliance with the Civil Rights movement, with the black people working for equality and justice, as an answer to their needs. This was truly a time of "black and white together."

In addition to the legal, political, and humanitarian forces that were affecting the lives of the southern rural black people in dramatic fashion, there was the impact of the afore-mentioned technological advances. In the final analysis it was the automation of the cotton industry that deprived thousands of black families of their only means of livelihood, thus forcing them to leave the plantations. As the machine took over the work previously performed by thousands of black hands, young and old, male and female, the former field workers had no choice but to move away in search of some new means of earning a living. Now just one or two men are all that are needed to work the machines that do all the field work. For the few black men currently working and living on the plantation, life is greatly improved. They are men who have a knowledge of machinery, men who by one means or another managed to acquire some technical training. On the whole their pay is fairly good, and as a result they live in comparative comfort, certainly in marked contrast to the way the mass of plantation blacks had lived for generations. As part of this improved situation the shacks in which they lived have been completely renovated or actually replaced by modern, attractive houses with every known convenience. For such homes they pay rent, but their salaries are such that they can afford this.

Riding around the dirt roads of the plantation country one now passes shack after shack standing empty, the windows broken, the porch sagging, the front door swinging crazily on one hinge, and the front yard overgrown with grass and weeds. No one resides here any more and the plantation owner has no use for or interest in these hovels. In some instances, a family that for one reason or another has not moved away may take parts of the deserted shacks to fix up their own home or just use the wood for fuel. In other instances, the owner permits people who do not have a home of their own or who think one of the empty shacks is better than what they currently live in to move the structure, sometimes charging them a pittance, sometimes giving them the "house" for nothing. In still other instances, the plantation owner burns the shacks down in order that even the minimal ground they occupy can be used for additional plantings. When one recalls the crowded homes, the children running back and forth from house to house, the adults calling to one another, the vibrant sense of life that once characterized the area, the overall impression is one of marked desolation.

For the few families who have remained on the plantations and whose men do not work the machines, conditions are of course even worse than they were previously. As the black people are no longer necessary for the production of the "white gold" as the cotton is termed, the white man has no need for them and in many cases he therefore shows no concern whatsoever about what happens to them. The attitude of the majority of the planters is marked by the hope that as a result of automation the black man will be compelled to move away, hopefully to the north. In this way the southerners see a solution to the "black problem" for their area of the country. In fact, when automation was first introduced these planters were heard to remark that one third of the fields would be mechanized each year for three consecutive years. Correspondingly, one third of the black population would be forced to leave each year until, at the end of the third year, no black people would be left.*·†

This hoped for "solution" of the black problem in the south has not worked out exactly as the southern white man anticipated. True, many black families have gone north, but many of them now crowd southern towns, and because there is little or no work for them, they seriously augment the welfare rolls. Certainly the white plantation owner no longer does anything for them if they stay on his property. Whatever limited repairs he formerly made when a shack became too old and decrepit to be lived in are no longer made. He no longer considers illness in the black family his business and does not concern himself about the hunger or the other problems that plague the black people.

Deprived of even the limited necessities that they had previously

---

*There is a certain irony in the fact that it was machinery, namely the discovery of the cotton gin, that made slavery such a lucrative business; and now once again it is machinery that is having such an overwhelming impact on the lives of the black people.

†It has been the policy of the white man in this country to destroy what he cannot use, what has no value for him, and to exploit to the limit whatever serves his purpose. Hence in the case of the Indian the white man resorted to genocide, while in the case of the black man, at least until very recently, he encouraged the production of large families.

known, whether they are living in a town or have remained on the plantation, the majority of blacks must now look to state and federal agencies
for help, and welfare in the south is an especially bad scene, with every
possible road block thrown in the way of those seeking to remain alive.
One man tells of going to a Welfare agency to get assistance for the care of
three children who had no parents and were living with aging grandparents
who had no work. The official in charge of Aid for Dependent Children
said she would look into the case and have an answer in thirty to sixty
days. The man's response was that in thirty to sixty days the children
would have starved to death.

Actually the black man is no stranger to "welfare," having long depended on the plantation owner for help in time of need. However, his
relationship to the boss man was of a very different order than his current
relationship to the Welfare worker. On the basis of his work on the plantation, his faithfulness and his conscientiousness, his readiness at all times
to please the white master in spite of the limited return he received for his
services, the black man felt he was entitled to the care that was provided
for him and his family when this was needed. In fact, in a sense this was
part of the bargain that obtained between the worker and his boss. Certainly it was not seen by the black man as charity and did not carry with it any
greater humiliation than what he habitually experienced. However, when
he was compelled to go to the Welfare agency he was confronted with a
strange and often unsympathetic, suspicious worker who asked many
questions and tried in every possible way to trap him and prevent him
from receiving any government aid.

As for food stamps, one of the most unfortunate aspects of that program
was and is the fact that those who need stamps the most are often the ones
least likely to receive them. The poorest people often do not have enough
money to buy the stamps or any way of getting to the place where the
stamps are being distributed. Some of them are also unaware of the day
they have to be present in order to secure stamps.

Even though the people are experiencing many hardships they are also
heartened by what they hear is taking place in many parts in the country.
What they learn is producing in some of them a type of assertive, demanding behavior seldom before practiced by rural southern black people. In
the development of this behavior, technology is once again playing an important part, this time in the form of the radio and the TV. Even in the
most impoverished black communities there is almost always at least one
radio or TV available, and so the people hear something of what is going
on in different parts of the country, particularly what other black people

are doing. They hear about marches and riots, and about resistance to oppression and discrimination. They also learn that black men are being elected to office in the south as well as the north. So the black people are learning to ask for, even to demand, needed change in such matters as schooling, housing, sewage, welfare, etc. When these requests are not even heard and not answered they are very likely to be followed by demands and then by more drastic action. For instance, for the first time in the history of the Mississippi cotton country, a group of southern black cotton pickers went on strike. This event took place in 1965 when these people refused to work for three dollars for a twelve hour or even longer day. Of course as soon as they made their request for higher pay they and their families were thrown off the plantation which meant that they not only were without work but without homes. Despite the hardships they endured for almost a year they finally managed to establish a community called "Strike City." Here they built houses and now live with the help of jobs, their gardens, and poultry that they raise. Their children attend integrated schools and some of them have gone on to college. How they feel about their life on the plantation as compared with the way they live today is very well conveyed in the reaction of an adolescent girl when she was asked how she would feel if for some reason all the families had to leave Strike City and go back to the plantation. She looked directly at the questioner and without hesitation said, "I'd kill myself."

In another instance, in 1968, in a small town in Mississippi a teacher was dismissed from an all black high school because he had the temerity to teach his pupils something about Afro-American history. Because he supported the teacher the Vice Principal was also relieved of his position. The students and many of the black townspeople immediately demanded the reinstatement of these two individuals. However, the Principal of the high school, also black, sided with the white superintendent and the all white school board, rejecting this request. Whereupon the high school students left the school, refusing to return until their demands were met. Out of twelve hundred odd students only forty-three showed up the first day of the school boycott, and these forty-three also gradually dropped out.

At the same time that the students boycotted the school the black townspeople, under the leadership of a highly effective, intelligent young mother, formed an Education Committee which immediately took a number of important steps. They began by requesting the removal of the black principal who had failed to support his own people. This request was backed by the school boycott and other demonstrations and consequently two days later the principal resigned.

A boycott of the town's white owned stores was then introduced. Since at least half the town's population was black and the stores depended heavily on black patronage, in a very short time the white merchants were really feeling the effects of the boycott. Maintaining the boycott was not an easy matter for the local black citizens since it required them to travel fifteen or twenty miles to the next town to do their marketing. Yet morale was good and difficulties met by forming car pools, commandeering buses, etc. The boycott began in April and continued all through the summer, long after school was no longer in session. During all that time the Education Committee was very active, holding the people together largely through the medium of rallies. They also put out flyers explaining the reasons for the boycott and what the goals of the black people were. One flyer read, "We are declaring open war on black racism. If you are tired of being treated as though you were not the son of God, and if you feel that it is wrong for the white man to run the Negroes' lives with no concern for what they want, then you should come to this meeting . . . . Join us in this WAR. It is your fight also. If you can fight for this country you can fight for yourself." By September the town was willing to meet the black people part way, and while they certainly did not win all the concessions they sought, the black people did achieve some of them. Furthermore, two years later for the first time in its history, a black man was elected to the local school board, an achievement that in itself was worth all the effort that had been expended during the boycott and school strike.

The example set by the black people in this particular town naturally became known throughout the area. Hence, two years later in a town twenty-five miles away, another boycott was organized. This one developed as the result of the incredible sewage conditions in the black section of the town. There actually was no sewage system where the black people lived. There was a very limited number of outhouses in this area, no indoor plumbing, and a city ordinance forbade the building of any more outside facilities. Consequently, waste matter, mingled with accumulated garbage, ran through the streets where people resided and children played. For several years the black people of the town had tried to convey to the town officials the health hazards inherent in such a state of affairs. Their representations were met with all kinds of excuses and promises, but the situation remained unchanged. Finally, in desperation, a boycott was initiated. As in the case of the boycott two years earlier in another town, the problem was to sustain the morale of the local black people and provide them with ways to do their marketing and shopping elsewhere. Rallies held the people together and kept spirits high, and cars were volunteered for the shopping expeditions. Transportation was less of a problem than locating merchants in other towns who would extend credit and take food stamps from people they did not know. However, in most instances it was possible to arrange this.

As a result of the spirit generated by the boycott, the sense of black solidarity it produced, at the next election a black man was nominated for the office of mayor. Although he did not win the election it certainly gave the white people of the area a taste of things to come, and brought home to them the importance of listening to the black community and giving their needs appropriate consideration.

There is no question that the white people of the rural south are disturbed, even frightened by what is happening. The majority of them cannot reconcile what is taking place with their life-long perception of and beliefs about the black man and his place in the overall scheme of things. As they saw it and still see it, the black man was inadequate and inferior and therefore had to be kept in his place. Now the events that are taking place all around them, the indications that the black man is giving of his ability to think and act in independent, constructive fashion, and the support that his efforts are receiving from the federal government and other sources, is most upsetting to the white people. So they struggle to maintain the *status quo*. At the same time the white people are well aware, as the black people are, that in many areas of the south the black people outnumber the whites. If violence should erupt it could undoubtedly eventually be put down by state and federal forces, but not before many white people would have paid for centuries of black exploitation. The black people, or at least the thinking, controlled elements of the black population, are also aware that in the long run they would be no match for the state militia or the armed forces of the United States government. So both sides have up to a point avoided direct violent confrontations, though no one can forget the church bombing which took the lives of four little girls in Sunday school, as well as many other such incidents, including the massacre at Jackson State college in 1970.

It is this fear of a holocaust that places restraints on both sides. Consequently, when the black people hold rallies in support of a boycott, the white police ride up and down the street where the rally is taking place but make no move to interfere even when the assembled blacks spill over into the street and interfere somewhat with the flow of traffic. Likewise, the black people make loud, uncomplimentary remarks about the police officers, but this activity is generally limited to verbal attacks to which the white officers give no response. When real conflict or violence erupts it is usually caused by some die-hard white who simply cannot and will not tolerate the current self-assertive, independent and reasonably confident behavior of the black man. For instance, during the course of one rally a white man drove into the town in a pickup truck with a shotgun lying across his knees. He was immediately surrounded by a large number of black people participating in the rally who asked him why he was holding the weapon. They indicated that they were unarmed and were not considering violence. They also stated that they were not afraid of him and they wondered why he was afraid of them. At the end of the exchange the white man put his gun in the gun rack behind him and drove away.

In general then, the relationship between the black and white populations is marked by stress and tension. However, at this time, individual skirmishes rather than all out warfare seem the order of the day. Furthermore, in many instances the emphasis is on the ballot rather than on violence. At this time neither group appears anxious for a knock-down, dragged out show-down. So unless some new element in the form of extremism on either side enters the situation it is possible that the interaction between the blacks and whites in the south will continue to be mutually distrustful and irritating but not completely irreconcilable and destructive.

# CHAPTER 11

# *The New Order*

What is happening to the southern rural black people at this time can of course be viewed from several different vantage points. Conspicuous are the markedly increased economic hardships that many of them are undergoing, the difficulties they are experiencing in finding new homes and jobs, and, failing this, of coping with the various local and federal relief agencies. There are also a whole series of psychological problems that these people have to face as they move from a traditional way of life to an entirely unfamiliar scene. Certainly the southern white man who had gone to such lengths in brainwashing the black man so that he would accept his role as the compliant field hand now did nothing to prepare him for his new life when his services on the plantation were no longer needed.

Ill-equipped though they may be for their new life circumstances and experiencing a great deal of confusion, anxiety and conflict, from the long term point of view the positive features inherent in the present traumatic upheaval taking place among the black people of the south appear to outweigh the negative ones. While he lived on the plantation and worked as a field hand, the black man's way of life was firmly set for him. Little ever changed and therefore there was relatively little need for deep consideration, planning, or adjusting on his part. He knew what he had to do and how he was expected to do it. He knew what he could expect from his own people and on the whole he knew what he could expect from the white community. So he had developed a life style that fitted him for his relatively static existence. Although his was not by any means a truly satisfying kind of life, at least it was familiar, and he was in some measure spared the anxiety that unfamiliarity generates.

172

Now his world has taken on an entirely new aspect and the reality to which he must adjust is very different from the one he and his people had lived with for centuries. Now he has to decide for himself where to live, where to look for work, how to keep a roof over his head and food on his table. Quite suddenly he has been evicted from his old home and his familiar way of life, economically and psychologically; and with little or no knowledge of the wider world into which he has been thrust, and without any preparation for maintaining himself in that world, he has been left to his own devices, expected to care for himself and those who are dependent on him.

The story of a forty-five year old field hand who could no longer obtain work picking cotton is fairly typical of what is happening economically to many of the people who knew no life other than that of the plantation. This man had several children of his own to care for as well as four small grandchildren whose mother had died giving birth to her youngest. Determined to support himself and his family he searched vigorously for a job throughout the entire area in which he lived. At one time he almost had a job at a small airport in his neighborhood, working as a kind of general factotum, sweeping the floor, stacking unclaimed luggage, etc. Unfortunately, at the last minute he was denied the position when it was discovered that he could not even write his name. In the long run he was lucky, certainly luckier than many of his former friends and neighbors. He eventually did find work driving a bus for Head Start, and during those times when Head Start funds were cut off he did odd jobs and to date has been able to avoid seeking Welfare. What is more, he has a daughter attending college.

In addition to the economic problems that currently confront the former field hands, there are all the other problems the black man has to solve, all the other responsibilities he has to meet and decisions he has to make. He has to decide how to cast his vote, where to send his children to school, whether he should stay in the south or move north, etc. For someone who never before had to make such decisions or assume such responsibilities all this can be quite upsetting. Yet the very existence of these issues and the fact that the black man must face them has at long last provided him with an opportunity for growth. As Dewey puts it "Learning begins at a forked road."

One of the most important decisions, very possibly the most basic one that the black man has to make at this time, the one that is relevant to everything he plans and does, concerns the question of trust — how much does he trust the various white men with whom he is now in comparatively frequent contact, and how much does he trust himself in determining the direction his life will take and in finding the means to carry out his decisions. The importance of this matter of trust cannot be too strongly emphasized since it affects the nature of the individual's adjustment in all areas.

Despite the importance that trust has in terms of the individual's functioning — its effect on his perceptions of himself and others — there is comparatively little in the literature on this matter. In fact, one can go through the indexes of hundreds of books on psychology, psychological research, and psychoanalysis and practically never find the words "trust" or "faith." Just a few authors discuss this concept and seem aware of its significance.

Erikson* calls "basic trust" "the corner stone of a healthy personality" and defines it as "reasonable trustfulness as far as others are concerned and a simple sense of trustworthiness as far as oneself is concerned." Schachtel† equates trust with a sense of familiarity, with the feeling of being with that which is known, thus causing one to feel at home. Steinzor‡ emphasizes the importance of trust being met with trust. Thus he says, "When one's trust is met with articulated trust and with communicated but not necessarily spoken reasonableness, faith is not blind."

Lynd's§ handling of the concept of trust is one of the most detailed. She states that "basic trust in the personal and physical world that surrounds him is the air that the child must breathe if he is to have roots for his own sense of identity and for the related sense of his place in the world." She also points out that when trust is shaken, doubt and fear take over.

In response to the care and the love that he received in the early months of his life (page 54) the black child on the plantation certainly acquired a sense of trust. He trusted those around him and he began to develop a sense of trust in himself. However, much that happened to him once he passed the stage of babyhood tended to modify, even destroy this sense of trust. And for many of the black people their recent experiences have gone a long way toward shaking but not totally destroying whatever faith they may have had in themselves or in anyone else.

Because the black man was forced to leave the plantation, there were

---

*Erikson, E. Growth and Crises of the Healthy Personality. Chapter in *Personality in Nature, Society and Culture*. Kluckhohn, C., Murray, H., and Schneider, D. (Eds.) Alfred A. Knopf, New York, 1968.

†Schachtel, E. *Metamorphosis*. Basic Books, Inc., New York, 1959, p. 184.

‡Steinzor, B. *The Healing Partnership*. Harper & Row, New York, 1967, p. 237.

§Lynd, H. *On Shame and the Search for Identity*. Science Editions, Inc., New York, 1961, p. 45.

now few people and few experiences that were as they had been, few things that were familiar to him, and therefore few that he could trust. In the past there had been trust in the Lord and his promises regarding a rewarding after life and there had been trust in relatives, friends, and neighbors. Now for some of the people, especially the younger ones, trust in the Lord was no longer an important part of their thinking and feeling. And for many an adult even trust in those who had been closest to him was likely to be shaken as the earlier spirit of co-operation was gradually replaced by disagreements, arguments, conflicts, and competition. Faced with new and hazardous experiences, there was no longer a common form of behavior, a common way of perceiving and responding, among the black people. Instead, each individual had his own ideas about how the new circumstances should be approached.

There were among the black plantation people those who felt that the only way they could survive, the only way they could avoid disaster and possibly even obtain some help from the white community, was by continuing to present a passive, subservient facade to the white world. On the other hand, there were those who were convinced that only by asserting themselves could the black people have any chance of improving their condition, and, as they saw it, now was the time for such assertion. Between these two extremes were the largest number of black people, those who were not sure which way to turn and who were torn with doubt and anxiety, or who simply went along with whatever occurred, living from day to day, without giving the matter much thought.

As might be expected it was mainly the older people who clung to the old ways, who were most comfortable when they could react as they always had. For almost all old people it is very difficult to alter life-long habits, and for the black people this was particularly so, since their experiences had taught them that unless they followed in the paths laid down for them by the white man and transmitted to them by their own ancestors, their lives were in danger. This conviction was reinforced by their memories of burning crosses, night riders, bombings, and senseless, brutal murders. At one time or another in the course of their lives they had all been eyewitnesses to such events, and they had also heard all kinds of tales from others about the past and present atrocities being perpetrated on the black people. So it was impossible for them to lose their fears, to develop trust, and then alter their life style.

The following episode well illustrates the extent of the black man's fear and distrust of the white man and how it hampers his functioning at all times. In a small southern town, over a hundred black people came to a meeting called by the leaders of the black community. Various school and community matters were to be discussed. The meeting was chaired by a man who had been very active in the Civil Rights movement and who was devoting his life to improving the lot of his people. He very much wanted to see the black people assert themselves and function in independent fashion. At one point during the meeting a vote was called, but only a handful of the more than one hundred people present actually voted. When this happened the chairman became incensed. He banged on the table in front of him and shouted, "How many of you ever heard of Medgar Evers?" Only a few members in the audience indicated that they knew who Evers was. "Damn you," the chairman cried, "that man died so you could vote, and now, here in the safety of your own building among your own people, you are afraid to express yourselves." Years of near-slavery conditions have certainly made it impossible for many of the old people to overcome their fears and effect radical changes in their habitual response patterns.

That old people are very likely to have difficulty changing their life styles and learning new ways is certainly nothing new. The Bible states that after the children of Israel escaped from Egyptian bondage they spent forty years wandering around the desert instead of going straight to the Promised Land. According to the Hebrew sages, this delay in settling in the Promised Land was necessary to provide time for the older generation to die out. The theory was that the old people would not be able to change their response patterns, would not be able to function like free men, and therefore would not make the necessary adjustments in their new life.

Unable to alter their life styles, many of the older people from the rural south are very much disturbed, even bewildered by much that is taking place around them. They are particularly disturbed by the behavior of the young people. They not only fear that harm will inevitably befall the young people because they are no longer reacting to the white man in docile fashion, but they are very much concerned because many of the young people are no longer deeply involved or even interested in the church and its activities. Although the church continues to be the mainstay for most of the older people and for some of the younger generation, large numbers of the latter are indifferent and even negatively oriented toward the church and toward religious practices in general. Many of the young people have stopped attending church and no longer allow religious concepts to play a part in their lives. As they see it, it is not possible at one and the same time to assert yourself and turn the other cheek. Some few of the young people, despite the respect and positive feeling they still have for their elders, are so driven by frustration and anger that they even seek to destroy the hold that the church has on the old people. So they try to point out to the oldsters the futility of their religious beliefs. As one young man put it, "You've been praying and singing for almost four hundred years and where did it get you? Isn't it time you tried something else?" Yet it is virtually impossible for the older generation to give up the one thing that throughout their lives afforded them some feeling of hope and worth.

In contrast to the young man who insisted that "praying and singing" would get them nowhere was the behavior of a sixty-five year old man attending a meeting of the black people in his town. The meeting had been called to discuss the feasibility of initiating a boycott of white-owned stores because the white town fathers were doing nothing about the dreadful sewage conditions that existed in the black section of the town (page 169). Until recently this old man had been an important figure in the black community, and under his direction the affairs of the black people had been conducted in accordance with his general philosophy, namely that black people survived by being passive and compliant. Now the young people were taking over and as a result the tone of the meeting was quite different from what it had previously been. Nevertheless the old man came to the meeting. Shortly after the proceedings got under way he rose and protested, "I feel bad. I can't do business like this. I have never attended a meeting that did not start with a hymn and a prayer." With somewhat poor grace the young people who were conducting the meeting interrupted the proceedings in order that the old man might offer a prayer. Prayers on such occasions are likely to be quite long and personal, and such was the case in this instance. The old man not only prayed for the success of the boycott they were about to launch, but he also beseeched the Lord to soften the hearts of the young people and turn them back into the ways and the religious beliefs of their fathers.

It is the young people, people in their middle and late teens, and people in their twenties and thirties who are convinced that the time is now, and who therefore advocate an assertive, even an aggressive stance *vis à vis* the white people. Nevertheless in this age group, as among the older people, there is a wide range of opinions and reactions. For instance, when one young man of twenty was addressed as "Sir" by a northern white woman he stared at her in disbelief and anxiety, and then quickly countered with, "I'm no sir."

Although the young people are not unanimously in favor of self-asser-tion it is certainly in their ranks that the leaders of the movements for black rights and black opportunities are to be found. And even though all the young people do not possess leadership qualities the majority of them possess a growing desire for independence, resulting in behaviors that would have been impossible in the south just a decade ago. For instance, there was the reaction of a young black mother to the behavior of the little white girl in the playroom of a southern Health Center (page 53). When this mother went to pick up her little boy he was at that moment the chief target of the white child's aggression. After observing the interaction between her son and the white child she turned to one of the Center's white professionals who had just come to intercede in the matter, and without hesitation said, "She's hateful." For a black woman in the south to be able to tell a white woman (no matter how understanding and sympathetic she might know the white woman to be) that a white child was hateful was a dramatic sign of change in the black woman's concept of herself and her role. It was something that her grandmother, even her mother, would not have dreamt of saying.

In another instance a fourteen year old black adolescent who had just given birth to her first child was explaining to a white woman why she was glad the child was a girl rather than a boy. The white woman worked in the hospital and was regarded by the black patients and the black professionals as a "friend." She had indicated that as far as she knew most people liked to have a boy first and then a girl, and she wondered why the patient preferred having a girl. After a moment's hesitation and a long searching look at the questioner the young mother replied, "It's the girls that carry on the race." Again, this was not the kind of statement that a black person would have made to a white person just a few years ago.

The black people who are no longer completely tied to the old ways but who are not yet able to assert themselves in consistently vigorous fashion are the ones who are experiencing the most stress and strain. They are the people who do not really have faith or trust in themselves, in other black people, or in white people. They want to trust, want to find stable, comforting, supporting figures in the midst of the current upheaval, but they are too riddled with doubts and questions to accept such figures, black or white, even when they are available.

Uncertain, anxious, and threatened, there are those black individuals who strive for security by over-identifying with the very people they fear. Among all groups there are those who feel endangered and helpless and who respond to such feelings by "identifying with the enemy." Certainly there have always been black men and women who bowed and scraped to excess in order to prove to the white man that they were "good niggers."

There are a number of reasons why frightened, threatened people may resort to such behavior. One of course is fear for one's life and by acting exactly as the powerful enemy wants, there is the possibility that one may be spared, that one may go on existing if not actually living. Again, by being the "good child," by heaping up credits as it were, there is the chance of receiving some recognition, earning some reward. The fears that lie behind such behavior cut across all lines, age, sex, race, socio-economic level, education, etc.

The individual who adjusts by recourse to "identification with the enemy" does not necessarily betray his people, at least not deliberately and overtly. Nevertheless his behavior can and does harm other members of his group. Such, for example, was the case of a young black man who had a master's degree in counseling psychology and held the position of guidance counselor in an integrated Junior High School in the south. When the question of school integration was discussed with him his reactions placed him strongly and unequivocally on the side of the southern white segregationist. It was evident from everything that he said that his major concern was for himself, and everything he did was directed toward pleasing the school authorities so that he would be permitted to keep his job. Consequently, as far as he was concerned, black students who did not feel that their admission to a previously all white school was a great honor for which they should be most grateful were deviant, even disturbed individuals for whom he had little understanding, patience, or sympathy. Likewise he reacted most negatively toward any black student who did not comply in all ways and at all times with the school regulations, regarding such a student as a source of trouble, someone who might well make his, the counselor's position difficult. He was so determined to demonstrate his "whiteness" that at one point in what was really a nightmarish conversation he went so far as to say, "Imagine teaching little children to say 'Black is beautiful'."

In another instance, a man who had been the principal of an all black high school and who currently has an even more prestigous and better paying position, could not admit to himself or to anyone else how he really felt about black-white relations. In the town in which he lived a group of black adolescents had for various reasons thrown stones at the homes of certain white people living in the area. Asked how he felt about this he insisted that he did not condone violence in any form, no matter who the perpetrator was. When the issue was pushed, when he was asked if, even though he did not go along with violence, he had not for the moment at least felt a certain sense of satisfaction that for once the white people rather than the black people were on the receiving end, his answer was, "I don't let myself think about things like that."

Where a black individual stands in regard to the many radical changes taking place in the black world today is not just a matter of age, but the result of everything that happened to him during the entire course of his life — while he lived on the plantation and after he left it; there were the things he had heard and learned about in the privacy of his own home, there was the attitude of the overseer and plantation owner for whom he worked, the teachers he had had, and the outlook and opinions of the clergyman whose church he attended. All these matters play a part in determining how he now perceives and responds to the new world in which he finds himself. Regardless of what has shaped his current stance, when one realizes how many black people are ready at this time to make almost any sacrifice, to endure beatings, imprisonment and possibly even death in order to gain the freedom they seek, it becomes apparent that the "cutting down" efforts of their elders and of the white community were not nearly as far reaching and effective as they were thought to be.

A study of the backgrounds of a number of the more effective black leaders reveals some interesting data. The majority of them are of better than average intelligence, and in spite of all the humiliations they have suffered and all the hardships to which they have been subjected, have managed to maintain a positive image of themselves. In most instances, although not all, they came from what have been described as "organized" homes, that is, homes where limits are set, duties and responsibilities defined, and order prevailed. Even if there was only one parent in the home, that one was a strong, stable, trustworthy figure. In practically all instances the parent or parents were religious people, and a number of the fathers were preachers. In only a few instances did an effective leader come from a disorganized home, a home without system, purpose, and hope.

The fact that the majority of black leaders have come from intact families and have manifested some of the values and traits characteristic of the white people has led some whites to emphasize the importance of getting all black people to accept the white man's way of life. While it is true that a number of black leaders had backgrounds similar in many respects to those of middle-class white men and in certain respects accepted and shared some of the white man's concepts and values, the congruence between black and white ways of perceiving and organizing their experiences is relatively limited. Black leaders are certainly not suggesting that the black people adopt all of the white man's values, goals, and life styles. What the black people are being asked to do is to think for themselves, to recognize what their past has been, what their heritage has left them; to determine where they want to go now and how they can best get there. At the moment they are being urged to face current realities and to adjust to these without succumbing to white domination. In many respects therefore the new culture that the black man is developing once again differs from that of the white man.

Greatly adding to the uncertainty, even confusion, that large numbers of the southern rural black people are currently experiencing is what is happening with their children. Many of the parents, largely from force of habit, are still "cutting down" their young ones, dealing with them as though they were still going to spend their lives on the white man's plantation. Actually conditions in the rural south still require black people to be cautious in their interactions with the white community, careful of what they say to a white person. However, the extreme repression of all spontaneity formerly demanded of the black children is no longer necessary. Yet, the parents are not always convinced of this. Their uncertainties in this respect are aggravated by what goes on in the various schools that the young children attend, and by what they learn from friends and neighbors. The majority of the small children go to Day Care Centers or Head Start schools. In some instances the workers in these schools try to give the children a sense of worth and feelings of self-respect, in other instances they stay with the old concepts, emphasizing silence and conformity. So in some schools children are quite spontaneous and active, in others they sit quietly with folded hands. Similarly, some of the children come home to parents who want them to be quiet and submissive, while other parents encourage self-expression. So when children who attend different schools get together their reactions and concepts are no longer completely in accord with one another. Similarly, children from different homes — homes that may be adjacent to one another — are no longer being taught the same things or expected to act as their neighbors do. For both the children and the adults this can at times be very upsetting. It is certainly very different from what went on a decade ago on the plantation.

The bewilderment experienced by both the child and parents is likely to be aggravated when a teacher visits the home and discusses with the mother her way of dealing with her child. The same thing may happen when a parent attends a Parent-Teacher meeting at the school. What she is hearing or what she is being told is often in direct opposition to what the mother firmly believes is in her child's best interests. When a teacher visits the home what very often occurs is that because the teacher, black or white, is perceived by the mother as an authority figure, she is met with an acquiescent response. However, after the teacher goes away and the mother is left alone with her child, she is very likely to resort to her habitual way of coping with the child, regardless of what authority has decreed. "Yessing" authority figures and then doing whatever seems best when no one is around is an old technique among the black people. This was one way they could earn a little peace, could satisfy the boss man while yet doing what they wanted to do. So a white person, man or woman, would give an order and be told in most respectful tones that what was asked would be done, only to discover later that it had not been done, or not done as required. In fact, this was so much a part of the black man's way of life that white authority figures came to expect such reactions and tended to attribute them to the black man's stupidity and/or laziness. Most white people never realized that this was one small way in which the black man could defy him, could indirectly wield some power; and it certainly did not trouble the black man that as a result he was often described as shiftless and untrustworthy.

Because of the newness of their current situation, black children who in their home and/or their school were encouraged to lift up their heads and have pride in themselves could and did get into trouble. This was particularly the case with young children whose judgment about when to make a stand and when it was wiser "not to hear" was not always as good as it might be. Such was the story of an eleven year old boy living in Mississippi in a town of ten thousand people, half black and half white. This little boy was arrested on the complaint of two white women who charged him with making "indecent oral sexual advances" to them. What actually happened was that as he was walking along the road minding his own business these two women shouted to him, "Hey there, nigger boy." Resentful at being accosted in this fashion he replied, "You can kiss my boottie" (bottom in black patois) whereupon the police were summoned and the child taken to court.

Then there are the problems created by the integration issue. Many families are divided over the question of where the children should go to school, to the integrated school or what the black people call the white school, or the all black school. Most parents feel that in the integrated school the child would probably receive a better education than he would in the black school and this is what they want for him. Theoretically the concept of the integrated school could be beneficial to the black child. In practically all instances the teachers in the integrated school have been better trained than the black teachers and more money is spent per pupil, for salaries, for books, building care, needed equipment, etc. in the white school than in the black school. So if the schools were truly integrated, if the white school boards and school personnel were sincere in their attempts to accept and assist the black children coming to the previously all white school, if they made every effort to provide them with a good education, then there would be distinct advantages in sending a child to such a school. In some instances the efforts of the personnel in the white schools have been sincere and constructive, but in many they have not. Instead, the reactions of many white teachers, principals, guidance counselors, etc. have at best reflected their token acceptance of what has become the law of the land, and everything that can possibly be done to sidestep, bend, and break that law is being done. Southern whites spend an incredible amount of time and ingenuity in such efforts, and as soon as one plan is vetoed by the courts they are ready with another. When the climate is not a positive one, when the school staff does nothing to help the black children overcome the handicaps caused by their earlier poor training, then the children will not only fail to benefit from the teaching to which they are exposed in the integrated school, but will feel negative and resentful because they will be aware of the denigrating attitude that is being taken toward them. Obviously under such conditions they will not profit to any great extent from the teaching they receive.

In one school district in Mississippi the efforts of the white community at maintaining segregated schools consisted of requiring all children in the area to take a specific test (California Test of Mental Ability). The children were to be grouped according to the test results, that is all children who scored above a certain mark would be in one class, while children with scores below the stipulated mark would be in a different classroom but in the same grade. It was of course anticipated that the black children who had until this time been attending the black school and whose homes rarely offered them the advantages that the white children enjoyed, would do poorly on the test and would therefore not be in the classroom to which the white children would be assigned. It did not take the black people very long to recognize what was happening and they refused to be part of such a trick — refused to allow their children to be humiliated in this fashion. Instead, they decided to keep the children in the all black school. However, when they did not bring the children for testing the authorities announced that any child who had not been tested would not be admitted to any school, black or white. So the black children were brought for testing but they had been instructed to do poorly on the tests, to give incorrect answers even when they knew the right ones. The result was that the majority of the children stayed in the black school.

Many of the black children in the south who do attend integrated schools are unhappy, disappointed, and angry at what is taking place. They are rarely accepted by their white classmates, and because the white children have had so many advantages they have been denied, their school work is often not as good as that of the more fortunate white pupils. So they are frequently looked down upon and ridiculed by both pupils and teachers. They are also very unhappy because they have no chance of being elected to a class office, of taking part in a school play, or even being on the ball team — all things they could and did do when they went to the all black school.

In one instance, an eight year old was so unhappy with her placement in the "white" school that she went to exaggerated lengths to bring her discomfort to the attention of the authorities. In school she sat sideways in her seat with her head averted and spoke to no one. Even when the teacher called on her directly she gave no response. After this behavior had persisted for some time the teacher contacted the child's mother and suggested that she seek help for the little girl who she was convinced was a disturbed child. When the child was brought to a local clinic she was referred to the psychologist who was white. As the mother and child walked into the office the little girl took one look at the psychologist and then sat in exactly the position the teacher said she adopted while in the classroom. When the psychologist tried to make contact with her she was as unresponsive as she was in school. So the matter was not pushed and the mother was interviewed rather than the child. According to the mother's account the child's first two school years had been spent in the black school and just this year she had been sent to the white school. While she was in the black school there had been no problems. The mother stated that she got along well in school and was liked by her teachers and the other children. The picture seemed very obvious and so the psychologist suggested that she be transferred back to the black school. At this point the child turned around, faced the white psychologist and with a broad smile on her face and with obvious satisfaction said, "That's right."

In still another instance a twelve year old black girl was being coached by a white teacher, a volunteer from the north. Although the girl was actually quite bright she could not really benefit from the coaching because of a certain withholding attitude on her part. Although the teacher was aware of this, there was nothing she could do about it. One day Mary asked for help with her reading assignment. The teacher knew that Mary was actually a very good reader, that it was in arithmetic that she needed help. She therefore did not understand why Mary wanted to go over the reading lesson, but of course she agreed to do so. The reading assignment dealt with a group of white high school students who had been required to read the Declaration of Independence and then discuss it among themselves. Then the student reading the story was asked to express his opinion about the Declaration of Independence. When this point in the lesson was reached Mary sat with her head down, offering no comment. The teacher who was coaching her urged her to express her opinion, to tell what she thought, but Mary insisted that she didn't "think nuthin." The teacher persisted, saying she knew Mary was bright and did think. When no amount of coaxing, cajoling, urging, or pleading had any effect the teacher finally said, "Mary, when you read that about 'liberty and justice for all' didn't you think it was a big fat lie as far as the black people were concerned?" The child lifted her head, looked at the teacher quietly for a moment, and then smiled sadly as she answered "Yes." From that time on the restraint that the teacher had felt in her work with Mary no longer was present, and learning proceeded much more rapidly than it had before this episode. The teacher also realized that Mary had asked for help with her reading in order to test the teacher, to find out just where the teacher stood in relation to the black people, how much of the black man's problems she really appreciated.

All the incidents cited here focus about the issue of trust. The southern black man's lack of trust derives not only from his experiences with the plantation owner for whom he worked and who had such control over him, but from all his other experiences with white people and white agencies, public and private, both in the past and in the present. Among the more recent ones that have certainly left the black man with grave questions about the federal government was what happened when the plantation owner was paid large sums for *not* planting cotton, while no provision whatsoever was made for the field hands whose very existence depended on what they could earn planting, chopping, and picking.

Again, there have been the black man's experiences with the various relief agencies. On the basis of his contacts with them he could only believe that the chief purpose of most of these agencies was to avoid helping him rather than providing him with the supplies that he and his family so desperately needed. Similarly, in the case of food stamps and supplementary food, there always seemed to be a great deal of red tape and a constant shifting of the regulations, so that a person could never be really sure if he would get anything, or what he would get.

As for Head Start and other such schools and Centers, they too had a kind of "on again, off again" quality. Sometimes the funds were there, sometimes they were reduced, sometimes withdrawn altogether for a period of time. Consequently, neither those who worked in the schools nor the mothers who sent their children to them knew whether or not the situation would last.

Once they left the plantation, relatively large numbers of the southern rural black people took off for the northern cities. Some of them did this as soon as they left their homes, others tried southern towns for a time and then decided to go north. In all instances they hoped to find greater economic opportunity and greater freedom than were available to them "out in the rural," to use their phraseology. The remark made by a principal of an all black high school gives some indication of the extent of this migration. As he put it, "The day after graduation everyone who has the price of a bus ticket to Chicago is on that bus." So with the coming of the new order the issues covered in the preceding pages, including the issue of trust, as well as the adaptations that have to be made, are no longer limited to the south and determined largely by southern customs. The plantation people are now invading the north and involved in interactions and adjustments affecting both black and white, north and south.

When a southern black man, with or without his family, arrives in a northern city he is very likely to feel overwhelmed and lost, particularly if this is his first visit to a large metropolis. Sometimes he is met by a friend or a relative, sometimes all he has is the address of someone to whom he can turn for help in getting located. In some instances he is able rather quickly and easily to make certain necessary modifications in his behavior; sometimes this is difficult and slow in coming. Sometimes he finds work in good time and tries to live with his family in the same respectable, God-fearing fashion he has lived in the south. However, in many instances, securing work is not easy and sooner or later at least some of the people resort to one of the various illicit practices — numbers, pimping, prostitution, etc. — that people in the ghetto pursue in order to keep body and soul together. Large numbers of course seek Welfare. On the whole their feelings about life in a northern city are mixed. They resent the fact that in the north they receive no more consideration and respect than they received in the south. But at the same time they no longer have to watch every word they say lest they provoke the white man and cause him to act in retaliatory fashion. One of the people in Lyford's "Airtight Cage"* explains how the people feel. As she puts it, "There's

*Lyford, J. P. *The Airtight Cage*. Harper & Row, New York, 1968, p. 55.

a different way of living up here. You're more free; you can get into an argument and call each other names and you don't go to jail and get beat up or turn missing. Here you can sit where you want to and eat what you want to eat. Down south you have to eat out of a window, standing up."

Once in the north and aware of the opportunity at least to speak his mind, the black man's long repressed feelings of rage find many targets. What particularly triggers that anger is the white man's insensitivity in his interactions with the black people, his inability to understand how the black people feel and what they want, and above all his refusal to give them real freedom, the freedom to control their own destinies. As one very angry young black college student asked, "Why won't the white man let go, why won't he give up his control of the black man?"

It is amazing how many white people fail to realize that, in addition to all the material things he needs and wants, all the economic and educational opportunities he seeks, the black man desperately longs for the one thing that has always been denied him, real freedom. It is not just freedom from slavery or even the pseudo-freedom of the cotton fields, but the freedom to live his life as he sees fit, the freedom to do everything the white man does without having to weigh the dangers inherent in such behavior, to be free of the white boss, the white agency, the white institution, etc. No white person can possibly appreciate the importance of this need for real freedom and of the part it plays in the perceptions and feelings of the black people. Instead, the white man continues to deny the black man this freedom, continues to deal with the black man as though he were a child or an inferior type of adult who really did not know what was best for himself. This attitude on the part of northern whites is strangely like that of the white southerners who justified their treatment of the black people by insisting that they were not capable of caring for themselves.

That the black people can quickly learn what is best for them and make the adjustments needed to achieve constructive goals is well illustrated by what took place in a public school in New York City. The control of this particular school had been placed in the hands of the community and was directed by a Community School Board. The Board's emphasis was on "freedom" and so initially the children were permitted to run all over the school, into the halls, into the school yard, and out into the street, while the classrooms remained empty and the teachers powerless. After about two months of this, the Board members realized that such freedom was not only meaningless but actually harmful as far as the children's education and future achievement was concerned. So a new policy was introduced, with freedom tempered with reason and limits established.

Now the children are in their classrooms and learning, but they are also content. Likewise, the community is satisfied and certainly wiser about the meaning of "freedom." The important thing is that the people had the freedom to experiment with the educational process and in so doing learned a great deal about running a school and providing good education, along with individual satisfaction. The people now have a much clearer idea about what their children require and they are therefore able to make constructive recommendations on the basis of what they learned from this experience.

The white man's unwillingness to turn over authority and power to the black man and let him work out his problems in his own way finds expression over and over in a variety of ways. For example, a large university was the recipient of a great deal of money that it was expected to use in developing programs for the black community in the city in which the university was based. A committee of interested, concerned, and somewhat knowledgeable faculty members was established to consider the matter and make recommendations. Hours were spent in discussions about "what we should do." When one committee member suggested that it might be a good idea to approach the black community and learn from the people what they regarded as their primary needs and how they thought such needs could best be met, indeed to have several black people on the committee, this foolhardy committee member was greeted with amazed and amused looks, and after a moment of silence the discussion continued as though there had been no interruption. The reactions of the university people clearly implied that they did not believe that the black people knew what they needed or how their needs should be answered. So programs are launched and funded, but they often have no meaning for the people they are intended to serve and consequently rarely achieve what they set out to accomplish.

It is this attitude on the part of the white community, this refusal to allow the black people to administer and carry out the programs that theoretically at least are intended for their benefit, that makes them so skeptical about the white man and his "helping" and remedial projects. The very words that are often used in describing such programs, words like "helping," "upgrading," etc. are irritants as far as the black community is concerned. Obviously the implication is that the black people are lacking, are inferior, and therefore need the help of the white man. As long as one person is in the position of the "giver," is someone who feels he "knows" and therefore qualified to dispense advice and knowledge, the person to whom he is giving this "charity" is inevitably regarded as inept and therefore dependent on and very possibly subservient to the individual in control.

Currently there are in operation many programs, publicly and privately funded, all directed toward improving the black child's and frequently the black adult's scholastic achievements. There is certainly nothing wrong with trying to teach people to read and figure more effectively than they do, and to add to their general knowledge and understanding, particularly if the people themselves have asked for such help. However, in many instances, the people running such programs recruit their students rather than waiting to be asked for their services. There are even instances where classes have been filled by suggesting to the people that if they do not attend classes they may not get the jobs they seek or may not retain the jobs they currently hold; or that children who do not come to special classes will be left back or transferred to less desirable schools, etc.

Even when such is not the case, the teachers often fail to realize that the teaching methods and the techniques they use to motivate white students are not likely to be effective with many of the black pupils. Few white teachers, and sometimes even black teachers, appreciate the fact that, as a result of their way of life, the black students perceive and approach the learning situation, as well as many other experiences, differently than many of the white students do. Yet most "remedial" programs are based on what the white man sees as important and relevant. The black child and adult have a very different concept of what is important or relevant for them. Certainly it must be borne in mind that "getting ahead," or "achieving," etc. does not have the same meaning or significance, the same motivating force for many black students that it does for white ones. The black student has not been imbued from his earliest days with the importance of competition, of being better or more successful than the next guy. Furthermore, there is always his conviction that, even if he did achieve, even if he studied hard and did learn well, his chances of competing successfully with the white man and getting ahead of him are very limited.

Adding to the black man's doubts about the value of working hard and getting ahead is his conviction that in spite of his economic advantages the white man is not really happy, is not at peace with himself. He also knows that there are many young white people who want no part of today's white culture, who are sharply opposed to an Establishment that strains for control and power regardless of the cost in human lives and human happiness. Although the young people are probably the largest group of whites in opposition to the current white life styles, there are actually many white people of all ages and from all walks of life who are also very much opposed to things the way they are, who resent being caught up in and made a part of the conflict, confusion, and irrationality that characterizes today's middle-class white world.

There are other factors that teachers in remedial programs for black people should recognize. One is the whole question of language and communication, spoken and written. It is an area of great difficulty both for the teacher and the student. Until very recently, the white teacher, whether she taught in the elementary school, high school, or college, recognized only one acceptable form of English, namely the English used by educated, middle-class white people. There was and in many instances still is no realization on the teacher's part of the existence of another language, namely the language that the child learned long before he came to school, the language of his people, a language that has its own vocabulary and its own rules. Because he does not know this the teacher communicates or attempts to communicate with the child in what he considers "correct" English, unaware that for the child he is speaking a foreign language and that therefore much that he is trying to convey to his pupil is not understood. Were the teacher to speak to him in his own language and were the books from which he is expected to learn to read written in a language familiar to him, his school progress would probably be considerably better than it is.

Once the child has learned to decode in his own language it then seems logical and even necessary that he learn the language of the country in which he lives. An American business man who settles in France would not be very successful if he did not learn to speak French. So too the black child should learn the language used by the prevailing culture. However, "standard English" should probably be taught to him as a foreign language is generally taught. It must also be recognized that when two languages, although different, have many points of similarity, acquiring the second language is generally more difficult than it would be if the two languages were totally dissimilar.

All kinds of programs are being employed all over the country in efforts to teach the retarded reader, and particularly the black student, how to read. In a number of instances the programs fail to indicate whether it is decoding or comprehension that is being emphasized. Neither is the age or the sex of the pupil always taken into consideration.

Possible approaches to the issue of decoding include recourse to the "buddy system." In such a program an older child, a child in an upper grade or even in high school, who reads comparatively well and is of the same ethnic background as the retarded reader, does the coaching. In such a situation there is a shared background and shared mode of communication. The coach having himself once struggled with the decoding process has an appreciation of what his pupil is experiencing and can give him the benefit of whatever cues or system he developed in his successful efforts at learning to read. In some instances such a program has not only improved the reading of the slow child but has served to enhance the coach's interest and involvement in learning.

Then there is the whole question of comprehension. Being able to read has little value for a student if the words and sentences he is reading convey no ideas or generate no thoughts. The issue of comprehension goes far beyond reading. It affects the pupil's entire approach to formal learning, his ability to deal with symbolic and abstract concepts, to acquire new ideas and broaden his understanding.

Because many black people who have not had the benefit of extensive and adequate schooling are on the whole concrete minded, the approach to the whole matter of comprehension should begin at that level. To this end acting out of simple stories or incidents, followed by a discussion of the ideas generated by the story, why the characters acted as they did, how they felt, etc., is one way of eliciting involvement and producing ideas. For example, with very young children, children in the first and second grades, the story of the bully in the barnyard might be told, then role played and discussed, and then told by the pupils. For older children and adults there are any number of appropriate tales that could be used for this purpose. As new words enter the discussion they can be explained and used until they become familiar, but the chief purpose of this approach is to enhance comprehension, to further the student's identification with and appreciation of the thoughts and feelings of the characters in the stories, and thus gradually give them some insights into their own feelings and attitudes, as well as to widen their horizons and their understanding of of the world of people and ideas.

When an older child or an adult comes to a remedial reading program it is important to find out from him his reason for coming, what he hopes to achieve through his attendance in the class, what his particular interests are, and what his general attitude toward formal learning is. There is a great difference in the overall reactions and adjustment of the student who comes to the reading class because he has been more or less compelled to do this as compared with the individual who really wants to learn to read and who enjoys studying. Until such matters have been clarified and there is openness and understanding between the pupil and the teacher no constructive program can be planned and learning is unlikely to proceed in as effective and rewarding a manner as it otherwise might.

The value of individually tailored programs is well supported by the experiences of the pupils and teachers in a small southern town. A number of local black teenagers who had just graduated from high school had requested a remedial reading program. These adolescents were going on to college or vocational training programs in the fall and they were well aware of their need to improve their reading skills. The IQ's of the teenagers involved in the program ranged from the low 70's to 95, reading rate and reading comprehension from the fourth to the eight grade.

After their concern about their reading and their concept of what could be accomplished in the eight week summer program had been carefully discussed with them, the students were taken to a local book store and invited to select for his or her use those books that interested them. In one case a student who was planning on a nursing career chose a book on biology, another with an interest in art made a very different but highly appropriate choice. Some took books on black history. In class each student reported on what he had read and any unfamiliar word that he came across in the course of his reading was explained, discussed and used in a number of ways until each student felt comfortable with it. Basically they were encouraged to read for content even if an occasional word was strange. At the end of the eight weeks the group had gained a little over a year in reading rate and a year in comprehension.

It is also most important for the teacher to recognize that in some instances her enthusiasm about imparting skills may not be matched by that of her pupils. For students who are tired, hungry, and possibly anemic, who live in rat-infested homes and flats and who have no way of altering these conditions, the emphasis on learning seems strange and misplaced. Focusing on the acquisition of cognitive skills when there is little food, no money and meager prospects for acquiring these is a little reminiscent of Marie Antoinette's reaction when she was told that the people had no bread, a little like "let them eat cake." It is certainly true that without cognitive skills the child will not get far in today's world, but if he is to acquire these skills and use them effectively he must have a home in which he can enjoy a good night's rest, he needs adequate nourishment so that he will be able to concentrate and not be restless and irritable much of the time, and he definitely needs to develop a positive image of himself, so that he will have faith in himself and his future.

Because of the special nature of the circumstances involved in remedial teaching of black pupils many programs are not as successful as it is hoped they will be. Unfortunately, the reasons for this lack of success are rarely appreciated, rarely seen for what they are. Instead, when the black child or the black adult participating in a particular program does not show the gains that were expected, the reactions of those in charge of the venture are such as to imply that it is the black students who are at fault because they are truly unable or unwilling to learn. Then the effort may be abandoned in despair, or the proponents of a different school of thought, professionals with a different philosophy about the education of the "disadvantaged," may take over. New methods are then introduced and a new group of white professionals "get into the act."

One of the major problems in the educational area is the fact that the models available to the black student have been and in many cases still are of a very different order than those that the white pupil has. If the whole concept of models is meaningful, then the fact that among the black people the parental attitude toward learning has by and large not been one that stressed school achievement is of the utmost importance. Until very recently very few black adults saw much relevance or importance in formal schooling. Certainly it was not high on their list of priorities, and most of the black children were led to believe that earning a few cents in any way they possibly could was far more important and acceptable to their parents than getting a good mark in school. The erratic nature of the employment available to black people, especially black men, likewise did nothing to impress on the child the importance of an orderly, disciplined approach to whatever task was being emphasized at the moment. There is a world of difference in an individual's concept of the meaning and importance of work, be it school work or other kinds of work, when there is a chance to move up the ladder and "get ahead" and when such a possibility is non-existent.

Given models who see little advantage in formal learning and who do not make sustained efforts at coping with their work, it follows that the children respond sporadically to the teaching efforts to which they are exposed. Even when they are reasonably well motivated it is most difficult for large numbers of these students to pursue learning tasks for long periods of time. This is simply not in the range of their training and experience. Instead, they respond in erratic fashion, at times involved and trying to do what they are asked to do, at other times seemingly not with it. Many teachers who are engaged in the teaching of students who plan to go to college and who are being given a year of coaching so that they can cope with college work are appalled at what takes place in their classes. They describe the students as motivated but vacillating between positive and negative reactions, seemingly interested yet frequently getting up and walking around the room or out of the room, gazing out of the window, failing to carry out assignments, etc. Once again it can only be stated that such students are the product of their early environment, and it will take a great deal of understanding and patience on the part of the teacher to modify this approach to the learning situation.

When a remedial program does not achieve its purpose there is not only waste of time for both teacher and pupil, but negative feelings that both parties develop. The teacher is discouraged and doubts her pupil's ability to learn, while the student becomes increasingly indifferent toward learning, and very possibly less sure of himself and his ability than he had been. The learning failures certainly widen the gap that already exists between the black and white communities. When a program is not a success the black people are aware that the white teachers see them as uneducable and "hopeless," yet they are convinced that the white people who set up and administer many of the programs are the hopeless ones. From the black point of view the white people do not know what they are doing, but they go ahead and initiate programs that are bound to fail, yet all the while earning salaries that seem like fortunes to the black trainees. The black people also know that the government has set up a large bureaucracy that plans and implements programs intended to help black people educationally and economically. Yet the black people are sure that if the money used to maintain the bureaucracy and the money used to run the programs were turned over to them, they could make far more effective use of it than the white professionals do.

In many instances the white professional is actually likely to be hampered by his training rather than helped by it in his work with a black person. His training has prepared him to teach, counsel, or do therapy with people who perceive and experience themselves and their world much as the professional does. Yet for the black pupil or black patient the realities he perceives and experiences are often likely to be of a very different order. Such is even likely to be the case if the teacher or therapist is a middle-class black person who has never known the plantation or ghetto life. It follows then that if the black child is to learn or the black adult benefit from counseling or therapy, the teacher and the therapist should be someone from the rank and file of the black people, not someone whose experiences and training have removed him from the every day world of the persons he is seeking to interact with, otherwise there will be no real communication.

Still another area of frustration and anger for the black community is the increasing number of richly funded research projects that use black people as subjects. They have quite a few objections to such investigations. One of course is the resentment they feel at being used as guinea pigs, and at having their privacy invaded. Only because they are financially desperate do they consent to such investigations. The few dollars they make acting as research subjects are important to them but they feel that they are being exploited, and they see research as putting them in a position not very different from what they experienced when they worked on the plantations. In the cotton fields they were exploited by the plantation owner for his economic gain, and in the research situation they are being exploited by the researcher for his advantage. They almost never benefit from the investigation beyond the few dollars they are paid. They seldom know what the research is about and are almost never told the result. The whole operation does little for them, and certainly does nothing to enhance their self-respect or provide them with a better future. It is not they but the researcher who benefits from the whole enterprise. He is paid a good salary to do the study; he publishes a paper, and makes a name for himself. The argument of the researcher is that it is customary to pay subjects for their participation in a study. However, most subjects are rarely as desperately in need of money as many of the black subjects are. Students are often the subjects of psychological, educational, and sociological researches. Sometimes they participate in a study out of curiosity or genuine interest, without being paid. Now there are large numbers of black people in Harlem, Bedford Stuyvesant, Watts, and other areas where black people are concentrated to whom the word research is anathema.

One of the most serious indictments of much of the research currently focusing on the black people is that what the study ultimately reveals is, in many instances, already well known, and that even with such knowledge little if anything is done to modify or alter the conditions that, according to the investigation, are responsible for what is seen as an adverse environment. Neither is the responsibility for the harmful conditions placed directly on the doorstep of those who have created and perpetuated such conditions. The Moynihan Report* is an example of the kind of study that incenses the black people and causes them seriously to doubt the intentions of the white intellectual and the white researcher. When a people has had to live for generations as the black people have been compelled to live, not through any fault of their own but because of the rapacity and prejudice of the white man, they do not need to be told that their way of

*Moynihan, D. The Negro Family: The Case for National Action. Office of Policy Planning and Research, United States Department of Labor, March 1965.

life, a way that has caused many black men to leave their homes and families (page 79), is not satisfying or satisfactory, in fact is even harmful and does not produce what, according to white standards, is a "normal family life." Instead, the black people want to know what those who wield power and who create public opinion are going to do to change the conditions that account for the fatherless families. Certainly they do not want to be regarded as a sociological phenomenon to be investigated because of circumstances that were not at all of their own making. If studies like Moynihan's emphasized the need for basic social and economic change in the black man's circumstances and the way that change could be implemented, the black people might regard research more positively than they currently do; but unfortunately most studies end up making the black man responsible for his differences, his failure to learn, to get ahead, to delay present satisfaction for the sake of future gain, etc. rather than indicating that it is the white man who is the culprit.

One of the most distressing forms of research is the kind that seeks to explore the child's learning ability and enhance his cognitive and verbal skills by sending paraprofessionals into the homes to "teach" his mother how to interact with him. Home visits by trained aides are very much in vogue right now. They are the result of still another myth about the black people, namely that black mothers do not know how to play with and interact with their children! What the sponsors of these programs do not take into account is that a mother with five or more children, all living in a two or three room rat-infested flat, very often on an upper floor of a rickety old tenement building, a mother who probably does not receive nearly enough vitamins and iron in her daily diet, is a tired, harassed woman who has no energy for anything but the essentials needed to maintain herself and her family. What she needs is not instruction in how to play with her children, but decent housing where she and the children can move about without falling over each other, where there is room to keep toys, to have an adequate diet, and some hope for the future. As it is, unless help in playing with her child has been specifically requested, there is something very wrong, something lacking in respect and basically incredibly insensitive, even blood-chilling, about going into a home and "teaching" a mother, black, white, red, or whatever color she may be, how to relate to and play with her child. How would the people who devise such procedures feel if someone came into their home and proceeded to tell them how to deal with their children? If mothers were not exhausted and without hope they would respond to their children just as most mothers do; and the rare mother who did not do so, the occasional insensitive, disturbed mother that can be found in any community, cannot be "taught" how to love her child and how to play with him in constructive fashion simply through the medium of home visits.

The designers of such programs and the teachers who carry them out rarely seem to recognize that there is a resigned acceptance of this intrusion on the part of many of the mothers, once again accepted because they need the money that they are paid for participating in such a study. Neither are they aware that once they leave the home the mother seldom pursues the behavior the teacher has sought to impress on her. Neither the mother nor the child really trusts the teacher or believes that she understands them or truly cares about them or what happens to them. If she were really concerned she would do something about their housing and monetary needs, and about the feelings of frustration and insecurity that plague them, instead of worrying about the child's acquisition of verbal and cognitive skills. The argument can be made that the acquisition of such skills will pay off in the long run, that the child who speaks well and thinks logically will eventually be able to take a place in the world that will provide him with the material and possibly even the psychological satisfactions he needs. However, such a time is a long way off — as much as fifteen or twenty years off — and the child and his family have to live *now*. They certainly cannot live on distant future hopes and promises. In this connection the inconsistencies in the thinking of the white professional planning such programs is particularly conspicuous. Convinced in most instances that the black man cannot delay gratification, does not plan for the future (page 40) they nevertheless frequently use future satisfactions and rewards as the means of motivating those whom they are seeking to help.

It is also important for the professionals researching "learning" programs to recognize that a child cannot digest learning that is offered to him in concentrated doses. The white middle-class child who learns about space, time, distance, and other concepts does so almost unconsciously, in response to what is taking place in his life, day by day. As the situation presents itself he is casually told about the objects and the people in his world and so the learning has a relevance and an appropriateness that is often lacking in the attempts being made to provide such training in the case of the "deprived" black child. One cannot make up to a child in a few months, possibly not even in a few years, for the cultural deprivations he has suffered. Efforts at so doing with concentrated doses are very like what might be done with a starving child — someone who has not had nearly enough food for a long, long time. Suddenly to stuff such a child at one sitting would most likely cause him to regurgitate and turn away from food.

It is not always white people who are guilty of such "stuffing." The efforts of a well-educated black mother in relation to her eighteen month old son were most revealing in this connection. This woman had had a number of children prior to the birth of the little boy. In fact, he was born when all her other children were in their late teens or older. Between the time that her older children were in school and the arrival of her latest baby she had taken a Master's degree in Educational Psychology at a northern university. She had been impressed with the importance of developing the child's cognitive skills and of involving him in verbal exchange. Her need to give her youngest boy what she had not realized was important when she was raising her other children led to such excesses of "teaching" on her part that the child could not experience her as a warm, loving mother, as her other children had. Instead, she spent as much time as she could giving him concentrated doses of "learning." Her conversation with him was largely in terms of the things she had been led to believe were important. So the child was told, "Put the ball *on* the chair," "Put the truck *under* the table," and so on. It was impossible for this little boy to digest everything she was offering him, and the slightly puzzled, worried little frown that he always wore certainly suggested that he was not really secure or happy. His cognitive skills will probably be of a high order, but at what a price!

In another family the stress on the acquisition of cognitive skills produced a different problem. In this case an aide visited the home in order to "teach" the mother how to "talk to" and "play" with her three year old little girl. While this activity was taking place, two older girls, aged six and seven—sisters of the three year old—came home from school. They were not invited to join the mother, teacher and little sister who were all sitting on the floor exploring a toy the aide had brought with her. Instead, they had to sit quietly in the corner of the room observing their little sister receiving all this attention. It is hard to believe that they did not feel resentful and angry toward the teacher, the mother, and the baby sister. Although the little sister may possibly acquire some skills as a result of this "teaching," what of her siblings' reactions and the whole familial relationship?

When these and other criticisms of the home intervention program were presented to a class of white university students, the reaction of a number of them was, "If we don't intervene and present them with models they will develop an entirely different culture." It is amazing that these well-educated people had failed to recognize that the black people long ago developed and, of necessity, have for centuries lived with a different culture. White people were not concerned about this difference until black people began to emerge from their state of subservience and powerlessness. It was then that the different outlook and life style pursued by the black communities really penetrated the white man's awareness, really registered . Until then, with few exceptions, how the black man lived and what he thought and felt was of little concern to most white persons. Now, however, the difference between the black man's outlook and values and those of the white community tends to disturb, even frighten some white people. Now the black man's way of perceiving and reacting is having an impact on white lives and can no longer be shrugged off and forgotten. So now there are studies geared toward "understanding" the black man and his culture, and programs that will hopefully persuade him to model himself after the white man. As might be predicted, the black people are both distrustful and resentful of the white community's attitudes and behaviors.

Still another reason why there should be a halt to researches with black subjects is the fact that such studies frequently lack validity. Such is often the case simply because the subjects do not react in their ordinary fashion when they find themselves in the research situation. Obviously the presence of the observer makes a difference, and even when the observer is not present, when the subject is watched through a one way screen or his behavior recorded on TV, the fact that he is taking part in a study and that he is in a strange set-up affects his mode of responding. In some instances the subject very much wants the investigator to see him as an able, co-operative person even though this may not be at all his usual attitude. In other instances the subject's reactions will be atypical simply because he has not really understood what is wanted. Nevertheless, what he does as a consequence of his failure to comprehend is taken by the researcher as a valid sample of his customary behavior. There are also those subjects, black and white, who understand very well what they are supposed to do but who make a very deliberate effort to fool the investigator. For the black man this is the same kind of game he used to play when he deceived the plantation owner or the overseer whenever this was possible. Few researchers are aware that they are the victims of a "put-on," or that for some other reasons the material they are obtaining from their subjects is not valid. For example, in a large northern city there is research in progress at this time involving white investigators who go into black homes and observe the interaction between the mother and the child. The likelihood of obtaining any valid material under such conditions is of course practically non-existent. It was suggested to the investigator in this particular study that it be entitled "Interaction between a Black Mother and Her Child in the Presence of a White Observer."

The "put-on" is a mechanism by means of which the black man seeks to maintain some self-respect, some sense of autonomy and self-determination. If he succeeds in fooling or "snowing" the white man he can, for the moment at least, feel himself in control of the situation. For someone who all his life has been told what to do, and when and how to do it, in other words, who has been consistently pushed around, the opportunity to be oppositional and negative even in relatively small, unimportant ways, can be very satisfying. So the "put-on" is an extremely important technique for the black person and one to which he is very likely to resort whenever the chance for so doing presents itself.

In view of the unique nature of the conditions governing researches by white professionals using black subjects, it seems very probable that truly representative samples of the subject's behavior are difficult to obtain. However, such considerations rarely stop the researcher from going on with his investigation and then publishing his findings, as well as drawing inferences from them. Yet if the findings are not valid how can the conclusions be meaningful? This whole issue was touched on previously (page 11) in relation to the myth regarding the limited verbal interaction that takes place among the black people.

The rigidity that so often characterizes the well-trained researcher is still another reason why so many studies involving the black people have so little validity or real significance. For instance, under the auspices of a medical school, a research concerned with the interaction that takes place between the black mother and her child, and the effect of this interaction on the child's school achievements and overall adjustment, is being planned. Parenthetically one cannot help wondering how many such researches, with some minor variations, are already under way in this country, how much money has been wasted on them, and why still another one is considered necessary. In this particular project the procedures were discussed with the members of the community from which the subjects were to be obtained. All arrangements, financial and otherwise, were described and settled. The only concern the mothers of the children to be studied expressed was in regard to what it might mean to the children to be brought to the hospital where the research procedures — the testing, interview, and observations — were to take place. When the psychologist on the project was asked why the adults had this concern she stated that she did not know, that she had not asked, but had simply sought to reassure the mothers in this connection. As she put it, the concerns of the black people seemed so "peripheral" to the purposes of the study! Since when is a mother's concern about her child "peripheral," particularly when what is being studied is the mother-child relationship? But because in this particular instance the research design did not include this natural, spontaneous reaction, it was brushed aside. It seems very possible that, had this matter been explored, the investigator would have learned more about how the mothers perceived and felt toward their children, and how they interacted with them, than by blindly following a predetermined research design.

In an article in the *American Psychologist,* Cole and Bruner* also stressed what they call "the inadequacy of present experimentation." The white investigator's gross ignorance of the life styles and the language of the groups he is attempting to assess accounts for the many misinterpretations and distortions that currently characterize the white scientist's and the white professional's concept of the black man, and the resulting ineffectiveness of so many "helping" programs. Comer† has discussed this matter at some length, asking "How can social scientists even know the questions to ask and variables to test without having spent a day in a black church. . . ?" In the same article, Comer also asks, "Have social scientists made as valuable a contribution as they might have made had they addressed themselves to their scientific blindspots? Have social scientists been as ethical and responsible with the data they have collected as they should have been? Careful consideration of these questions (without undue defensiveness) is indicated."

The whole issue of scientific freedom, the right to investigate when and what one considers appropriate, comes into question. What today's researcher describes may be of great importance in years to come, but there are also the ethical issues that must be considered in relation to the subjects of the study. Just as one would not administer new and very possibly harmful, even lethal drugs to human subjects, no matter how important such experiments might seem to be, so one should not use subjects for studies which serve to derogate and harm them.

The sudden plethora of research studies dealing with the black people raises a number of questions. Why has such research become so popular in the past few years? There is the suspicion that, regardless of whatever other reasons there may be for this current interest in black populations, funding for such studies is, or until very recently has been comparatively easy to obtain. There is also the fact that because interest in the black

*Cole, M. and Bruner, J. Cultural Differences and Inferences about Psychological Processes. *American Psychologist,* Vol. 26, October 1971, No. 10, pp. 867–876.

†Comer, J. F. Research and the Black Backlash. *Amer. J. Orthopsychiat.,* Vol. 40, No. 1, January 1970, pp. 8 and 10.

people is fairly new, such research is tapping virgin territory and consequently the chances of turning up new findings relatively good.

Nothing that has been said here should be interpreted as anti-research. Research certainly needs no defense. The criticism is directed against inadequate research methods, misinterpretation of findings, and disregard of the rights of the research subjects. Furthermore, although such is not considered the function of a researcher, there is something strange about a psychologist, research or service oriented, who when he unearths conditions inimical to the physical and psychological health of his subjects, fails to follow through and try to alter such conditions. Likewise, studies undertaken by research workers who have not the slightest familiarity with the people they are studying is hardly likely to be of value. The anthropologist who wants to learn about people whose culture differs from his own does not set up laboratory situations for this purpose, but rather goes and lives with the people he wants to know and understand.

Once again then, the issue of trust comes into the picture. Yet given conditions as they currently exist, how can this be achieved? Here is an area that psychologists might explore with profit rather than some of those in which they are currently involved. Trust, like respect and love, is something that cannot be asked for or demanded. It develops when the climate for its growth is favorable, when there is understanding between the two parties concerned; and it certainly will not bloom when the relationship is marred by attitudes of condescension, patronage, or open hostility. There can be no trust when one party in the situation feels and acts superior — presents himself as though he were doing the other person a favor. Yet this attitude is so often present in the interaction that takes place between blacks and whites. It is certainly not an equal relationship when the white person sees himself in control. But this condition tends to prevail in almost all the teaching and research programs described above. The instructor or the researcher is seldom aware that his black pupil or black subject could teach him a great deal about economics, family life, social and interpersonal relationships, could open his eyes to constructive ways of living, different from those he has known. Instead, he is generally so set in his ways, so determined to perceive the black man through the screen of his professional orientation, that he fails to recognize the relationship as one in which both parties could profit, as one in which the people involved have equal status. As a result the black man can only see the white man as constantly trying to put him down rather than respecting him, and so he certainly does not trust him. One cannot help speculating on the possibility that, in addition to all the many reasons why the black child and black adult do not benefit as it was hoped they would from the many teaching programs to which they are exposed, there is not yet one more reason, namely that by digging in their heels and resisting such educational efforts they are desperately seeking to assert themselves, and in the only way available to them, establish a certain equality in their relation with the white man, and so retain some measure of self-respect, pride, and dignity.

Trust would require conveying to the black people in very concrete terms that the white man considers him quite capable of taking care of his own affairs without outside intervention or supervision. This means letting the black people plan and run their own programs, and through their various organizations, giving them the money and the facilities to do this. They would set up, staff, and carry on programs needed to foster certain kinds of skills in black children, they would develop black businesses and solve housing problems. In view of the contributions that the black people have made to the wealth of this country, contributions for which they have never been paid, the money they need for their programs is certainly due them. As it is, there are instances when a few black men and women are invited to serve on a committee setting up a program for black people. Despite the presence of these people during the planning sessions, the final character of the project almost always betrays its white origin. The white people dominate the committee and in most instances are able to persuade the black people present that the white plan is best. In fact, until very recently it has almost always been the black people who tend to think as the white people do, whose perceptions and ideas coincide with those of the white community, who have been asked to serve on or even constitute such planning boards or committees.

Many people in authority, particularly those who are responsible for large sums of money earmarked for black programs and who must give an accounting to the government and the tax payer in regard to the disbursement of the money, are undoubtedly horrified at the thought of turning large sums over to people who have had no experience with money. There seems little doubt that, given this money, the black people will make mistakes, will do foolish things with it and that a good portion of the money will therefore be wasted. But why do we go on pretending that that never happens when white people are handling the money, that white people never make mistakes, and that a good part of the millions that are spent every year on welfare, research and "upgrading" processes are not a waste? Certainly it seems time that the people most closely involved in the various programs be given a chance to demonstrate what they can do, and given such opportunities both know-how and trust will develop.

Because the black people have not been permitted to control their own lives, but have instead been treated like inadequate children, they not only have no trust in the white man, but they are frustrated, resentful, and filled with rage. All the anger that for generations had to be repressed is now finding expression, primarily in the north, but increasingly in the south. And it is amazing how little this anger is understood by the white population. Surely intelligent, sophisticated, educated people must realize that when a whole race has been treated as the black people have been dealt with in this country only distrust, anger, and hate can result. Even when they know this intellectually the white people are not ready to accept this emotionally, and even their intellectual acceptance of this state of affairs is limited. So as they become the targets of the black man's hate looks, the recipients of rude and offensive remarks, and of actual violence, they become appalled and angry rather than understanding. They make no connection between this disturbing behavior on the part of black people and the way they themselves have long reacted to black individuals. One constantly hears stories from middle-class white women about how inconsiderate, insolent, brazen and so on the black people are, in the department stores, on buses and even in the home they work in. Most of these stories come from people who all along treated black people as inferiors, as "maids" and "boys," from people who at best were "tolerant" and who felt extremely righteous for being so "kind and forbearing."

In line with this lack of appreciation of what the black man has experienced there frequently goes the question "Who is stirring them up?" Surely people who have been subjected to the conditions that have for centuries marked the black man's life need no outside "stirring up." The anger and hate, along with the desire for a human way of life was always there, but it would have been little short of genocide to express these. Currently, however, there is a crack in the wall of the black man's prison and, as the light filters in, hope blossoms. And each black person finds his own way to express and implement that hope. It is hope and desire as well as anger that are stirring up the black man, emotions that are natural to every human being and that have always been the right of white people.

Right now there are more opportunities available to the black people than ever before — more schools, colleges, high level jobs, etc. But there is still a large number of black individuals who, for one reason or another, cannot avail themselves of these opportunities and who still live in the squalor that has always marked their lives. They, as well as some of the more fortunate black people, are irked by the slow pace with which change is proceeding; and above all else by the fact that, no matter what educational or economic gains the black man makes, the white man still does not regard him as an equal. Until this happens the relations between the two races will remain tense and strained. Focusing on the attitudes and behaviors of white populations and trying to alter these, rather than seeking for ways to change the customs and attitudes of the black people or engaging in studies that emphasize racial differences, would seem a more appropriate and constructive activity for psychologists to pursue at this time.

# CHAPTER 12

# *The New Order (continued)*

At this point it seems appropriate to explore the impact that the "new order" has had on those aspects of the black man's life that were discussed in the first half of this book, specifically what has happened to his perception of reality, to his family relationships and child-rearing practices, to his intellectual functioning, his educational opportunities, his health, his sense of identification, his identity, his self-concept and his role. At the very outset it must be recognized that the black community, north and south, rural and urban, is no longer as monolithic in its perceptions and reactions as it once was. While there were of course always individuals who departed from the common way of life, in previous times in any given area the majority of the people were in accord with one another on important issues. Currently among the black people, however, there are many differing ways of perceiving and reacting to themselves and their world, and on some issues they are far apart, actually in opposition to one another. What they have in common is their hope for a better life even though their ideas as to how this is to be achieved are not at all congruent.

The black man's departure from an agrarian way of life has wrought a decided change in his perception of reality. He now recognizes that his survival no longer depends upon his success in placating the plantation owner or any other immediate white boss, but on his ability to assert himself and to develop certain technological skills. He is aware that if he is to survive economically and psychologically in the new world in which he now finds himself, he must acquire certain necessary techniques and muster all the resourcefulness he can. His lack of education and experience with other than agricultural work, along with the prejudiced attitudes of the white people, hamper him considerably as he seeks to maintain and fulfill himself. Even when he possesses the necessary skills for specific jobs he finds the going difficult. He is denied membership in many unions and discriminated against when non-union jobs are available, "the last to be hired, the first to be fired."

In addition to the external forces that make the black man's adjustment to his new world most difficult, there are other forces, particularly his life-long way of functioning, his traditions and feelings, which are not at all in tune with many aspects of the prevailing culture to which he is now expected to adjust. While there are certainly some black men who engage in assertive, competitive forms of activity and who are quite successful in these undertakings, there are also many black people who are not at all happy with the pressureful, tense, highly competitive atmosphere in which they are currently living and working. Although many of them have learned in one way or another to accommodate to the cut-throat nature of the American economic life, they do not feel comfortable with it. Furthermore, this accommodation results in the loss of some of the most highly desirable, human qualities that were part of the black culture. However, desirable or not, the black man has little choice. He has learned and learned well that if he is ever to secure anything better than menial jobs or be relegated to Welfare he must do as the white man does, namely compete with his fellow workers and try to "get ahead" at any cost. In this connection, as in many others, the black community is of several opinions. There are those who have successfully entered the white man's world, who have become middle class. Then there are those who have tried to do this but have failed. Finally there are those who refuse to adopt the white man's way of life partly because they find it so unpalatable and partly because they are convinced that no matter how hard they try they will never be given a fair and equal chance by the white man.

While the work world has been a disappointment and a frustration for many black men, in another area his perception of reality has been of a more positive order. This is in relation to the role he plays as a political force. The black man now recognizes that his vote has an effect on the elections, local and national, and that the policies of the candidates are to some extent at least influenced by the black people, by what they think and feel. This is certainly a very different reality from the one he knew on the plantation when his voice was neither sought nor heard. He is now a force to be reckoned with, and this alters both his concept of himself and his concept of the environment and his place in that environment. Similarly, what he reads in the papers and what he sees and hears on TV and radio make him increasingly aware of his legal rights. Consequently, although there are definitely times when he is discriminated against, when he is mistreated by the authorities and poorly defended by inadequate lawyers, he no longer feels resigned or compelled to accept such conditions, at least not without protest and some effort at remedying them. It is from his sense of injustice, when his rights are repeatedly ignored and denied, that a good part of the black man's anger and his resulting recourse to acting out, even destructive behavior, stems. The answer to the question, how to do away with anger and violence, should certainly be obvious.

Another reality that has altered for the black man as a consequence of his migration to the cities is the nature of his family relationships. When he lived in the rural south the black man was a member of an extended family system, with all the members of that family living in very much the same way, sharing the same activities, the same hardships, the same pleasures, and the same ideas about the way their lives should be led. Now, although he may have old friends and relatives living in the same house or at least in the same neighborhood that he does, they often tend to go their separate ways. Furthermore, many of the people who live in the same building that he does were strangers to him until recently. These people, as well as those with whom he shared the past, frequently have ideas, outlooks, and attitudes very different from his own. This may cause him to feel uncertain and insecure or to become overly defensive and rigid about his concepts. As a result, although the black people still stand together in times of need and stress, the homogeneous way of perceiving and reacting to their experiences no longer prevails as it once did.

The black man's response to his current problems and the feelings of uncertainty and anxiety that accompany these problems are of a quite different order than they were before. While he lived on the plantations of the south he was mainly fearful lest he fail to exercise the control and judgment required in order to avoid angering the white man and so in most instances he resorted to passivity and subservience (page 23). Now, however, especially in the north but to some extent in the south, subservience is no longer the answer. The black man's altered concept of reality, his changed relationship with the white man, his growing awareness of himself as an individual with definite opportunities and rights, and his perception of himself as a political force, plus his mounting anger when he recognizes that the white man persistently resists his attempts to fulfill himself and only slowly and reluctantly gives ground when he cannot avoid doing so, all produce assertive, demanding reactions rather than passive, submissive ones. His aggressive behavior serves the black man in several ways. It definitely makes him visible, a force that cannot be ignored. At the same time, by asserting himself, he proves to himself that he has strength. This behavior becomes a way of denying feelings of dependency and fear, just as his earlier emphasis on laughter and joking was a denial of depression. At long last a change has taken place and the anger that was formerly contained and turned back against himself is now being directed outward.

Because direct release of anger against the white community is a comparatively new experience for many black people, it is sometimes expressed in inappropriate and ineffective fashion. To use anger, even justifiable anger, constructively requires time and experience. Currently, the satisfaction that they feel from a release of their resentment is all some black people hope to gain from their assertive behavior. In a sense, having moved from their child-like dependence on white authority, they are now reacting like rebellious adolescents whose main concern is to oppose the powers that be. This is a phase in the history of the black man's struggle for freedom and, like other phases, will gradually give way to the more mature and constructive behavior that will eventually help him attain his goals.

Even though many black men no longer live as closely and intensely with their neighbors as they did just a few years ago, and even though they are not always in accord on many matters, their identification with the black people remains strong. In addition to all the factors, past and present, that have contributed to this identification, there are the reactions of the white communities. Their failure to recognize and accept the black man as an equal has gone a long way toward sustaining and intensifying his identification. At the same time the black man's new life, his exposure to broader horizons and new opportunities have generated a sense of independence and autonomy in many black people. Consequently, they have acquired a sense of "identity" that is far stronger than it was before.

The black man's self-concept naturally still depends in large measure on his personal experiences, and especially the experiences he had in his early years. So, particularly among the older people, there is not too much likelihood that any great change will occur in the way they perceive themselves, although in individual instances this is not impossible. However, for the children and the younger people, the increasing freedom that they know, not always in their homes but in the community, their knowledge of what is taking place all over the country in regard to black people, inevitably affects their picture of themselves. Along with this more positive self-concept and a strengthened sense of identity there is, of course, a decided shift in the role that the black people now feel they must play. So the black people, and once again most particularly the younger black people, tend to adopt assertive, aggressive roles, because they feel it is to their advantage to do so as they try to win better opportunities for themselves. Furthermore this is the way they truly feel — aggressive and angry. As part of this stance there is now a hypersensitivity among younger black people when they come in contact with whites. They seem to have all their senses tuned to what is being said and done; all their antennae are out to pick up any little casual remark, any little action that might be regarded as a racial slur. And because so many white people are insensitive to the feelings of the blacks, and because there is so much latent prejudice, the black people's conviction that the white people neither understand them nor care about what happens to them is being constantly confirmed.

Obviously the way they perceive themselves, their current self-image, their perceptions of reality, and their concept of their role, affects the way parents cope with their children. So the universality that once marked the child-rearing practices of the black people no longer exists. On the whole, though by no means consistently so, older parents tend to abide by the old ways, partly from habit and partly from their continued belief that by so doing they are insuring their children's survival. Consequently, many children are still being told to "hush," even though they may be attending schools that are encouraging them to act otherwise. They certainly hear other children assert themselves and see such behaviors on TV. Where the home training brings the child in conflict with what he hears and sees outside the home, confusion along with loss of faith in his elders is very likely to occur. Therefore the generations are no longer as closely in tune as they once were. This is very likely to occur in "immigrant" families of all races and nationalities.

The problems of the children are varied, depending upon the education and economic status the father has attained, as well as on his political and social outlook. The children of those black men who are educated and economically successful have special cause for confusion. First of all there is the fact that although the father may have attained a position of importance, may be a teacher, a principal, a lawyer, or own a successful business, and is therefore regarded by many black people with awe and respect, other black people and especially those who are devoting their energy to enhancing the well-being of the entire black community, not just their own families, are likely to be contemptuous of and negatively oriented toward the father. Similarly, even though the father earns good money, lives well and is in a position to give his son the advantages that middle-class white children have, he is rarely accepted by the white community, at least not as a social equal. Furthermore, in many instances, such a father, although well aware of current theories regarding child development and constructive child-rearing practices, fears that unless his child assumes a highly compliant, conforming manner, especially in his contacts with the white community, his comfortable, prestigious job may be lost and with it all the material comforts the family enjoys. Under such conditions a child can feel very conflicted about himself and his parents.

Successful fathers are by no means the only ones who for a variety of reasons stress compliance and even servility. Many uneducated and unsuccessful black fathers and mothers believe that such docile behavior on their part and on the part of their children is the best way to avoid trouble and possibly win some favors from the white man. Yet such favors are rarely if ever forthcoming and trouble is ever present in one form or another. Their negative experiences, combined with what they hear from others and from the news media, cause many children to wonder about the need for and the value of such humility.

The children of "activist" parents are not likely to be cut down at home. Rather, both by percept and example, they are encouraged to take pride in themselves and stand up for themselves. Whether or not they can do this, and whether they are comfortable or anxious in so doing is an individual matter, depending upon such things as early relationships and experiences, temperament, etc.

Once again between the extremes of the overly timid and the markedly aggressive, or the overconforming and the overassertive, there is the great body of people who follow the middle of the road. As is typical of any community, their child-rearing practices vary according to the experiences and perceptions of each family. Similarly, each child in turn accepts, modifies or rejects the parental model, and responds accordingly.

What has taken place in relation to the whole question of the black man's intellectual functioning is in many respects very challenging and paradoxical. As was indicated above, there have been many studies, including those of Klineberg and Montagu (page 84) to indicate that environment plays a most important part in determining the intellectual level at which an individual will function. However, there are also a number of recent studies which suggest that a change or an enrichment of the environment does not necessarily raise the IQ. Are we to assume that the current compensatory programs, set up by white educators, psychologists and others for the benefit of the disadvantaged are less effective than what took place in the public schools thirty and more years ago? At that time there were no "compensatory" programs, yet according to the investigations of Klineberg* and Lee† children whose parents had come north gained IQ points in line with the number of years that they had spent in a northern environment. In other words, better teaching and exposure to a broader and somewhat freer world improved the functioning level of these children without the benefit of specially tailored programs. One reason for this difference may lie in the fact that the current pressures placed on the black children to achieve are very different from those they experienced in the thirties and forties. Right now every professional who develops a program and every teacher who implements it feels "on the spot," is overly involved and works for the success of the program rather than for the educational advancement of the child. The pupils cannot help being aware of this and consequently the whole scene is a very different one. Furthermore, two, three, and four decades ago, black children did not feel it necessary to establish their identity by opposing teacher efforts and frustrating her in her push for success — did not have to assert themselves by not learning (page 203).

One of the strongest and most effective factors in the educational experience of some black children and adults is the emphasis that certain programs place on the attainment of strong identity and pride in being black. So small children are being taught that black is beautiful, while older children, and high school and college students are involved in Afro-American studies. The Afro-American program is a most important one for the black student, and should also be included in the white student's course of study. Black history is part of American history and no individual's knowledge and understanding of this country can be complete if the whole story is not told. In addition, knowledge and appreciation of the black story is important if white people are ever to respect, admire and in certain aspects emulate the black people. One example of the many that might serve in this connection, is the story of Charles Drew. How many white people, children or adults, know that the blood plasma that has saved the lives of thousands of American soldiers in recent wars, as well as a high percentage of civilians, was developed by this black physician?

As might be expected, especially in the case of adolescents, the reac-

*Klineberg, O. *Ibid.*, p. 84.
†Lee, E. S. Negro Intelligence and Selective Migration: A Philadelphia Test of the Klineberg Hypothesis. *American Sociological Review*, April 1951, **16**, 227–233.

tions of some of the students to what they learn in their courses on Afro-American history is likely to be extreme. For example, in a psychology class being held in a small all black college in the deep south, a student was gloating over the fact that a number of black candidates had been victorious in a recent local election. Referring to the white people in the area she kept repeating in triumphant tones, "They hurting now, they hurting now." One can well understand why the thought of white people being frustrated, upset, and angry would cause this young lady so much satisfaction. However, as she continued in this way for some time her professor finally pointed out to her that whether or not the white people were hurting was not really the crucial issue. Yet the student could not halt her jubilant chanting. Finally the professor said, "Gwendolyn, you are too bright and too well educated to waste your time, effort, and ability on the white people and what they feel. How they feel is not really the point. You must use your assets to help your own people, not to get back at white folks." The student considered this for a moment, and then she and several other members of the class nodded their heads in understanding and agreement.

In another instance the instructor was not as mature and understanding, and so the reactions of his students were often not as constructive as they might have been. In his class, as part of his attempt to build up pride and self-confidence, he taught his students to say such things as "I have power." Unfortunately he did not tell them what this power was or how they could exercise it. Consequently, when the students got into arguments with other people, black or white. all they could do was repeat, in monotonous fashion, "I've got power." When asked to explain this, to tell what this power was and what it could achieve, they were unable to do so. As a result they ended up unsure of themselves and with their faith in their professor also eventually shaken.

In general, it can be said that the overall attitude toward education, how it is perceived and responded to by the black community is very different from what it had been when the majority of the black people lived in the south. There are some black people who still feel that formal education has little or no value for them, but such individuals are relatively small in number and growing smaller all the time. Almost all black people now recognize that if they are to survive in today's world they have to be educated. However, being educated means very different things to different people. To some of the black people it means learning a trade so they can earn a living, to others it means acquiring the skills and the knowledge of the white man in order to get ahead in the white world, while to still others it means using the white man's skills and know-how primarily to enhance and enrich the life of the black man.

Finally, what changes has the new order brought about in the area of health? Despite the absence of well-paying jobs and continuing poor living conditions, the opportunities for health care for the black people seem better than they previously were. Health Centers for the indigent have been established in many rural areas, and these provide free medical and nursing care, free contraceptive advice when this is requested, free drugs, etc. Such services have generally been available in urban areas for a long time, and although the overcrowded conditions in most cities today result in long clinic waits and irritable, insensitive reactions from pressured, harassed personnel, it is possible for a needy person, regardless of color, to be seen by a physician; and most children are receiving the various immunizations they should have.

As far as mental health is concerned, there are a number of factors that make any attempt at estimating the black man's condition in this regard unfeasible at this time. One such factor is the lack of understanding that characterizes the reactions of the majority of the white professionals working with black mental patients. Another is the fact that the black people are, as a group, going through a transitional period, and that this naturally has a considerable impact on their feelings of security and the level of their anxiety. In some instances the anxiety generated by the altered nature of his existence increases the individual's sense of tension and strain. For others, the release from the restraints that they had to exercise when they lived in the south has resulted in a reduction of anxiety. In other instances, however, it has led to an excess of acting out as the black man tests his new "freedom" to its limits. Such behavior must be explored and recognized for what it is, not immediately labeled "psychopathic." One problem that was minimal in the south but is conspicuous in the north is drug addition.

The lack of understanding and/or prejudices of the white diagnostician and therapist likewise render estimates of the mental condition of black people invalid. Unless the white professionals recognize that the black people are going through a transitional state at this time; and unless they are also familiar with black customs, black traditions, and accepted black life styles, the white professional's judgment about the degree of disturbance manifested by his black patient is likely to be quite wrong. For example, among the black people, especially those who grew up in the south or who have been exposed to the attitudes and customs of the southern black, hearing, seeing and responding to the appearance and the voices of dead friends and relatives is not an unusual happening. Unless such apparitions are extremely hostile and malevolent, the phenomenon is most likely to be a hysterical rather than a psychotic one. Again, sexual promiscuity in black women certainly does not constitute evidence of a character disorder or a psychopathic personality.

The diagnostician and therapist working with the black patient must not only be aware of the depressive condition that characterizes practically all black people, but must recognize states of depression that arise from causes other than racial ones. Similarly, there must be an awareness on the part of the professional working with the black patient of the caution and the distrust that are the inevitable products of the black man's experiences. Such caution and a tendency to suspicious, paranoid-like reactions must not be confused with a true paranoid condition.

Still another source of error for the white professional is the black person's recourse to the "put-on." Many black people are so accustomed to telling the white man what he thinks the white person wants to hear or what he thinks will produce the best results for him, and have become so adept at doing this that what he tells a psychiatrist, psychologist, or social worker is often in no way related to what he is actually thinking and feeling.

In determining an individual's psychiatric status it is usually the patient's history, his current behavior, attitudes and thought processes, and the findings of psychological tests that are taken into account. As far as history is concerned, the experiences of the black man are so different from those of the middle-class white man, educationally, socially, economically, and maritally, in fact in every way that is usually considered important, that it is questionable if the white diagnostician can accurately evaluate the material he is getting from his patient. The same is true in regard to the information he is getting about the patient's current behavior, attitudes, and thoughts. For instance, a diagnostician interpreted a patient's use of her full name and all her initials as evidence that she felt put down by him and wanted to build herself up and feel important. He had no realization that the use of the full name, with all the initials, is traditional among the southern black people. This is a minor matter but in the course of an interview between a white professional and a black patient there are many such "minor" misunderstandings which add up to a final gross misunderstanding of the individual the professional is trying to comprehend and help.

One of the most frequent sources of diagnostic error is the psychologist's failure to take into account the differences that obtain between black and white functioning. Certainly if the tester takes the IQ that the black patient makes quite literally then he is going to diagnose an inordinately large number of mental retardates. Again, there is a tendency on the part of psychologists to suspect central nervous system damage in a black patient because he rotates a number of the figures on the Bender Gestalt test. Yet such rotation can of course have other causes and is apparently a relatively frequent occurrence among black subjects. For example, when African children were asked to copy the designs that are part of the Army Alpha test* a large percentage of them rotated the figures. There are also the errors that can result from interpreting projective tests in the same way that one interprets the reactions of white subjects to these stimuli (pages 43, 144). In general, using the diagnostic criteria employed in work with white people is in many instances not at all appropriate with black people, particularly black people who have not lived all their lives in cities. Such individuals who have not been exposed to all the cultural opportunities that the city child and adult enjoy, function "differently." This difference is caused largely because the needs of the individual who did not grow up in the city were of an order which led to the development of skills other than those required for survival in an urban area. To focus on functions that insure survival is certainly an indication of good thinking, good judgment and competence, not of inferiority or illness.

The white professional's failure to appreciate the difference between the issues confronting black and white patients in at least one instance led to a serious conflict between a black clinical psychology student and his white supervisor. The student had tested a black hospitalized psychotic. On the Picture Completion Test of the Wechsler Adult Intelligence Scale the patient insisted that he did not recognize the map of the United States (with Florida missing) when it was presented to him. The student interpreted this behavior as an expression of the patient's negative feelings toward and rejection of the United States. However, his supervisor negated this idea unequivocally, describing it as a projection of the student's attitudes and feelings, not those of the patient. As far as the supervisor was concerned the response was simply another indication of the seriousness of the patient's condition. Had the patient's response to this item or any other test item been one which lent itself to the more usual interpretations of patient reactions, had it had sexual, familial, and other such overtones, the supervisor would certainly have

*Nissen, H. W., Machover, S., and Kinder, E. A. A Study of Performance Tests Given to a Group of Native African Children. *British Journal of Psychology* (General Section) XXV, Part 3, January 1935.

agreed that the content of a psychotic reaction is related to the issues that are troubling the patient. Yet in this instance, because what the patient produced was not in line with what is ordinarily obtained from white schizophrenics, its significance for the black patient was neither recognized nor accepted. This supervisor's insensitivity in regard to his black patients and black students was further reflected in his description of this episode and of his relation with his students. In talking over the matter with a colleague he indicated that his initial contacts with the black students had been difficult, but that since the particular incident just cited all had gone well. However, the version of the black students was rather different. As they put it, they gave up hope of ever getting through to this particular instructor, so they no longer argued and protested, but simply got what they could out of their contact with him.

In general, using the diagnostic criteria employed in working with white patients is often likely to be inappropriate and sometimes grossly misleading when working with black patients. In this connection, in order to be able to apply some corrective to his clinical judgments, the diagnostician should ascertain among other facts, how long the patient has lived in the city, where his parents grew up, what kinds of educational opportunities were available to him, etc. What must always be borne in mind is that the social and cultural, as well as the highly personal experiences of individuals vary markedly, and that the more disparate from the so-called norm of white culture the patient's culture is, the greater will be the difference in his needs and perceptions, and in his way of responding. This does not of course label him "retarded" or "mentally sick." Each individual learns what his culture has reinforced and the fact that he has learned what his particular society thinks is important indicates that he can learn.

Many of the same issues are of major importance for the white therapist who has a black patient. The therapist must be able to move away from his concepts of what is relevant and appropriate for a white patient and learn what is essential for the black patient. Unless he can appreciate what the patient's experiences have really been and what they have done to his perceptions, attitudes, and feelings, as well as the nature of the realities the black patient has to face, he cannot possibly plan an effective therapeutic approach with him. Instead, the white therapist's biases, positive or negative, his ideas as to where the black movement should go, may well cause him to miss the signals his patient is sending him. The well-intentioned, enthusiastic liberal white therapist working with the anxious, conservative black patient can be just as ineffectual and harmful, in some cases even more so than the conservative possibly somewhat negatively oriented therapist, working with the activist black patient. In discussing some of the issues involved in therapy when the patient and the therapist are of different races, Schachter and Butts* state that among a number of other possibilities that can affect the course of treatment "subculturally acceptable pathology or acting out may evoke overreactions in the analyst, while material fitting racial stereotypes may be ignored." Oberndorf† claims that "integration of the mentally disturbed individual can best be achieved if he is treated by one of those who understands his motivations, rather than by one considered expert in a particular form of mental illness." This is much like the idea that the black student often learns best from someone who though not necessarily trained in educational techniques understands him and speaks his language, rather than from some white person highly trained in educational processes.

In relation to therapy when the therapist is white and the patient black the whole issue of trust is once again of paramount importance. That the black people, including black patients approach the white people, including therapists with a degree of caution and suspicion is understandable and even normal. Hence the reasons why the patient has sought out the white therapist and his perceptions of and feelings toward him as a person must be explored and clarified if there is to be therapeutic progress. Similarly, the therapist must explore his own reasons and feelings for accepting the black patient.

*Schachter, J. S., and Butts, H. F. Transference and Countertransference in Interracial Analyses. *Journal of the American Psychoanalytic Association*, October 1968, **16** (4), 792–808.

†Oberndorf, C. F. Selectivity and Option for Psychotherapy. *Amer. J. Psychiat.*, 1954, **110**, 754–758.

# CHAPTER 13

# *Retrospect and Prospect*

Very early one morning during the summer of 1966 I was riding through the Mississippi Delta with a black friend. Even at six o'clock the heat was intense. We passed plantation after plantation where cotton was growing abundantly. Yet there was almost no sign of human activity, only mammoth machines waiting to be driven between the cotton rows, and monoplanes about to be launched so that they might spray insecticides on the fields below. Occasionally one came upon a solitary man preparing to drive a machine or plane. These men looked small and unreal, and the whole effect was of some strange automated world, very different from the way the countryside had looked just a few years earlier when all the planting, spraying, chopping, and picking had been done by human hands.

As we drove along we came upon a few small fields where black people were still doing the work for which their ancestors had been brought to this country. In mid-summer this work is primarily chopping or weeding. Suddenly a small black boy, six or seven years at most, shot across the road, directly in front of our car. Because of his haste his big straw hat, tied under his chin, was bobbing at the back of his neck instead of sitting on his head and sheltering him from the sun. He was carrying a hoe as big as he was, and on his face there was a most anxious look as he hurried toward the group of adults already assembled in the field. "He's a few minutes late and he's afraid he'll be docked and make less than the magnificent dollar he's supposed to get for working from sun-up to sun-down," my companion explained. And then he added in the angriest yet saddest tone I had ever heard him use, "Just about now the white children are turning over in bed, dreaming about the swimming pool or the air-

219

conditioned movie they're going to later on." Because I too was deeply touched by the plight of the little black boy and hundreds like him I answered sharply, "What do you want me to do? Bleed? I am bleeding. Inside I bleed all the time but what good does it do?"

Incidents of such a heartbreaking order take place all over the country, in one form or another, many times a day.* In all of modern history no form of slavery was as evil and degrading as that practiced in the southern states of the United States of America. In other parts of the civilized world slavery had been abolished before the Civil War in this country, and where it had been practiced it had been tempered by conditions which did not render the slave totally helpless. For example, in South America a slave could work toward and eventually buy his freedom, something that almost never occurred in this country.† While it is true that a few slave owners did free their slaves, the greatest number of them were held in bondage from the moment of their birth to the moment of their death. In the final analysis the only thing a slave had to look forward to was death, something well conveyed in the words engraved on Martin Luther King's tombstone, "Free, free, free at last. Thank God in Heaven I'm free at last."

Even in ancient times provision was made for a man to see the light ahead, to have some hope for the future. Thus in the Bible, in Exodus, Chapter 21, it says, "Now these are the judgments which thou shall set before them. If thou buy a Hebrew servant six years shall he serve; and in the seventh he shall go out free for nothing. If he came in by himself he shall go out by himself; and if he were married then his wife shall go out with him."

Unlike what happened among the ancient Hebrews or among modern civilized nations, the practice of slavery in this country was one which did everything possible to crush the black man and deny him any possibility of hope. Isolated from the outside world, unaware of what was going on apart from the events taking place in his own circumscribed world, without dreams and without hope, and without any real opportunity for independent thought, what has not been taken from the black man, what could not be taken from him, was his will to live. Consequently, despite all the dehumanizing to which he was and is subjected, he has

---

*Poor white children also experience severe hardships and deprivations. However, they were never enslaved and because they are white many doors are not inexorably closed to them as they are in the case of the black people.

†Elkins, S. M. *Slavery: A Problem in American Institutional and Intellectual Life.* University of Chicago Press, Chicago, 1959.

achieved what for many people seemed impossible. He survived, and what is more, developed and practiced some of the finest qualities mankind has ever known. He was kind, gentle, patient, understanding, empathic, and most willing to help, with an instinctive knowledge of how to be helpful. Aside from whatever else it may demonstrate, the contrast between the attitudes and behaviors of the black people on the one hand, and of their white overlords on the other, is an amazing example of the range of human potentialities and human reactions. Certainly one cannot resist asking, who were the true Christians?

Given the conditions under which they were forced to live, one of the burning questions is, of course, what enabled this oppressed group of black people to endure and survive. Any number of reasons can be postulated, one of the more obvious ones being constitutional superiority and natural selection, Jensen and others notwithstanding. Certainly those who survived must have been physically strong and intellectually alert and perceptive. The inference therefore must be that today's black population, like all persecuted minorities that survive, is of a superior order.

In view of their particular past and today's social, political, and economic picture, what of the future? Where do the black people want to go and how do they plan to reach their goal?

At the present time the issues that loom largest in the minds of the leaders of the black community are (1) the acquisition of control over their own economic and psychological destinies and (2) the retention of their own culture and their own identity. These have always been their chief concerns and in previous years it was also the concern of the white people who worked with the black people in the efforts to secure equal rights for them. In 1963 and 1964 members and supporters of The Civil Rights movement and such organizations as SNCC and CORE were not only concerned about securing justice for the black man but were convinced that the best aspects of black culture, the co-operative spirit that characterized their attitude as opposed to the competitive spirit so rampant in white communities, along with the love and care they extended to their fellow man, should be preserved and encouraged to infiltrate into the white culture. At that time their sentiments in this regard found expression in the oft-repeated statement, "The Civil Rights movement will save America." It was generally believed by the many white people working with the black communities that if the beauty of the black spirit were truly understood by the white people there might yet be hope for the future of white civilization.

Unfortunately, the relationship between the black and white people did not progress in the way that concerned Civil Rights workers had hoped it would. Instead, the movement has been in the opposite direction, with both blacks and whites angry and disillusioned. For the black people the movement toward establishing their rights has been much too slow and tortuous, and they no longer have faith in the white man and his intentions. They see him as handing out sop after sop in the form of various programs intended to benefit the black man, but never really letting him design his own future, never letting him take over such programs, and most of all, never making the basic changes in the whole social structure that are essential if he, the black man, is ever to enjoy true equality with the white man.

The white man on his part has felt endangered by the demands of the black man and by his insistence that change must take place *now*. He has become increasingly distressed and even fearful because of the pressure that the black man has been bringing to bear. He feels threatened by this pressure, by the increased competition he feels sure will result if the black man is in a position to become involved in all the economic and political activities that until recently have been the prerogative of the white man, and of course, many white men are angry and deeply disturbed by the violence that has erupted in some black communities. The increased tension that this state of affairs produces is by no means confined to the business or political world. Many young people who grew up in middle-class white liberal homes are currently expressing considerable resentment about what they perceive as the preferential treatment being accorded black students. They do not think it is "fair" that a number of these black students are being admitted to college when in some instances their marks have not been as high as those of some white students. They also resent the fact that in class, allowance is sometimes made for the black student's low, possibly even failing scores.

Finally, there are numbers of white people who are pleased that many whites, among them people who at one time were identified as "liberal," are now put out and even angered by what is regarded as the black man's intrusion into the white world. Such whites are even pleased when the black man resorts to violence because they see such violence not only as confirmation of their perception of the black people, namely that they are too primitive, too uncivilized, to be accepted in the white world, but as still another way to turn more whites against them.

Among the black people at this time the range of feelings and ideas as to the nature of their goals and the best way to attain those goals is extremely wide. There are those who hope for and continue to work toward peaceful co-existence. By this they mean that the black man will have the same opportunities as the white man but will in most respects remain apart from white communities, leading their own lives, socially, educationally, and even to some extent economically. To create such a world for himself the black man must have the financial resources which would enable him to develop industries owned and operated by black people, establish banks that are run by and cater to black clientele, and promote housing that enables people to live securely and with dignity. Naturally the schools that the black children would attend in such a state of co-existence would be staffed by black personnel and administered by the black community. It seems probable that if such a state of peaceful co-existence were established the line separating the black and white communities would not be as tight as the description of such a program makes it sound. In a way, all "outside" groups lived for a time at least apart from the established groups. It was not only because they were alien and impoverished that European immigrants when they first arrived in this country lived together, each in his own distinct little ghetto, but because it was the only way they could preserve a culture that was important to them and provided them with a sense of identification. Then gradually as the "newcomers" are accepted, the lines of demarcation are loosened.

In contrast to the black people who see peaceful co-existence as the answer to their problems, there are those who emphasize integration as the best solution. For those who stress this point of view this means an acceptance and a pursuit of the white man's way of life, becoming white in all but physical appearance. Under such conditions some aspects of black culture would inevitably be retained, but they would be subordinated to the conditions of white culture, and slowly disappear. Again this is what has happened to some individuals who came from cultures rather different from the typical American one, while other members of such groups have struggled and retained much of their original way of life.

In contrast to those who seek for peaceful co-existence and those who seek integration, there are the angry, mainly young black people, who are so impatient, so bitter and so disillusioned by the responses they have received from the white community that, although they insist that they are working for the good of the black people, their activities appear to be directed more toward harming white people than doing anything positive for black people. For them the reaction of the white power structure has been at best based on efforts at appeasement and at worst on frank racism. In their fantasies they either destroy the white world or withdraw totally from it. As one young black college man stated, "I can't even turn on my TV. I can't bear to look at nothing but white people." He was so blinded by his hatred that he simply ignored the black programs that do appear, actually denied their existence. He went on to say that he would like to go and live in Africa, but before leaving this country he would like to kill a large number of government officials and destroy government property. In this group of angry young people there are those who feel it is better to die, and even to let black children die, than to make constant concessions to white demands and go on living as they are forced to live. While their anger is understandable, they have little in the way of a positive answer to the issues that so trouble them, and their concern seems in many instances to be more for themselves as individuals than for the race as a whole. Their general attitude and their insistence that they "can't take it anymore" is a far cry from the attitudes and behaviors of their forebears who "took" much more than they are taking.

Although the statements, and in some instances the behaviors, of some of the very young and very angry black people are quite different from those of their ancestors, the reason for these differences is psychologically understandable. When the black man had no chance whatsoever of improving his lot he learned to resign himself to the inevitable and sought ways to hold on, to survive, under the most outrageous conditions. However, once such conditions were even slightly modified, once the door was opened even a little bit and the chance of a better way of life made available, it followed that any obstacles that stood in the way of achieving his goals were perceived as objects to be attacked and destroyed.

When a minority group, like the black people, has to struggle to attain equal status with the in-group, be it through peaceful co-existence, integration, or violence, it is apparent that the minority is considerably less powerful than the dominant group. Under such conditions peaceful co-existence is difficult to achieve, integration likely to result in a complete loss of identity, a case of the wolf swallowing the lamb, and violence end in genocide. Put this way the issue sounds almost hopeless, but the progress that the black people have made in many areas, while far from what it should be, far from the goals they seek to reach, indicates that in spite of all the obstacles that must be met and overcome, there is hope and that eventually the black man will win true freedom and equal opportunity. Right now, because of a rather strong white backlash, a conservative administration and economic difficulties the situation seems less promising than it did five or ten years ago. Such temporary set-backs are inevitable, are a case of losing a battle but eventually winning the war. It takes time, historical perspective, and infinite patience on the part of the oppressed to brook continued frustration and delay, but such patience and understanding have been among the black people's greatest strengths.

Judging by what happened to other minority groups in this country it seems probable that both integration and co-existence, to varying degrees, will characterize the future way of life of the black people in this country. Those black men who stress the maintenance of a strong identity will make every effort to retain certain traditions and customs, and they certainly will seek to have a large hand in the education of their children, just as certain white groups do, sending their children to special rather than the usual public school. The attitude of the people who feel strongly in this respect was well conveyed by a young black man who said, "We are the only people I know of who have been expected to place the education of our young in the hands of the enemy." The establishment of Community School Boards that determine educational policy and run neighborhood schools is one way in which this issue is already being met. Similarly, changes in teaching methods and in the composition of teaching staff, the introduction of Afro-American courses provide some answers to the issues. Likewise, in the business world, there have been some small beginnings toward helping the black business man get started and there is every likelihood that these efforts will grow. But no matter how hard the black people strive to bring about the changes that are needed, these cannot take place unless the white community recognizes the importance for such change and does everything in its power to bring it to pass.

The white community must support the efforts of the black people, not only because to do so is only just and right, but because it is to their, the white people's, interests to do so. For the white man there are actually two possibilities in so far as the black issue is concerned. He can fail to help the black people find themselves or even cause them to fail by putting all manner of obstacles in their path, or he can facilitate their attainment of the status of respected citizens who are part of the assets of a great nation. If he adopts the former stance the black people will become a perpetual irritant in the life of this country, a running sore that will drain the nation's strength and seriously interfere with its social, political, educational, and economic life. If the doors of equality and opportunity are closed to them the black people will continue to swell the ranks of the school drop-outs, of the unemployed, the criminal offender, etc., thus adding enormously to the tax burden and weakening the moral fiber of all the people as well as destroying our image all over the world. On the other hand, if the black people are perceived and treated as they should be, as people who have contributions to make and who will make them if given the chance, as people who through their behavior, their achievements, and their talents have shown a great humanness, then the country will be the richer for their full participation in it.

In considerable measure, therefore, what happens in the United States in the future depends on the understanding and the response of the white power structure *vis à vis* the black issue. What is involved in this connection is not "just a matter of money" as one erstwhile liberal put it. Neither is it just a question of jobs and housing, although these are part of the total issue, not only because they are essential to decent living and effective functioning, but because their presence or absence symbolizes a specific attitude on the part of the Establishment. As important as all these issues is the psychological one, the need that every human being has to be himself, to control his own life, to live without fear, to be truly free and independent, and to be recognized and respected as a man.

Because of the significance of psychological factors in this whole issue, it is especially disturbing when so many individuals in the psychological and allied fields are insensitive to the problems. It is also most distressing to realize that in years to come, when the history of this period is written, it will be psychology that will be seen as having contributed most to the "scientific" evidence used as justification for discrimination and racism. It would be a terrible thing indeed if, on the basis of inappropriate research methods and unsound conclusions derived from poorly conceived studies, psychology were the science that had supplied the bigot and racist with the ammunition he needs. Surely it would be far more constructive and more in line with the values and objectives of psychology not only to help the white community recognize the enormous part it has played in creating the black issue but to enable the white people to perceive the black people as they really are, to make them aware of the black man's many assets as well as his rights, and in this way facilitate rather than hinder his efforts to attain those rights. Psychology is certainly the science that can appreciate and communicate the meaning of individual and group differences without accompanying value judgments or emphasis on superiority and inferiority. If we can do this, then psychology will have made one of its greatest contributions.

# Bibliography

Allen, V. L. (Ed.) *Psychological Factors in Poverty*. Markham Publishing, Chicago, 1970.

Anastasi, A. Intelligence and Family Size. *Psychological Bulletin*, May 1956, **53**, 187–209.

Baldwin, J. *The Fire Next Time*. Dial Press, New York, 1963.

Baratz, J. C. & Shuy, R. W. (Eds.) *Teaching Black Children to Read*. Center for Applied Linguistics, Washington, D.C., 1969.

Bardolph, R. *The Negro Vanguard*. Vintage Books, New York, 1961.

Baughman, E. E. & Dahlstrom, W. G. *Negro and White Children*. Academic Press, New York, 1968.

Benedict, R. Continuities and Discontinuities in Cultural Conditioning. *Psychiatry*, Vol. 1, May 1938.

Bennett, L., Jr. *The Negro Mood*. Ballantine Books, New York, 1964.

Birch, H. G. & Gussow, J. D. *Disadvantaged Children*. Grune and Stratton, New York, 1970.

Brown, R. & Halpern, F. The Variable Pattern of Mental Development of Rural Black Children. *Clinical Pediatrics*, July 1971, **10**, 404–409.

Carmichael, S. & Hamilton, C. V. *Black Power*. Vintage Books, New York, 1967.

Cash, W. J. *The Mind of the South*. Alfred Knopf. New York, 1941.

Census of Negro Population in Bolivar County, Mississippi. Prepared by D. Yankelovich, Inc. for the Department of Preventive Medicine, Tufts University School of Medicine, 1967.

Chetnik, M., Fleming, E., Mayer, M., & McCoy, J. A Quest for Identity: Treatment of the Disturbed Negro in a Predominantly White Treatment Center, *American Journal of Orthopsychiatry*, January 1967, **37**.

Clark, K. B. *Dark Ghetto*. Harper & Row, New York, 1965.

Cleaver, E. *Soul on Ice*. McGraw-Hill, New York, 1968.

Cole, M. & Bruner, J. S. Cultural Differences and Inferences about Psychological Processes. *American Psychologist*, October 1971, **26**, 867–876.

Comer, J. F. Research and the Black Backlash. *American Journal of Orthopsychiatry*, January 1970, **40**.

Deutsch, M., Katz, I., & Jensen, A. *Social Class, Race and Psychological Development*. Holt, Rinehart & Winston, Inc., New York. 1968.

Dobzhansky, T. *Mankind Evolving*. Yale University Press, New Haven, 1962.

Duberman, M. *In White America*. The New American Library, A Signet Book, New York, 1965.

Dubois, W. E. B. *The Souls of Black Folk*. McClurg, Chicago, 1903, reprinted, Fawcett, New York, 1961.

Dubos, R. *Mirage of Health*. Doubleday & Co., Garden City, 1959.

Elkins, S. M. *Slavery: A Problem in American Institutional and Intellectual Life*. University of Chicago Press, Chicago, 1959.

Erikson, E. H. Growth and Crises of the Healthy Personality. Chapter in *Personality in Nature, Society and Culture*, Kluckholm, C., Murray. H. A. & Schneider, D. (Eds.) Alfred A. Knopf, New York, 1953, pp. 185–225.

Gesell, A. & Armatruda, C. *Developmental Diagnosis*. Paul B. Hoeber, Inc., New York, 1949.

Goldfarb, W. Psychological Privation in Infancy and Subsequent Adjustment. *American Journal of Orthopsychiatry.*, **15**, 247–255.

Grier, W. H. & Cobbs, P. M. *Black Rage*. Basic Books, New York, 1968.

Griffin, J. *Black Like Me*. Signet Books, New York, 1962.

Halpern, F. Psychotherapy in the Rural South. *Journal of Contemporary Psychotherapy*, 1970, 67, **2**(67), 67–74.

Halpern, F. How Things Might Be and How They Are. *The Clinical Psychologist*, Fall 1968, **22**, 22–29.

Halpern, F. Self-Perception of Black Children and the Civil Rights Movement. *American Journal of Orthopsychiatry*, April 1970, **40**, 520–526.

Hersey, J. *The Algiers Motel Incident*. Alfred A. Knopf, New York, 1968.

Hunt, J. McV. *Intelligence and Experience*. The Ronald Press Co., New York, 1961.

Hunt, J. McV. Parent and Child Centers: Their Basis in the Behavioral and Educational Sciences, *American Journal of Orthopsychiatry*, January 1971, **41**.

Jensen, A. R. How Much Can We Boost IQ and Scholastic Achievement? *Harvard Educational Review*, Winter 1969, **39**, 1–123.

Johnson, C. S. *Growing Up in the Black Belt*. Schocken Books, New York, 1941.

Kagan, J. In "The Child," Saturday Review, December 17, 1968.

Kardiner, A. & Ovesey, L. *The Mark of Oppression*. The World Publishing Co., Cleveland, Ohio, 1962.

Klineberg, O. *Negro Intelligence and Selective Migration*. Columbia University Press, New York, 1935.

Klineberg, O. *Characteristics of the American Negro*. Harper & Row, New York, 1944.

Klineberg, O. *Race and Psychology*. UNESCO Pamphlet, 1951.

Klineberg, O. Negro and White Differences in Intelligence Test Performance: A New Look at an Old Problem. *American Psychologist*. April 1963, **18**, 198–203.

Liebow, E. *Tally's Corner*. Little, Brown & Co., Boston, 1967.

Lyford, J. P. *The Airtight Cage*. Harper & Row, New York, 1966.

Lynd, H. M. *On Shame and the Search for Identity*. Science Editions Inc., New York, 1961.

Meier, A. *Negro Thought in America*. University of Michigan Press, Ann Arbor, 1963.

McCord, W. Howard, J., Friedberg, B., & Harwood, E. *Life Styles in the Black Ghetto*. W. W. Norton & Co., New York, 1969.

Montagu, M. F. A. The Intelligence of Northern Negroes and Southern Whites in the First World War. *American Journal of Psychology*, 1945, **58**, 161–188.

Moynihan, D. P. *The Moynihan Report*. Massachusetts Institute of Technology Press, 1967.

Nissen, H. W., Machover, S., & Kinder, E. A. A Study of Performance Tests Given to a Group of Native African Children. *British Journal of Psychology* (General Section) January 1935, **25**.

Oberndorf, C. F. Selectivity and Option for Psychotherapy. *American Journal of Psychiatry*, 1954, **110**, 754–758.

Passow, A. H. *Education in Depressed Areas*. Teachers' College Press, 1963.

Pettigrew, T. F. *A Profile of the American Negro*. D. Van Nostrand Co. Inc., Princeton, 1964.

Ploski, H. A. & Kaiser, E. *The Negro Almanac*. The Bellwether Co., New York, 1971.

Rae-Grant, G., Gladwin, T., & Bower, E. Mental Health, Social Competence and the War on Poverty. *American Journal of Orthopsychiatry*, July 1966, **36**, 652–664.

Rainwater, L. & Yancy, W. *The Moynihan Report and the Politics of Controversy*. The Massachusetts Institute of Technology Press, Cambridge, 1967.

Schachter, J. S. & Butts, H. F. Transference and Countertransference in Interracial Analysis. *Journal of the American Psychoanalytic Association*, October 1968, **16**, 792–808.

Silberman, C. E. *Crisis in Black and White*. Vintage Books, New York, 1964.

Silver, J. W. *Mississippi: The Closed Society*. Harcourt Brace, New York, 1964.

Smith, L. *Killers of the Dream*. W. W. Norton & Co., New York, 1949.

Storr, A. *Human Aggression*. Atheneum, New York, 1968.

Vosk, J. S. Study of Negro Children with Learning Difficulties. *American Journal of Orthopsychiatry*, 1966, **36**, 32–40.

Williams, J. A. (Ed.) *Beyond the Angry Black*. New American Library, New York, 1966.

Wright, R. *Native Son*. Harper & Row, New York, 1940

Yette, S. F. *The Choice: The Issue of Black Survival in America*. Berkeley Publishing Corporation, New York, 1971.

# Index

## TITLES IN THE PERGAMON GENERAL PSYCHOLOGY SERIES